MARK TWAIN
SPEAKS FOR HIMSELF

Samuel Langhorne Clemens

Speaks for Himself

EDITED BY PAUL FATOUT

PURDUE UNIVERSITY PRESS
WEST LAFAYETTE, INDIANA
1978

Front endpaper: *Mark Twain in 1869 at age thirty-four.*
(From The Mark Twain Papers, University of
California, Berkeley.)
Back endpaper: *Mark Twain in 1907 at age seventy-two.*
(From the collection of Franklin J. Meine, Chicago.)
Opposite beginning of text: *Mark Twain as a young man.*
(From the California State Library, Sacramento.)

Appreciation is expressed to the above-mentioned sources
for their courtesy in permitting use of these photographs
and others credited to them in this book.

Library of Congress Catalog Card Number
77-81462

International Standard Book Number
0-911198-49-0

Printed in the United States of America

FOR BILL TINDALL

TABLE OF CONTENTS

{ PREFACE }

his book evolved out of a number of trips to the University of California at Berkeley and many agreeable hours there in the Bancroft Library. Combing the Bancroft's extensive files of nineteenth-century western newspapers on the trail of whatever subject was of concern at the moment, I was like Autolycus in *The Winter's Tale,* a snapper-up of unconsidered trifles. Frequently I came across news stories lifted by California editors from the Virginia City *Territorial Enterprise* when Sam Clemens was a reporter on the paper, none of the items credited to him but some probably written by him. Those that looked promising I filed away for future reference. Since no file of the *Enterprise* is known to exist for those years, fragments reprinted elsewhere were a roundabout way of viewing the Virginia City of his time and occasionally, in comments about the *Enterprise* "Local," of getting a conjectural glimpse of the man himself.

After he had adopted the *nom de plume* of Mark Twain early in 1863 and had gained, by reason of exploits funny and outrageous, a measure of regional fame or notoriety or both, the pen name was often attached to editorial borrowings and his doings were more likely to be noticed than heretofore. Among his contemporaries, who expressed frank opinions about him as a person and as a writer, he was both admired and derided. His tall tale about the petrified man, published in the *Enterprise* soon after he had arrived in Virginia City, was received with amused favor, but a later hoax, the bloody massacre of the Hopkins family, was roundly condemned.

We hear of "this great and truly original, unapproachable humorist," also of "the distinguished humorist, traveler, correspondent and missionary." He was fulsomely complimented as "a refined humorist and a scholar" and as a man whose "fine sense of humor is surpassed by his acute moral perception." One reporter described his first San Francisco lecture in 1866 as "an intellectual draught from his inexhaustible fountain of mental lore."

Countering laudatory words is the dispraise of critics who looked upon him with a jaundiced eye. They called him "this miserable scribbler," "this wandering Bohemian," and "this desperate joker," compounded of "brass and triple cheek," whose writings were "so intolerably silly that they have not seemed like the production of a sound mind." One fellow said that Mark Twain was thinking of writing a book about "adultery, more and more of it," adding the scurrilous remark: "We know of no one more capable of writing such a book than Mark Twain." Another wit spoke of a projected drama entitled *One Night in Ten Bar-Rooms,* of which he said, "No doubt it will have a successful run, as Mark understands that subject to a dot."

Now and then a perceptive observer gives us a picture of Mark Twain in action, as in the following account from the Oakland, California, *News* of April 10, 1868:

> Yesterday afternoon . . . Mark Twain might have been seen rushing madly about in the neighborhood of the Oakland and Alameda ferry landings . . . inquiring in a bewildered manner of all whom he met, "which boat he ought to take in order to get to the place where the dinner is to come off?" "What dinner?" inquired a benevolent looking citizen, who seemed to think that something was the matter with the pilgrim from the Holy Land. "Well," responded Mark, with a bewildered look, "that's the question. I agreed yesterday, or the day before, or the day before that, or some time or other, to go somewhere to a dinner that was to come off to-day, or maybe to-morrow, or perhaps to-morrow night, at some d——d place, across the bay. I don't know exactly where it is, or when it is, or who I agreed with. All I know is, I'm advertised in the newspapers to be somewhere, some time or other this week, to dine, or lecture, or something or other—and I want to find out where the d——l it is, and how to get there."

That account may have been touched up by the reporter's fancy, but no matter. It is an engaging view of Mark Twain's absentmindedness, which was genuine and permanent.

Whether Pacific Coast editors approved of him or disapproved, they kept on printing stories by and about Mark Twain long after he had left California for good. Out there, his rise to eminence and fortune in the East seemed a surprising example of hometown-boy-makes-good, an event entirely unexpected in some quarters of San Francisco. Still in the air in the late twentieth century is an occasional hint of incredulity over such an unlooked-for occurrence.

Stray pieces of his writing gleaned from California and Nevada papers, together with others from eastern dailies, as well as weeklies and monthlies, are all part of this book, which is intended as a collection heretofore unpublished between covers. I cannot be certain that the claim is valid, but it is almost so. At this late date it is difficult to find anything by Mark Twain, printed anywhere, that has not been unearthed by diligent researchers, cataloged, and possibly resurrected to be republished, but the contents here, except perhaps for a few exceptions, have been hitherto uncollected.

So far as I am aware, there has been no systematic publication of his remarks to newspaper reporters, whose attentions became more pressing as he became more famous during rambles over the world for forty years. Included here are several examples, ranging from the conventional interview to brief observations. All suggest that the spoken word was as important to Mark Twain as the written one, if not more so. Consideration of the man as a writer can hardly ignore the talker, for the vernacular style of his best writing is fashioned upon the rhythms of speech. He considered English as a spoken language, and in top form he wrote as he talked or, as in *Huckleberry Finn,* as his characters talked. Even his idiosyncratic punctuation, which bothered editors, who enraged him when they tinkered with it, , accords with the word groupings, pauses, casual repetitions, and loose structure of conversational speech.

Spanning the years between his first days as a reporter on the *Enterprise* and the last months of his life, this anthology gives sporadic glimpses of almost his entire career as writer and talker. No ulterior motive prompts the presentation. It is not intended to advance a theory, psychological or literary, to confirm a thesis, or to defend a critical point of view. The purpose is only to recall from obscurity some of his little-known efforts, oral and written, out of which the reader, if so minded, may construct any hypothesis he chooses.

The chronological arrangement, however, offers grist to the mill of the inquirer seeking to trace some sort of development, in style, ideas, or whatever. Walter Blair remarks in his introduction to *Selected Shorter Writings of Mark Twain* (1962) that Mark Twain's short sketches are essential to any analysis of his development. "One who studies such works," says Blair, "perceives that, for all his apparent diffusion, Twain works best in small compass. . . . Varied though they are, works which—as wholes—show Twain coming closest to perfection all are short."

Waiving that point, the short pieces in this collection illustrate the man's versatility in turning his hand to a variety of topics, illuminate episodes in his life as well as facets of his character, and affirm opinions that are provocative even when wrongheaded. Mark Twain is observer and reporter, reflective moralist, teacher and preacher, advocate of causes, teller of tall tales, hoaxer, crusader for copyright, industrious writer of letters to the editor, ostensibly a casual talker who is more studied than casual when he talks for publication.

If any other reason be needed for rescuing fugitive pieces, it is this: that in almost anything written by Mark Twain, even his offhand journalism, some trace of his best style is likely to appear—as in Shakespeare's blood-and-thunder potboilers that pleased the groundlings—the right word, a striking phrase, a sharp figure of speech, a pungent remark that is uniquely his own and that momentarily gives the whole a lift. The authentic Twainian touch is equally the property of the *Enterprise* reporter and of the seasoned

writer thirty years later. The reader comes upon these
flashes with surprise and delight. As a longtime follower of
Mark Twain, I am as pleased by such finds as an old
prospector exhilarated by a show of color in the pan.

In this book the tone, infused with familiar satire and
irony, ranges from the grave to the frivolous.
Undercurrents of moral indignation, subdued rumblings of
disgust over the idiocies of what he called the damned
human race, moments of good humor that approach
serenity, and forays into nonsense: all manifest the variable
character of Mark Twain, an elusive sort of character that
evades easy classification.

Because of his variable character, I have not attempted
to follow the contemporary vogue of dividing him into
Samuel L. Clemens and Mark Twain. I cannot do it,
furthermore, because the line of demarcation seems to
me so vague and shifting, so blurrily defined that it is
difficult, at times impossible, to discern where Clemens
yields to Twain and vice versa. The division is credible, as it
is likely to be in any man as much in the public eye as he was
and desirous, like a campaigning office-seeker, of projecting
a popular concept of himself, but the two parts are often too
close for separation. If he was a one-man version of the
Siamese twins, who continually fascinated him, the ligature
is frequently invisible. Still, the divided personality, which
is of concern to scholars, is a tantalizing subject that merits
attention.

We are offered a medley of opposing personae: Mark
Twain, the public man, vs. Clemens, the private citizen;
Mark Twain, the popular funny fellow, vs. Clemens, the
serious thinker; Mark Twain, the careless bohemian, vs.
Clemens, the respectable pillar of society; Mark Twain, the
iconoclast, vs. Clemens, the conformist; and so on as the
ingenuity of the analyst may discover other conflicting
roles. The confrontation of opposing forces conveys the
impression that he shifted from one to the other as a driver
shifts gears, and that the behavior of one party to the
contest did not infringe upon the mode of the other.

Such compartmentation seems oversimplified for a complex entity like Mark Twain. He provides contrary views in his conceptions of the Siamese twins. In one of these, "Those Extraordinary Twins," a character called Angelo is an upright Methodist teetotaler joined to Luigi, a dissipated and shocking freethinker. Luigi's steady drinking does not affect him but makes Angelo drunk; Luigi's gluttony gives Angelo indigestion, and Angelo is generally blamed for Luigi's low pranks. Mark Twain acted out this fantasy for a few guests at a New Year's Eve party, 1906, in his home at 21 Fifth Avenue. He and a young man, their arms around each other, were bound together by a sash symbolizing the ligature. While Angelo (Mark Twain) tried to deliver a fervent temperance lecture, Luigi kept nipping from a pocket flask, making Angelo more and more unsteady as he staggered about and his lecture degenerated into hiccupping incoherence—a convincing performance that brought down the house.

Another version of the twins appeared when Mark Twain introduced James Whitcomb Riley and Bill Nye to a Boston audience (1889) as the Siamese twins, Chang and Eng. He elaborated upon the theme that one of the pair was dynamo or creating force, the other motor or utilizing force, and that these roles were interchangeable. Thus each complemented the other, the merits of Chang compensating for the shortcomings of Eng, and vice versa. Hence, said Mark Twain, "They must travel together, conspire together, hoe, and plant, and plough, and reap, and sell their public together, or there's no result."

In the light of such interpretations, Mark Twain as an example of twinship becomes perplexing. Did his two selves assist each other or obstruct each other? And which of the twins was he among his associates?

Of his two best friends, Howells called him "Clemens," and the Reverend Joseph Twichell called him "Mark," and he called them "Howells" and "Joe." The distinctions suggest duality of attitudes, yet Clemens-Mark was surely not an entirely different person for each of his intimates. Still, there were probably variations in behavior.

Twichell, as the audience for the first reading of that bawdy sketch "1601," which he thought hilariously funny, is in keeping with an easy association fostered by the neighborly habits of Nook Farm. Apparently their conversations were uninhibited, as befitted the casual camaraderie that existed between them. Twichell, a Civil War chaplain accustomed to the rough talk of army camps, was tolerant of his friend's earthy mode of expression and his spectacular profanity.

The relationship with Howells may have been more formal, but he testifies in *My Mark Twain* that his friend had "the Southwestern, the Lincolnian, the Elizabethan breadth of parlance, which I suppose one ought not to call coarse without calling one's self prudish." Since he is, in effect, calling himself prudish, very likely Mark Twain made a point of trying to shock his sensibilities; at any rate, he did not modify his language out of deference to squeamishness. Howells also remarks, "I was often hiding away in discreet holes and corners the letters in which he had loosed his bold fancy to stoop on rank suggestion; I could not bear to burn them, and I could not, after the first reading, quite bear to look at them." Hence, Mark-Clemens must have been something of both his twin selves for both of his friends. Or as if, at times, Mark Twain and Clemens spoke with the same voice and used the same words.

One tenet of the divided personality theory is that the man called Mark Twain played a role of his own creation. No doubt. He was his own best public relations advocate, and we all know how diligently a PR man labors to fashion an attractive image of his client. In an after-dinner speech to a Boston club in 1907, he said: "One must keep one's character. Earn a character first if you can, and if you can't, then assume one." The inference is that he had done just that.

In another speech (1902), he told of riding on an elevated train and of being approached by a stranger who said, "I have never seen Mark Twain, but I have seen a portrait of him . . . and I can tell you . . . that you look enough like Mark Twain to be his brother. Now, I hope you take that as a compliment." Mark Twain replied:

Certainly, I take it as more than a compliment. Yes, this is the proudest moment of my life to be taken for Mark Twain, for most men are always wishing to look like some great man, General Grant, George Washington, or like some Archbishop or other, but all my life I have wanted to look like Mark Twain. Yes, I have wished to look like that synonym, that symbol of all virtue and purity, whom you have just described. I appreciate it. . . . In my desire to look like that excellent character I have dressed for the character; I have been playing a part.

Perhaps that story was one of his stretchers. Nevertheless, we may ponder its implications, as well as the hint in yet another speech (1902) when he said: "As a rule, we go about with masks, we go about looking honest, and we are able to conceal ourselves all through the day."

These several allusions support the argument that Mark Twain created an image, which, it is generally assumed, was at odds with his genuine being, whatever that was. Possibly he himself was not sure what it was. As Hawthorne says of Dimmesdale in *The Scarlet Letter,* "No man, for any considerable period, can wear one face to himself, and another to the multitude, without finally getting bewildered as to which may be the true."

If Mark Twain was puzzled, we should not be surprised that outlines become indistinct and that outward image and private image merge and exchange places. In this volume some pieces signed *Mark Twain* are fraught with sober purpose, as if he were the serious thinker; others, signed *S. L. Clemens,* are flippant as befits the jester. Episodes like that in the Hartford home when householder Clemens entertained guests with a hoedown, and later in New York, as previously mentioned, with a burlesque temperance lecture, reveal him in the role of Mark Twain, public showman working for laughs.

Reversal of roles increases confusion, which might be partially dissipated if we concede that the character known as Mark Twain may have been as close to the core of reality as the man called Clemens. When he introduced himself to audiences on the lyceum circuit as "the lecturer of the evening, Mr. Clemens, otherwise known as Mark Twain," he implied that the two names were interchangeable, one as accurate as the other. We might also inquire whether attributes ascribed to Mark Twain are also visible in Sam Clemens before he adopted the pen name and became a public figure in need of an image.

The foregoing paragraphs about Clemens-Twain are not strictly relevant to the contents and purpose of this book. They are a digression into a sort of amateur psychoanalysis, interesting to me but not really necessary. If somewhat skeptical about dualism, I am not beyond conviction. Nevertheless, to me the man has always been Mark Twain, and that name I have used throughout, recognizing the contradictions, inconsistencies, and exasperating vagaries of his enigmatic character.

──{ *ACKNOWLEDGMENTS* }──

am grateful to everybody in the Bancroft Library, which, when I was there, was under the amiable direction of John Barr Tompkins, now retired. Operated by a helpful staff, it was a most pleasant place to work. Another pleasant place was The Mark Twain Papers in the general library of the University of California at Berkeley. Best thanks to Fred Anderson and aides there. For supplying textual material and other assistance, I am indebted to Christine R. Longstreet, University of Chicago; Alfred N. Brandon, New York Academy of Medicine Library; Dorothy Brickett, Hartford Public Library; the people of the Purdue University Library and of the West Lafayette, Indiana, Public Library. My wife, Roberta, has assisted with encouragement and forbearance. She is also a sharp-eyed proofreader and skillful at inducing a typewriter to work when it becomes sullen and stubborn. Finally, I appreciate the help of William J. Whalen, director; Diane Dubiel and Verna Emery, past and present managing editors; James McCammack, graphic designer; and others affiliated with the Purdue University Press.

After abortive mining adventures in Nevada Territory, Sam Clemens arrived in Virginia City in the latter part of September 1862 to become a reporter on the Territorial Enterprise. *On his first day on the job, as he tells the story in* Roughing It, *he filled his two nonpareil columns by embroidering elaborate fiction upon a minimum of fact. Observing one hay wagon, hardly a newsworthy object, he multiplied it by sixteen, brought it into town from sixteen directions, and "got up such another sweat about hay as Virginia City had never seen in the world before." Happening upon a saloon brawl in which one man was killed, he wrote up the episode with suitable embellishments. Finding a wagon train that had encountered Indians, he talked to an emigrant, then invented lurid details of scalpings and killings that, he says, "put this wagon through an Indian fight that to this day has no parallel in history." The account which follows may be that story. No conclusive evidence suggests the manner of the future Mark Twain, but the report was published in the* Enterprise *soon after his arrival, and it is sensational enough to merit the description in* Roughing It. *It is offered here as perhaps one of the new reporter's earliest contributions to the paper.[1] Virginia City referred to here and later on was also known as Virginia.*

THE INDIAN TROUBLES
ON THE OVERLAND ROUTE

VIRGINIA CITY *Territorial Enterprise,* OCTOBER 1, 1862;
REPRINTED IN MARYSVILLE, CALIFORNIA, *Daily Appeal,*
OCTOBER 5, 1862

Twelve or fifteen emigrant wagons[2] arrived here on Monday evening, and all but five moved on towards California yesterday. One of the five wagons which will remain in the city is in charge of a man from Story County, Iowa, who started across the plains on the 5th of May last, in company with a large train composed principally of emigrants from his own section.

From him we learn the following particulars: When in the vicinity of Raft River,[3] this side of Fort Hall,[4] the train was attacked, in broad daylight, by a large body of Snake Indians. The emigrants, taken entirely by surprise—for they had apprehended no trouble—made but a feeble resistance, and retreated, with a loss of six men and one woman of their party. The Indians also captured the teams belonging to thirteen wagons, together with a large number of loose

1

cattle and horses. The names of those killed in the affray are as follows: Charles Bulwinkle, from New York; William Moats, Geo. Adams and Elizabeth Adams, and three others whose names our informant had forgotten.

The survivors were overtaken in the afternoon by a train numbering 111 wagons, which brought them through to Humboldt.[5] They occasionally discovered the dead bodies of emigrants by the roadside; at one time twelve corpses were found, at another four, and at another two—all minus their scalps. They also saw the wrecks of many wagons destroyed by the Indians. Shortly after the sufferers by the fight recorded above had joined the large train, it was also fired into in the night by a party of Snake Indians, but the latter, finding themselves pretty warmly received, drew off without taking a scalp.

About a week before these events transpired, a party of emigrants numbering 40 persons was attacked near City Rocks by the same tribe of uncivilized pirates.[6] Five young ladies were carried off, and, it is thought, women and children in all to the number of fifteen. All the men were killed except one, who made his escape and arrived at Humboldt about the 20th of September. This train was called the "Methodist Train," which was not altogether inappropriate, since the whole party knelt down and began to pray as soon as the attack was commenced.

Every train which has passed over that portion of the route in the vicinity of City Rocks since the 1st of August has had trouble with the Indians. When our informant left Humboldt several wagons had just arrived whose sides and covers had been transformed into magnified nutmeg graters by Indian bullets. The Snakes corralled the train, when a fight ensued, which lasted forty-eight hours. The whites cut their way out, finally, and escaped. We could not learn the number of killed and wounded at this battle.

In the same issue, the Enterprise *also published the following account, but whether it was part of the foregoing story is not clear.*[7]

Mr. L. F. Yates, who arrived in this city a few days since from Pike's Peak, has given us the following particulars of a fight his train had on the 8th of last August, about one and a half miles this side of the Lander's Cut-off and Fort Bridger roads. Their train consisted of 15 wagons and 40 men, with a number of women and children. The train was attacked while passing along a ravine by a party of Indians being concealed in among a thick growth of poplar bushes.

When the attack commenced, most of the front wagons were some 80 rods in advance. They formed in corral, and intrenched behind their wagons, refused the slightest aid to those who were struggling with the savages in the rear. The party thus left to fight their way through the ambushed Indians numbered but nine men, and there were but four guns to maintain the battle. Five of the nine were killed and one wounded. The names of the killed are as follows: Parmelee, James Steele, James A. Hart, Rufus C. Mitchell, from Central City, Colorado Territory, and McMahan, residence unknown; the name of the man wounded is Frank Lyman. He was shot through the lungs—recovered.

The thirty-one men who were hidden snugly behind their wagons, with a single honorable exception, refused to render the slightest assistance to those who were fighting for their lives and the lives of their families so near them. Although they had 27 guns they refused to lend a single gun, when at one time four men went to seek assistance. The cowards all clung to their arms, and lay trembling behind their wagons. A man named Perry, or Berry, was the only one who had sufficient courage to attempt to render his struggling friends any assistance. He was shot in the face before reaching the rear wagons, and was carried back to the corral. The fight lasted nearly two hours, and some seven or eight Indians were killed, as at various times they charged out of the bushes on their ponies. Several Indian horses were killed, and at length the few left alive fought through to where their thirty heroic friends (?) were corraled, leaving the killed and two wagons in possession of the Indians. Thirty bigger cowards and meaner men than those above mentioned never crossed the plains; we are certain that every man of them left the States for fear of being drafted into the army.

1. *No file of the* Enterprise *is known to exist for the years of Mark Twain's stay in Virginia City, but a scattering of material from its columns can be recovered from reprintings in other papers. Editors in Nevada and California borrowed freely from one of the best known and most quoted dailies in the West.*

2. *Emigrants followed the Oregon-California trail, which ran along the south bank of the Platte River from Fort Kearney through what is now Nebraska, then into Wyoming and through South Pass to the great bend of the Snake River. There the trail divided, one fork heading northwest to the Oregon country, the other southwest to California. Sam Clemens and his brother Orion traveled over part of this trail on their stagecoach journey across the plains in the summer of 1861.*

3. *The river is located in what is now Cassia County, Idaho, one of the southernmost tier of counties.*

4. *In the eastern part of Idaho, the fort was not far from the Snake River in what is now Bingham County.*

5. *This mining district was about 175 miles northeast of Carson City, Nevada. The principal town was Unionville.*

6. *The expression faintly suggests the manner of the future Mark Twain. The reference to the "Methodist Train" is also suggestive, and the description of riddled wagon covers as looking like "magnified nutmeg graters" is typical of his imagery.*

7. *Remarks—occasionally bracketed, mostly unbracketed—inserted in italic type within the body of the text are those of the editor of this book.*

From the start of his Enterprise *career, Sam Clemens began to build up a reputation as a journalist of originality. The earliest story that is indubitably his was the account of the petrified man, published on October 4, 1862. Lifted by other papers all over the West, the hoax was followed by further items often audacious enough to attract the attention of papers elsewhere. After about four months on the job, he adopted the* nom de plume *of Mark Twain. The next article, which has Twainian tone and mannerisms, is almost certainly his. Although it was reprinted without a byline, the Stockton* Independent *credited it to the local editor of the* Enterprise *at a time when Mark Twain was temporarily filling that position in the absence of the regular local, Dan De Quille (William Wright). Other indications of Mark Twain's style, mentioned in the notes, go far to authenticate the authorship.*

SILVER BARS—HOW ASSAYED

VIRGINIA CITY *Territorial Enterprise,* N.D.; REPRINTED IN
STOCKTON, CALIFORNIA, *Daily Independent,* FEBRUARY 26, 1863

We propose to speak of some silver bars which we have been looking at, and to talk science a little, also, in this article, if we find that what we learned in the latter line yesterday has not escaped our memory. The bars we allude to were at the banking house of Paxton & Thornburgh, and were five in number; they were the concentrated result of portions of two eight-day runs of the Hoosier State Mill on Potosi rock. The first of the bricks bore the following inscription, which is poetry stripped of flowers and flummery,[1] and reduced to plain common sense: "No. 857; Potosi Gold and Silver Mining Company; Theall & Co., assayers; 688.48 ounces, gold, 020 fine, silver, 962 fine; gold $572.13, silver $1,229.47." Bars No. 836 and No. 858 bore about the same inscription, save that their values differed, of course, the one being worth $1,800, and the other a fraction under $1,300. The two largest bars were still in the workshop, and had not yet been assayed; one of them weighed nearly a hundred pounds and was worth about $3,000, and the other, which contained over 900 ounces, was worth in the neighborhood of $2,000. The weight of the whole five may be set down in round numbers at 300 pounds, and their value, at say, $10,000. Those are about the correct figures. We are very well pleased with the Hoosier State Mill and the Potosi mine—we think of buying them.

From the contemplation of this result of two weeks' mill and mining labor, we walked through the assaying rooms, in the rear of the banking house, with Mr. Theall, and examined the scientific operations there, with a critical eye. We absorbed much obtuse learning, and we propose to give to the ignorant the benefit of it. After the amalgam has been retorted at the mill,[2] it is brought here and broken up and put into a crucible (along with a little borax), of the capacity of an ordinary plug hat;[3] this vessel is composed of some kind of pottery which stands heat like a salamander;

the crucible is placed in a brick furnace; in the midst of a charcoal fire as hot as the one which the three Scriptural Hebrew children were assayed in;[4] when the mass becomes melted, it is well stirred, in order to get the metals thoroughly mixed, after which it is poured into an iron brick mould; such of the base metals as were not burned up, remain in the crucible in the form of a "sing."

The next operation is the assaying of the brick. A small chip is cut from each end of it and weighed; each of these is enveloped in lead and placed in a little shallow cup made of bone ashes, called a cupel, and put in a small stone-ware oven, enclosed in a sort of parlor stove furnace, where it is cooked like a lost sinner; the lead becomes oxidized and is entirely absorbed by the pores of the cupel—any other base metals that may still linger in the precious stew, meet the same fate, or go up the chimney. The gold and silver come from the cupel in the shape of a little button, and in a state of perfect purity; this is weighed once more, and what it has lost by the cooking process, determines the amount of base metal that was in it, and shows exactly what proportion of it the bar contains—the lost weight was base metal, you understand, and was burned up or absorbed by the cupel.

The scales used in this service are of such extremely delicate construction that they have to be shut up in a glass case, since a breath of air is sufficient to throw them off their balance—so sensitive are they, indeed, that they are even affected by the particles of dust which find their way through the joinings of the case and settle on them. They will figure the weight of a piece of metal down to the thousandth part of a grain, with stunning accuracy. You might weigh a mosquito here, and then pull one of his legs off, and weigh him again, and the scales would detect the difference. The smallest weight used—the one which represents the thousandth part of a grain—is composed of aluminum, which is the metallic base of common clay, and is the lightest metal known to science. It looks like an imperceptible atom clipped from the invisible corner of a piece of paper whittled down to an impossible degree of sharpness—as it were[5]—and they handle it with pincers like a hair pin.

But with an excuse for this interesting digression, we will return to the silver button again. After the weighing, melting and re-weighing of it has shown the amount of base metal contained in the brick, the next thing to be done is to separate the silver and gold in it, in order to find out the exact proportions of these in the bar. The button is placed in a mattrass filled with nitric acid, (an elongated glass bottle or tube, shaped something like a bell clapper) which is half buried in a box of hot sand—they call it a sand bath—on top of the little cupel furnace, where all the silver is boiled out of said button and held in solution, (when in this condition it is chemically termed "nitrate of silver"). This process leaves a small pinch of gold dust in the bottom of the mattrass which is perfectly pure; its weight will show the proportion of pure gold in the bar, of course. The silver in solution is then precipitated with muriatic acid (or something of that kind—we are not able to swear that this was the drug mentioned to us, although we feel very certain that it was), and restored to metal again. Its weight, by the mosquito scales, will show the proportion of silver contained in the brick, you know.

Now just here, our memory is altogether at fault. We cannot recollect what in the world it is they do with the "dry cups." We asked a good many questions about them—asking questions is our regular business—but we have forgotten the answers. It is all owing to lager beer.[6] We are inclined to think, though, that after the silver has been precipitated, they cook it a while in those little chalky-looking "dry cups," in order to turn it from fine silver dust to a solid button again for the sake of convenient handling—but we cannot begin to recollect anything about it.

We said they made a separate assay of the chips cut from each end of a bar; now if these chips do not agree—if they make different statements as to the proportions of the various metals contained in the bar, it is pretty good proof that the mixing was not thorough, and the brick has to be melted over again; this occurrence is rare, however. This is all the science we know. What we do not know is reserved for private conversation, and will be liberally inflicted upon anybody who will come here to the office and submit to it.

After the bar has been assayed, it is stamped as described in the beginning of this dissertation, and then it is ready for the mint. Science is a very pleasant subject to dilate upon,[7] and we consider that we are as able to dilate upon it as any man that walks—but if we have been guilty of carelessness in any part of this article, so that our method of assaying as set forth herein may chance to differ from Mr. Theall's, we would advise that gentleman to stick to his own plan nevertheless, and not go to following ours—his is as good as any known to science. If we have struck anything new in our method, however, we shall be happy to hear of it, so that we can take steps to secure to ourself the benefits accruing therefrom.

1. *The remark has a Twainian ring.*

2. *In hard rock mining, amalgamation is the process by which the precious metals are separated from pulverized ore by combining with quicksilver, from which they are again separated by heat or pressure.*

3. *This image is typical of Mark Twain. Others are "stands heat like a salamander," "cooked like a lost sinner," "a sort of parlor stove furnace," and the fanciful description of the aluminum weight that "looks like an imperceptible atom clipped from the invisible corner of a piece of paper whittled down to an impossible degree of sharpness."*

4. *Mark Twain frequently alluded to scriptural episodes and quoted biblical passages.*

5. *A tag he put into his writing as a reporter, using it so often that it became an annoying habit.*

6. *Since thirst for lager was almost universal in Washoe, this reference does not conclusively identify Mark Twain, but he was known in Virginia and elsewhere as a connoisseur of the brew. A brewery announced in the Como, Nevada, Sentinel of June 4, 1864, that its beer was "the best in the Territory, as we can prove by 'Mark Twain,' who has sat in the brewery and drank 'gallons and gallons' of it without arising from his seat." A remarkable feat in more ways than one.*

7. *The informality throughout, the rhythms of easy talk, the mixture of objective fact and imaginative editorializing—all are in the manner of Mark Twain, who was not a conventional reporter. The whole has an air that may be difficult to define precisely, but it bears the stamp of his casual style. The account is more lively than his explanation of assaying in chapter 36 of* Roughing It, *but there are similarities, and the method of procedure is the same in both.*

Joe Goodman, editor of the Enterprise, *kept a loose rein on his talented staff, who had more freedom to express themselves than is generally permitted in a city newspaper office. The circumstances suited the temperamental Mark Twain, who would much rather write about something that never happened than to relate the humdrum story of mining equipment and statistics. When he struck up a friendship with another reporter, Clement T. Rice, dubbed "the Unreliable," of the Virginia Union, both took potshots at each other in their respective papers, carrying on a mock feud that went on for some time in 1863. This fragment of the pseudo-obituary is part of one round in the exchange of salvos.*

MARK TWAIN ON "THE UNRELIABLE"
Virginia City *Territorial Enterprise,* n.d., Reprinted in
Marysville, California, *Daily Appeal,* February 28, 1863

He became a newspaper reporter, and crushed Truth to earth and kept her there; he bought and sold his own notes, and never paid his board; he pretended great friendship for Gillespie,[1] in order to get to sleep with him; then he took advantage of his bed fellow and robbed him of his glass eye and false teeth; of course he sold the articles, and Gillespie was obliged to issue more county scrip than the law allowed, in order to get them back again; the Unreliable broke into my trunk at Washoe City, and took jewelry and fine clothes and things, worth thousands and thousands of dollars; he was present, without invitation, at every party and ball and wedding which transpired in Carson during thirteen years. But the last act of his life was the crowning meanness of it; I refer to the abuse of me in the Virginia *Union* of last Saturday, and also to a list of Langton's stage passengers sent to the same paper by him, wherein my name appears between those of "Sam Chung" and "Sam Lee." This is his treatment of me, his benefactor. That malicious joke was his dying atrocity. During thirteen years he played himself for a white man; he fitly closed his vile career by trying to play me for a Chinaman.

He is dead and buried now, though; let him rest, let him rot. Let his vices be forgotten, but his virtues be remembered; it will not infringe much upon any man's time.

Mark Twain

P.S. By private letters from Carson, since the above was in print, I am pained to learn that the Unreliable, true to his unnatural instincts, came to life again in the midst of his funeral sermon, and remains so to this moment. He was always unreliable in life—he could not even be depended upon in death. The shrouded corpse shoved the coffin lid to one side, rose to a sitting position, cocked his eye at the minister and smilingly said, "O let up, Dominie, this is played out, you know—loan me two bits!" The frightened congregation rushed from the house, and the Unreliable followed them, with his coffin on his shoulder. He sold it for two dollars and a half, and got drunk at a "bit house"² on the proceeds. He is still drunk.

M.T.

1. *William M. Gillespie was a native of New York, who arrived in Virginia City in 1861. He was clerk of the first Nevada territorial legislature (1861); a delegate from Storey County to the constitutional conventions of 1863 and 1864, also acting as secretary; and a representative from Storey County to the third territorial legislature (1864).*
2. *A "bit house" was a saloon that dispensed cheap whiskey at one bit (12½ cents) per drink. Although historians do not clearly state how much was in it, the standard Washoe barroom tot was 2½ ounces.*

Mark Twain's status on the Enterprise *was something like that of the modern columnist, who writes on any topic that strikes his fancy. The next item is identified by Orion Clemens as coming from "Sam's Column." Orion kept a scrapbook of clippings, which is now in The Mark Twain Papers, University of California, Berkeley.*

NEW YEAR'S DAY
Virginia City *Territorial Enterprise*, c. January 1, 1864

Now is the accepted time to make your regular annual good resolutions. Next week you can begin paving hell with them as usual. Yesterday, everybody smoked his last cigar, took his last drink, and swore his last oath. Today, we are a pious and exemplary community. Thirty days from now, we shall have cast our reformation to the winds and gone to cutting our ancient shortcomings considerably shorter than ever. We shall also reflect pleasantly upon how we did the same thing last year about this time. However, go in, community. New Year's is a harmless annual institution, of no particular use to anybody save as a scapegoat for promiscuous drunks, and friendly calls, and humbug resolutions, and we wish you to enjoy it with a looseness suitable to the greatness of the occasion.

Gunplay, knifing, and brawls occurred so frequently in Virginia City that newspaper accounts of murder and mayhem became perfunctory, as in the following story of events reported in one issue of the Enterprise. *The story has no particular touches characteristic of Mark Twain, yet, sharing the local beat with Dan De Quille, he may have had a hand in it. In the office they wrote at the same table, traded items, and very likely added bits to each other's copy. Possibly the account here is undramatic because straight reporting did not excite the imagination of Mark Twain. Inured to the chronic violence of Virginia, perhaps even bored by it, he may not have extended himself beyond a bare recital of the facts. At any rate, whether written by Mark Twain or Dan De Quille or both, the story describes the turbulent milieu in which the wild humorist of the Pacific slope served his literary apprenticeship.*

A BRISK BUSINESS IN THE SHOOTING AND SLASHING WAY IN WASHOE[1]
Virginia City *Territorial Enterprise,* March 8, 1864

About 1 o'clock yesterday afternoon P. H. Dowd, proprietor of the "Gem" saloon, South C street, was shot and probably fatally wounded by William Janes, a barkeeper in Daley's saloon. Janes and Dowd were formerly partners in the Gem saloon, but owing to some disagreement dissolved their partnership, Janes leaving and finding employment in Daley's establishment. Yesterday Janes went to the Gem, and after taking a drink commenced talking something about some business matters still remaining unsettled between himself and Dowd. They quarrelled, the lie passed, when Dowd threw a glass tumbler at Janes. This compliment Janes returned in kind by throwing a tumbler at Dowd. At this the parties drew their weapons and Janes fired two shots in quick succession at Dowd, the last of which struck him in the left breast, a little above the nipple, and glancing downward, broke the seventh rib and passed into his body in the region of the stomach.

At this stage of the affray Patrick Cox, a man employed about the saloon by Dowd, seeing his master shot, seized a 6-shooter and fired at Janes. Janes fired a shot or two at Cox, and was in the act of firing again when he was seized by Officer Leckey, and Marshal Perry at the same time arresting Cox. Janes pulled the trigger of his pistol just as it was caught hold of by Leckey, and the hammer came down and caught the officer's hand, slightly bruising it. No wounds were received by either Janes or Cox. Janes was lodged in the county jail and Cox in the city lock-up, though Cox was shortly released, as it did not appear that he did more than any other man would have done under similar circumstances. One of Janes's shots passed through Cox's vest, but without touching his person.

About 11 o'clock last night Dowd was reported to be dying. Drs. Bryant and Green were attending him, and from the first neither of these gentlemen had but small hopes of his recovery. Dowd is about 33 years of age, a native of county Langford, Ireland, though he has resided in the United States since boyhood. He is a single man, and has been on the Pacific Coast since '50; he has been in the Territory about four years, is chief owner of the well known "David" mine, and was for some time employed as a carpenter by the Central Mining Company.

A shooting scrape occurred at the Clipper Saloon, B street, on Sunday night, between Jack McNabb and a stranger whose name we could not learn. According to the story of an eye-witness, the stranger was abusing a harmless individual known as "Drunken Jimmy," when McNabb came up and remonstrated against such treatment of an inoffensive man. The matter ended there and all parties adjourned to the saloon to take a drink, but while standing at the bar, the stranger made an insulting remark to McNabb, who promptly replied in kind. The stranger drew a revolver, fired two shots, received one in return, and then cleared out. One of the stranger's shots damaged McNabb's vest to some extent, and passed through a couple of letters in his pocket, but did no injury to his person, while the ball from the latter's pistol peeled a strip from the stranger's forehead which a small amount of doctoring will restore. After the occurrence McNabb gave himself up to Marshal Perry.

Last evening about 8 o'clock Mike Haley got into a dispute with another man on C street, above Taylor, about a chicken fight, and words no longer sufficing as argument concluded to resort to the soft persuasion of the derringer.[2] In drawing or in cocking the tool, it was by some means discharged, and its contents passed through the palm of his left hand, breaking the bones of the two middle fingers and badly mangling the hand. He was brought to the station-house and Dr. Bryerly called for, who gave his hand the attention it required. During the evening he was released, and went off to where he could better nurse his pet hand.

John Boyd, engaged in wood-chopping, on what is known as Newton Canon, about 7 miles north of this city, was found in his cabin on Saturday last, murdered and mangled in a horrible manner.[3] A bloody axe was found in the cabin, which was doubtless the instrument used in doing the fiendish deed. Boyd appears to have been at supper when attacked, as his legs lay partly under the table when his body was discovered, and food was still on the table. One of his arms was almost severed from his body; his head showed on the back part a gash as though the whole bit of an axe had been struck into it; and his head was nearly cut off by a blow across the neck.

The murder is supposed to have been committed by a California Indian, who was in Boyd's employ, and whom he brought from California, as the Indian, a pair of blankets, a large butcher knife and a lot of bread is gone. The murder was first discovered on Saturday evening, after dark, by a negro man named William Jackson, who was employed by Boyd, and who had come to this city the night before to buy an axe. Arriving at the cabin after dark, on entering, Bill stumbled over something on the floor, which appeared like a body, and which he supposed to be the Indian, as it was near the spot usually occupied by him when sleeping. On lighting a match, however, he discovered the dead and mangled body of Boyd, and immediately ran off to a neighbor's house and gave the alarm.

Several persons went to the cabin and examined the body and its surroundings. There was a considerable quantity of blood on the table, as though it had spouted out from a wound received while standing. The blood on the table and scattered around the cabin was quite dry, and showed that the murder must have been committed about Friday evening. Bill, the colored man, says that Boyd had $9 in coin, $5 of which he gave him to bring with him to town, to buy an axe and pay his expenses while in the town, and the balance of which $4, he put into his pocket. When Boyd's body was found, his pockets were turned inside out and the four dollars gone.

An inquest was held on the body on Sunday by the Coroner of Washoe county, the verdict being, we presume—though we have not heard it—in accordance with the above. Boyd was from Napa county, California, where he has a considerable amount of property, and where he has a wife and family. He was a very clever and industrious man, and all who knew him speak well of him. There are many persons in the city who were well acquainted with him in California. The Indian who is supposed to be his murderer was from Eel river, and is known to persons here. Dispatches have been sent to California for his arrest, should he pass over the mountains by any of the principal routes.

There was something of a muss Sunday night in a C street hurdy-house.[4] Grand result, a whipped Mexican and a victorious Irishman. No arrests—no cards.

The voters of the Fourth Ward behaved in an orderly manner yesterday.[5] They didn't fight a single fight and gave no cause for a single arrest.

A man was arrested on Sunday, on B street, who was crazy drunk, and rushing about the streets with a big knife, offering to attack everybody who came in his way. He was placed in the lock-up after some difficulty, though he was so wild that it took the Sheriff and some three or four men to get him to the station-house.

Gortey, the man who was shot a few nights ago by the fellow Siefetill, is now in a fair way of recovery, and his physicians express the belief that he will not die, at least for the present; notwithstanding that he has been reported dead several times, and his slayer reported hanged by the Vigilance Committee.

1. *In the West, Nevada Territory was generally referred to as Washoe, the name probably derived from the Indian word* washiu, *meaning "a person," also from the Washo Indians, a small tribe that lived along the Truckee and Carson rivers and around Lake Tahoe. California papers delighted to publish stories of Washoe disorder, then to sermonize, rather self-righteously, on the shocking state of society over there. The San Francisco* Evening Bulletin, *which reprinted the above* Enterprise *story on March 10, 1864, and which, for lack of space, omitted a midnight robbery and a woman-whipper, remarked that the items made "a pretty catalogue* for one day's reporting *of crimes of violence against the person," and concluded: "It would be hard anywhere to beat this record, even in the worst days of San Francisco."*

2. *The expression faintly suggests the manner of Mark Twain.*

3. *The mangled corpse and the item about the wild man looking for somebody to carve up with a butcher knife are reminiscent of Mark Twain's "Bloody Massacre," a hoax he published in the* Enterprise *on October 28, 1863. It is the gory and fictional tale of P. Hopkins who, in a fit of insane rage, kills his wife and seven of his nine children with axe and club, then rides into Carson with his throat cut from ear to ear, and falls off his horse, dead, in front of the Magnolia Saloon. Widely reprinted throughout the West, the story was received with shock and horror until the hoax was exposed; whereupon a tempest of indignation and reproof burst upon Mark Twain.*

4. *A "hurdy-house" was a dance hall. It was an essential institution in a mining town, along with the saloon and a red light sisterhood. Virginia was well supplied in all departments. On duty in a hurdy-house was a corps of girls who were taxi dancers, paid for each dance, often a bonus when a man was in a happy mood. Unlikely to be glamorous, the feminine partners were usually buxom and sturdy, as they had to be to withstand a long evening of being swirled around by miners and stepped on by heavy boots. A hurdy-*

house was likely to be noisy, frequently rowdy, but it was not more iniquitous than other gathering places in a town like Virginia, and the girls were not professional trollops. In musical language, a hurdy-gurdy was a flutelike stringed instrument that produced sound by the friction of a resined wheel turned by a crank, but the dance music in a hurdy-house was more likely to be provided by a fiddler or piano player or both. In mining terms, a hurdy-gurdy was a water wheel propelled by the direct impact of a stream of water upon its paddles, but that device had nothing to do with a hurdy-house.

5. The brief reference to law-abiding citizens illustrates the journalist's credo that innocuous propriety was not—and is not to this day—as newsworthy as violence. Dismissing in two short sentences the peaceful voters who "behaved in an orderly manner" strikes a note of irony typical of Mark Twain and Dan De Quille.

Although the next squib is not positively identified as Mark Twain's, indications of his authorship are there. It may serve as a mild example of the drubbing in print he administered now and then to various citizens, politicos, and others, who had aroused his ire. These assaults, we are told, were often virulent enough to make him disliked and feared. Because of such blasts and his fondness for tall tales, he became known as a wild and unpredictable humorist.

GASHWILER AND FUNK
VIRGINIA CITY *Territorial Enterprise*, N.D., REPRINTED IN AMADOR, CALIFORNIA, *Weekly Ledger*, APRIL 30, 1864

Yesterday morning Gashwiler and Charley Funk, citizens of Virginia City and of the Territory of Nevada, and officers of the great Virginia and Gold Hill Water Company,[1] came rushing into our office in a state of excitement bordering on lunacy, and pointed out to us the following advertisement in the *Evening Bulletin*,[2] with a fierce demand upon us to read it and render unto them our opinion concerning it:

In the last day, that great day of the feast, Jesus stood and cried, saying: If any man thirst, let him come unto me and drink. St. John, vii, 27.

Whosoever drinketh of the water that I shall give him shall never thirst; but the water that I shall give him shall be in him a well of water springing up into everlasting life. St. John, iv, 14.

The lamb, which is in the midst of the throne, shall feed them, and shall lead them unto living fountains of waters, and God shall wipe away all tears from their eyes. Rev., vii, 17.

We ask, now, in all candor, if there is a man in all Virginia who is competent by reason of his extraordinary natural or acquired stupidity, to guess what these gentlemen found in the above extracts to fill their souls with rage? As we hope for mercy past and present, they thought it was an attempt to ring in an opposition water company on the people! We call that infernal ignorance[3]—and if we could think of a stronger term Gashwiler and Charley Funk should have the benefit of it. When men get so far gone that they do not know the Sermon on the Mount from a bid for a water franchise,[4] it is time for them to begin to reform and stop taking chances on the hereafter.

1. *Just over the Divide a few miles from Virginia City, Gold Hill was close enough to be something like a suburb.*
2. *Founded in 1863, the* Evening Bulletin *gave Virginia three daily papers, not bad for a town of its size. The* Democratic Standard, *founded by southern sympathizers in 1864, made a fourth, but the paper died after about two months.*
3. *Infernal was a favorite adjective of Mark Twain. He used it so often that it became a stereotype.*
4. *As already noted, Mark Twain was familiar with the Bible, a lifelong reader and satirical critic of scripture. See Allison Ensor,* Mark Twain and the Bible *(Lexington: University of Kentucky Press, 1969).*

In May 1864, Mark Twain's newspaper career in Virginia City ended abruptly when he became involved in an altercation with James Laird, editor of the Virginia Union, *and was inveigled into issuing a challenge to a duel. No shots were fired in this ridiculous affair, but Mark Twain hastily departed for California to avoid being apprehended for violation of Nevada's antidueling law. In San Francisco, he was a reporter for a time on the* Morning Call, *but bored as usual by a routine job, he was not an enthusiastic newsman and after a few months left the paper, probably by request. The following story, evidently not written for the* Call, *shows Mark Twain in a typical dual role of reporter and editorializing moralist.*

IMMORALITY IN SAN FRANCISCO
DOWNIEVILLE, CALIFORNIA, *Mountain Messenger,* JULY 1, 1865

Immorality is not decreasing in San Francisco. I saw a girl in the city prison last night who looked as much out of place as I did myself, possibly more so. She was petite and diffident, and only sixteen years and one month old. To judge by her looks, one would say she was as sinless as a child. But such was not the case. She had been living with a strapping young nigger for six months! She told her story as artlessly as a schoolgirl, and it did not occur to her for a moment that she had been doing anything unbecoming; and I never listened to a narrative which seemed more simple and straight-forward, or more free from ostentation and vain-glory. She told her name and her age to a day; she said she was born in Holborn, City of London; father living, but gone back to England; was not married to the negro, but she was left, without any one to take care of her, and he had taken charge of that department and had conducted it since she was fifteen and a half years old very satisfactorily. All listeners pitied her, and said feelingly: "Poor heifer! Poor devil!" and said she was an ignorant, erring child, and had not done wrong wilfully and knowingly, and they hoped she would pass her examination for the Industrial School and be removed from the temptation and opportunity to sin. Tears—and it was a credit to their manliness and good feeling—tears stood in the eyes of those stern policemen.

O, woman, thy name is humbug! Afterwards, while I sat

taking some notes and not in sight from the women's cell, some of the old blisters fell to gossiping, and lo! young Simplicity chipped in and chattered away as lively as the vilest of them! It came out in the conversation that she was a hail fellow well met with all the old female rapscallions in the city, and had had business relations with their establishments for a long time past. She spoke affectionately of some of them, and the reverse of others; and dwelt with a toothsome relish upon numberless reminiscences of her social and commercial intercourse with them. She knew all manner of men, too—men with quaint and suggestive names, for the most part—and liked "Oyster-eyed Bill," and "Bloody Mike," and "The Screamer," but cherished a spirit of animosity toward "Foxy McDonald" for cutting her with a bowie-knife at a strumpet ball one night. *She* a poor innocent kitten! Oh! She was a scallawag whom it would be base flattery to call a prostitute! She a candidate for the Industrial School! Bless you, she has graduated long ago. She is competent to take charge of a University of Vice. In the ordinary branches she is equal to the best; and in the higher ones, such as ornamental swearing, and fancy embroidered filagree slang, she is a shade superior to any artist I ever listened to.

After leaving the Call, *to the satisfaction of both employer and employed, Mark Twain was a free-lancer, contributing to the* Californian *and the* Golden Era, *best known weekly on the West Coast. In the* Era *from July 2 to August 27, 1865, a series of eight articles credited to S. Browne Jones were undoubtedly written by Mark Twain. The first one, which follows, is very much in his vein of Washoe humor. The second, on July 9, entitled "An Astounding Fraud Practiced Upon Us," reveals that one "Marcus Twain" or "Swain" had imposed upon the* Era *by fraudulently writing under the name of S. Browne Jones. The third article, published on July 16, is a "Full Report of the Proceedings upon the Examination of Mark Twain on the Charge of Fraud, in the Police Court." After damaging testimony from several witnesses, the defendant, represented as editor of the nonexistent San Francisco* Bohemian, *changes his plea to guilty and is sentenced to forty-eight hours in the city jail. The rigmarole is characteristic of Mark Twain, who was fond of hoaxes.*

A NEW CONTRIBUTOR
SAN FRANCISCO *Golden Era,* JULY 2, 1865

We take pleasure in announcing to our readers that we have secured the services of the eminent Smith B. Jones, Esq., whose arrival by the last steamer has already been announced, and who will henceforth contribute weekly to our columns.

Mr. Jones needs no introduction from us. His brilliant effusions have charmed the *literati* of both Europe and America, and are familiar to all. Although the literary services of Mr. Jones have been procured by us only at a large pecuniary outlay—as will be seen by the subjoined correspondence—yet we heartily congratulate ourselves as well as our readers on the acquisition of our new contributor.

On Tuesday last, we addressed Mr. Jones the following note:

Editorial Rooms "Golden Era,"
San Francisco, June 27th, 1865

Smith Brown Jones, Esq., Consequental Hotel

Dear Sir: Seeing your name in the list of arrivals by the steamship *Sacramento,* we take the liberty of addressing you at this early moment, to secure, if possible, the productions of your pen for the columns of the Era.

Pardon us for the business tenor of this note, and for any seeming intrusion upon your privacy. We are aware that the immense literary labors to which you have been subjected for years past have somewhat impaired your health, and that you have come to our golden shores to seek, in quiet and retirement, that rest so much needed; but our standing as the first literary paper of the Pacific coast—if not of the world—demands of us that we should not allow the opportunity to pass unheeded.

What we ask is but a mere dash of your pen. Our readers will be grateful for a weekly contribution—half a column or more in length—to suit your own convenience of course—and for which we will be glad to pay you at the rate of two hundred and fifty dollars per week.

We hope other engagements will not preclude your acceptance of our offer. Should our terms not meet your approval, please bind yourself to no periodical until we have had an interview.

Very Respectfully,
Editors Golden Era

In reply, we received the following somewhat incomprehensible production, which, however, we place before our readers, conscious that what flows from the pen of the gifted Jones—however erratic—must be esteemed as beyond price.

Consequental Hotel
San Francisco, June 28th, 1865

Editors Golden Era—

Gentlemen: In reply to your kind and flattering note, allow me to say at once that I accept your offer of the Senatorship. I do it advisedly, and without fear of contradiction.

Hon. John C——s[1] says, "Close at once with them!" John is a friend of mine—came out on the steamer—and, as I before remarked, advised me to appoint you next Senator—no—I mean you remarked me to advise you to appoint him in succession to Senator to be me. I'm afraid that is not quite clear. The fact is, I'm laboring under a slight indisposition, arising from change of water, I presume, although I've taken but very little. It's funny about that water. I felt the change before we got in sight of the Heads. C——s affects me in the same way, too. I mean, he affects the water in the same way. No, that's not it, either. What I mean to say is, the water affects him. I know it does. Said he, with tears in his eyes, "Jones, I love you. You are the apple of my eye—may we always be friends! Jones, vote for me!"

I assured him I would—that I always had from infancy. Shook my hand affectionately and asked me to go below. Immediately descended to his stateroom, in second cabin, and took a glass of lemonade at my expense. Talked of old times—of our adventures on the voyage—last day board ship—grew convivial, and took a glass of lemonade for which I paid. Said he was our only sober Senator, and sent for some lemonade—kindly allowed me to pay for it. Went on deck. John said, "There Jones! Can you see the Heads?"

Felt annoyed—thought John was too familiar—was indignant—rebuked him. "Lemonade doesn't affect me in that way, of course I can see ahead!"

Think that went home. John smiled sarcastic—said, "Don't mean can you see ahead—but can you see the Heads?"

Told him couldn't see anything else unless I stood on tiptoe, or went on upper deck—which Cap'n didn't allow to second-class passengers.

Saw at once lemonade affected my friend—laughed immoderately—said I had made a joke. Abjured me above all things to vote for him. Called my attention to Lime Point. Said he was concerned in the swindle—or at least he thought 'twas him. Said United States wanted to buy Lime Point—owners anxious to sell—in fact very anxious to sell—big price—big thing—pulled wool over U.S.—U.S. agreed to buy. Then he and Broderick[2]—but especially he—thought so at least—stepped in—advised U.S. not to buy—stood by U.S. like a brother. U.S. backed out—didn't buy—saved millions—didn't make a cent out of it himself—didn't, 'pon his word.

Asked me if I saw Meigg's wharf on right—Meiggs his friend but unfortunate. Said that was Alcatraz on my left. Immediately turned to gentleman on my left—Mr. Alcatraz—was happy to meet him—sorry friend John hadn't introduced him before. Think gentleman on left had a pain in stomach. Said intoxicated beast made him sick. Looked for intoxicated beast—didn't see him—saw John—John looked silly—asked me if I was sick, and if I didn't want to go ashore—said he'd introduce Gov. Low[3] to me—Gov. was friend of his—anxious to see him—I could vote for him, but he was tricky. Thought we'd better take a hack and he could dumfoozle Gov. every time.

Called hack. Hack said twenty dollars. Told him I'd see him first! John said to hush—said he'd make contract with hack—was great on contracts. Then we made contract. Hack said where did he want to go. Told him yes, we would, and how did he know it? Man said we would take him, ten dollars and the Russ House to us for three trunks—best carriage in State—both white—had preference for fast carriages that were white—always drove 'em.

Told man ten horses too much, would he give us fifteen. Man

with carriage impertinent. Think was intoxicated. Said he was
no member of Congress, and had no poor relations. Know man
was intoxicated. Tried to be funny—said I was drunk. John asked
him to sing—carriage and I was to come in heavy on the chorus.
Man failed to come to time. Said he couldn't sing except on flute.
All of him laughed—thought he was funny carriage—fact was,
all six of him was drunk.

John said 'twas time to go home—but would have one more
game—ten cent ante and his deal. Low's chance wasn't worth a
copper—he'd taken his straight. Also said he was sick—wished
he hadn't come, and asked policeman if he was on it and to
beware of bowl—intoxication was best policy, and he'd been a
missionary once himself. Policeman very attentive. John wanted
policeman to sing. Had great difficulty in getting policeman in
carriage. John felt bad—wanted to know where Gov. Low was—
said policeman was dearest friend—gave policeman his spectacles. Began to think John was 'toxicated. Said never min' ole
boy—may be happy yet. Wanted to know if Russ Hotel dead-
headed me—didn't cost him cent—asked policeman to dine with
him. Said if I paid, I'd better go to Consequental Hotel—chock
up house—and pay greenbacks.⁴ Said he was glad the war was
over and would call policeman Gen. McDowell⁵ and was glad to
see him.

Gen. McDowell—I mean policeman—borrowed two and a
half of me and said I was all right. Think he had been drinking
some, but apologized to him. Consequental House arrived—said
good-bye to John—John wept bitterly, and I am here, some
sickly, but

Truly yours,
S. B. Jones

1. *John Conness (1821-1909) was an American politician. An immi-
grant from Ireland, he was a forty-niner who was miner and merchant in
California before going into politics. In the state legislature(1853-54, 1860-
61), he was the Union Democratic party's candidate for governor in 1861,
but lost the election. He was United States senator from California (1863-
69), then gave up politics and later moved to Massachusetts where he
engaged in farming operations.*
2. *David Colbreth Broderick (1820-59) was an American politician. As
a young man in New York, he was a stubborn, self-centered, Irish saloon
owner schooled in the political tactics of Tammany Hall. In Congress*

(1846), he was a forty-niner who soon entered California politics. Elected to the state senate (1849), he became known as the unscrupulous boss of the Democratic party of California. When he became United States senator (1857), he attacked the Buchanan administration for its Kansas policy and became strongly antislavery. Thereafter he was more humane, advocating legislation of broad social significance. He was said to have been well read in history and a devotee of literature, Shelley being his favorite poet. His demise at an early age was the result of a duel with David S. Terry, a leading proslavery advocate of the United States Supreme Court.

3. Frederick Ferdinand Low (1828-94) was an American politician, diplomat, and banker. A native of Maine, he was a forty-niner who was a prospector on the American River, then merchant and banker in Marysville and San Francisco. After serving as Congressman-at-large from California (1862), he was governor (1863-67) and won a reputation for fearlessness and sound judgment. He aided in founding the University of California and kept Golden Gate Park out of the clutches of landgrabbers. He was United States minister to China (1870-74), then ended his career as joint manager of the Anglo-California Bank (1874-91). Low was not a brilliant man, but he was highly esteemed for good sense, honesty, courage, and friendliness.

4. Legal tender notes first issued by the United States government in February 1862 to defray the cost of the Civil War. Other issues of July 1862 and March 1863 raised the total to $450 million. As fiat money without adequate gold support, greenbacks immediately depreciated in value, sometimes being worth only 35 cents on the dollar. Nevertheless, agrarians and others organized a Greenback Party (1874), which advocated unlimited circulation of paper currency. In a 1902 sketch, "A Letter to the Secretary of the Treasury," Mark Twain, complaining of the high cost of fuel, orders forty-five tons of old dry government bonds for furnace use and "twelve tons early greenbacks, range size, suitable for cooking."

5. Irvin McDowell (1818-85) was an American soldier who attended West Point and became a brigadier general (1861). He organized the Army of the Potomac, then was reluctantly induced to attempt to dislodge Confederate forces at Manassas Junction. The resulting battle of Bull Run, almost a victory, ended in rout for McDowell's army. He was reduced to divisional commander assigned to the defense of Washington, and after the second Bull Run, he was relieved of field duties. In San Francisco (1864-68), he returned in 1876 and remained thereafter. McDowell was an able but unfortunate officer, an abstemious man, and a good disciplinarian, but as a leader he did not possess the temperament to inspire enthusiasm or warm admiration.

Following his short-lived and not very agreeable experience as a reporter for the Call, *Mark Twain, after an interlude out of town at Angel's Camp and Jackass Hill, became San Francisco correspondent of the Virginia City* Enterprise. *The job grew irksome, as routine tasks generally did, but for some months he kept at it, sending daily letters that were often reprinted by other papers. This story is one of those contributions.*

ROMANCE IN REAL LIFE

Virginia City *Territorial Enterprise,* n.d., Reprinted in
Redwood City, California, *San Mateo County Gazette,*
January 6, 1866

You all recollect young Stephenson, the actor, ballad singer, and sometimes stage manager, perfectly well—he who was lately blown up on the Yo Semite and killed? He is one of the heroes in the romance, and his infant son is another. I shall tell the story as I heard it, and aver that I believe it to be substantially correct and true in every particular.

Stephenson's real name was Carnagie, and he was the son of a wealthy Scotch gentleman—William Fytte Carnagie, of Edinburgh. His mother was divorced from his father and married Col. J. D. Stevenson, the ancient pioneer of "Stevenson's Regiment" notoriety. Young Carnagie grew up here, and fell in love with one of the pretty waiter girls employed in Gilbert's Melodeon,[1] in the days when such clerks were permitted in such places, and married her, in the face of the bitterest opposition on the part of the mother, and step-father. They at once discarded him, and he was obliged to go on the stage in order to gain a livelihood; he began as a ballad singer and assumed the name of his step-father as a stage name. His parents tried hard to get the marriage annulled, and brought the matter in court, charging that young Carnagie's wife was a prostitute before he married her. They failed to prove anything against the woman's character, however, and the marriage remained a valid contract. Carnagie continued on the stage to the time of his death, and was always a pleasant, kind-hearted and very quiet gentlemanly young fellow, and a useful actor, though not a genius.

I might as well mention, just here, a fact which you knew before—that the vengeful hatred of the parents survived the son's death and was visited upon the corpse. When the actor, Woodhull, called and told them that Carnagie was dead they manifested no feeling whatever—at least no sorrow for the event, and refused to receive or bury the corpse. The actors had the body of their late comrade shrouded and coffined, and left it at the undertaker's. In the meantime the papers shamed the parents into burying their despised son with their desecrating hands, and when the actors came next day with uncounterfeit sorrowing friendship to follow their dead comrade to the grave, they found that less worthy hands, but of nearer kin, had carried away the body in the night and consigned it to the earth.

News has just come over the sea from Scotland that the father of the dead actor has departed this life and left a fortune of half a million of dollars to his heir. Carnagie would have been sole heir to the property, but he being dead, his infant son, now four years of age, is heir to the whole fortune.

Now this would be but a tame romance if Mrs. Carnagie could clear right out to Scotland and put her hand on the money and deposit it in the bank and sit down and enjoy ease and affluence for all time to come. Fortunately for my story, though, she cannot inflict any such tameness upon it. It takes money to go to Scotland, even when one is going after money, and happily for the dramatic symmetry of this romance, the young widow Carnagie has no money. She is surrounded by difficulties. She could go if she had money if she could get hold of her late husband's wardrobe and sell it. But she cannot. She says her late husband boarded and lodged at the home of an actress well known on this coast—Miss Sallie Hinckley—for some time, and that Miss Hinckley refuses to give up the theatrical wardrobe, claiming that he had only the use of it, and that it did not belong to him. Mrs. Carnagie contends that it did belong to her husband and that Mr. Maguire also says he owns it.[2]

Now you have the romance. It is a very good one as it is, but it would be still better if somebody would run off with the child and scrape all the mysterious strawberry marks off its person so that it could never be identified by any one.

1. *A melodeon was a place of entertainment something like a music hall, noisy and generally rowdy. As implied by Mark Twain's comment on "such places," genteel people looked upon a melodeon as not quite respectable.*

2. *Thomas Maguire was the principal theatrical impresario of the West Coast. Proprietor of Maguire's Opera House in San Francisco, he brought in touring companies and imported from the East celebrities like Artemus Ward and Adah Isaacs Menken. He also established an opera house in Virginia City.*

Of his life in San Francisco from 1864 to 1866, Mark Twain's account in Roughing It *tells of a hand-to-mouth existence, in which he was occasionally solvent, often broke, living on credit, and reduced to the seedy status of a bum on skid row. The story, if inaccurate in detail, is in keeping with his checkered career in the Bay City and with his character as a man who liked to live well and who, when he was in funds, seldom laid anything by for a rainy day. Being a daily* Enterprise *correspondent might be a boring job, but he stayed with it until, he says, "At the end of five months I was out of debt." To fill his letters to the paper, he wrote about all sorts of minor experiences.*

MARK TWAIN AT
THE ORLEANS HOTEL, SACRAMENTO
Virginia City *Territorial Enterprise,* n.d., Reprinted in Grass Valley, California, *Union,* March 7, 1866

I got down stairs at ten minutes past twelve, and went up to the landlord, who is a large fine-looking man, with a chest on him which must have made him a most powerful man before it slid down, and said, "Is breakfast ready?"

"Is breakfast ready?" said he.

"Yes; is breakfast READY?"

"Not quite," he says, with the utmost urbanity; "not quite, you have arisen too early, my son, by a matter of eighteen hours, as near as I can come at it."

Humph! I said to myself, these people go slow up here; it is a wonder to me that they ever get up at all.

"Ah, well," said I, "it don't matter—it don't matter. But ah—perhaps you design to have lunch this week, some time?"

"Yes," he says, "I have designed all along to have lunch this week, and by a most happy coincidence you have arrived on the very day. Walk into the dining room."

As I walked forward I cast a glance of chagrin over my shoulder, and observed, "Old Smarty, from Mud Springs, I apprehend."

And he murmured, "Young Lunar Caustic, from San Francisco, no doubt."

Well, let it pass. If I didn't make anything off that old man in the way of "sass," I cleaned out his lunch table, anyhow. I calculated to get ahead of him in some way. And yet I don't know but the old scalliwag came out pretty fair, after all; because I only staid[1] in his hotel twenty-four hours, and ate one meal, and he charged me five dollars for it. If I were not just ready to start back to the Bay now, I believe I would go and tickle him once more. If I only had a fair chance, that old man is not any smarter than I am. [I will risk something that it makes him squirm every time I call him "that old man" in this letter. People who voted for General Washington don't like to be reminded that they are old.] But I like the old man; and I like his hotel, too, barring the d— barring the fountain, I should say.

1. *The spelling of* staid *is one of Mark Twain's idiosyncrasies. Although allowed by Webster's Unabridged as a variant of* stayed, *the latter is customary, but Mark Twain, who prided himself on his spelling, consistently used* staid.

Upper left: *"The American Humorists"* (left to right) *Josh Billings, Mark Twain, and Petroleum V. Nasby in a photo published by G. M. Baker of Boston circa 1869. (From The Mark Twain Papers.)* Lower left: *Mark Twain in early middle years. (From the Franklin J. Meine collection.)*

In his Enterprise *correspondence, Mark Twain probably put into any one letter a variety of topics and wrote about several incidents, real or imaginary. The method was convenient for editors of other papers who lifted segments of suitable length to fill their columns. The following item may have been part of a medley based upon his visit to the capital.*

A REMINISCENCE, BY MARK TWAIN

VIRGINIA CITY *Territorial Enterprise,* N.D., REPRINTED IN UNIONTOWN, NEVADA, *Humboldt Register,* MARCH 10, 1866

And speaking of steamboats reminds me of an incident of my late trip to Sacramento. I want to publish it, as showing how going north on the river gradually enfeebles one's mind, and accounts for the strange imbecility of legislators who leave here sensible men and become the reverse, to the astonishment of their constituents, by the time they reach their seats in the Capitol at Sacramento. John Paul, Lieutenant Ellis and myself went up with Captain Poole to his room on the *Antelope* at 10 o'clock last Saturday night,[1] and by way of amusement we instigated an intellectual game. John Paul recited the first line of "Hohenlinden":[2]

"On Linden, when the sun was low,"
I recited the second:
"All bloodless lay the untrodden snow,"
Lieut. Ellis the third:
"And dark as winter was the flow"
John Paul the fourth:
"Of Iser, rolling rapidly."

Lieut. Ellis began the next verse, and we went through it regularly, as before.

Bill Stevenson was umpire. He held the watch, allowed a man ten seconds to recollect the line, and if he couldn't, called "Time!" and "passed the deal" to the next, and the delinquent had to send for the whiskey. Or if a man misquoted a word, Bill checked the mistake on his memorandum, and it was good for four drinks. Well, we went through the whole poem, and only one mistake, of a single little word, was made. The drinks were ordered. We went through it again; result, one mistake, and whiskey. We repeated the operation; result, three misquotations, and three whiskies all around. We stayed with that poem all the way to Sacramento, arriving there at three in the morning, and here is the way the first verse of "Hohenlinden" stood the last time we recited it:

Myself: "On London when the tray was low—"
John Paul: "The curfew tolled the knell of parting day:"
Lieut. Ellis: "This world is all a fleeting show—"
Myself: [Hic!] "Berer dog'n ole dog Tray!"

Bill Stevenson said: "Texas, bring four quarts of whiskey and charge to these gentlemen—such stupidity as this must be severely punished!"

1. *During flush times in California, the* Antelope *carried so much gold dust and bullion down the Sacramento River from the mother lode that she became known as "The Gold Boat."*

2. *The poem was the work of Thomas Campbell (1777–1844), a prim Scotsman who lived most of his life in London and wrote poetry that appeared in American schoolbooks of the nineteenth century. No doubt Mark Twain had heard "Hohenlinden" recited by schoolmates in Hannibal and perhaps had memorized it himself, along with others of Campbell's poems, like "Lochiel's Warning" and "Ye Mariners of England."*

The following story is of an incident that supposedly occurred on the maiden voyage of the steamship Ajax *to the Sandwich Islands. Lewis Leland, the central character, was manager of the Occidental Hotel in San Francisco, a popular haunt of newspapermen and other writers. On the second voyage of the* Ajax, *which began on March 7, 1866, Mark Twain himself embarked for the islands as correspondent for the Sacramento* Union. *He sent back long letters about the islanders, their country, customs, and so forth, later incorporating much of the material in chapters 62–78 of* Roughing It. *He found the balmy climate, lush vegetation, and tropical languor so enchanting that always thereafter he thought of the Sandwich Islands as an earthly paradise.*

THE MAIDEN VOYAGE OF THE AJAX
VIRGINIA CITY *Territorial Enterprise*, N.D., REPRINTED IN
EUREKA, NEVADA, *Humboldt Times*, MARCH 17, 1866

Lewis Leland, of the Occidental, was a passenger. There was some savage grizzly bears chained in cages on deck. One night in the midst of a hurricane, which was accompanied by rain and thunder and lightning, Mr. Leland came up, on his way to bed. Just as he had stepped into the pitchy darkness of the deck, and reeled to the still more pitchy motion of the vessel (bad), the captain sung out hoarsely through his speaking trumpet, "Bear a hand aft, there!" The words were sadly marred and jumbled, by the roaring wind, and Mr. Leland thought the captain said, "The bears are after you there!" and he "let go all holts" and went down into his boots. He murmured, "I knew how it was going to be—I just knew it from the start—I said all along that those bears would get loose some time, and now I'll be the first man that they'll snatch. Captain!—Captain!—can't hear me—storm roars so. Oh, God, what a fate! I have avoided wild beasts all my life, and now to be eaten by a grizzly bear in the middle of the ocean, a thousand miles from land! Captain! Oh, Captain!—bless my soul, there's one of them. I've got to cut and run."

And he did cut and run; and smashed through the door of the first stateroom he came to. A gentleman and his wife were in it. The gentleman exclaimed, "Who's that?" The refugee gasped out, "Oh, great Solomon, those bears are loose and are just raising merry hell all over the ship!'' and then sank down exhausted. The gentleman sprang out of bed and prepared for a siege. After a while, no assault being made, a reconnaisance was made from the window and a vivid flash of lightning revealed a clear deck. Mr. Leland then made a dart for his own stateroom, gained it, locked himself in, and felt that his body's salvation was accomplished, and by little less than a miracle.

Now I have told this story as I heard it from a passenger, who said he would vouch for every part of it except the language, which is stronger than Mr. Leland ever indulged in. The next day the subject of this memoir, though still very feeble and nervous, had the hardihood to make a joke upon his adventure. He said that when he found himself in so tight a place (as he thought) he didn't bear it with so much fortitude, and when he found himself safe at last in his stateroom, he regarded it as the bearest escape he had ever had in his life. He then went to bed, and did not get up again for nine days. This unquestionably bad joke cast a deep gloom over the ship's company, and no effort was sufficient to restore their wonted cheerfulness until the vessel reached her port and other scenes erased it from their memory.

When Mark Twain returned to San Francisco after a stay of some five months in the Sandwich Islands, he used material in his letters to the Sacramento Union *to compose a lecture, which he delivered in Maguire's Opera House on October 2, 1866. Then he took off on a speaking tour of mining towns in California and Nevada, winding up with a farewell lecture in San Francisco on December 10. At the time, official Washington was disturbed by the establishment in Mexico of a government headed by an emperor who was the Austrian Archduke Maximilian and supported by Napoleon III, as well as the presence of French troops. In February 1866, Secretary of State Seward, invoking the Monroe Doctrine, had dispatched to the French government a firm demand that its forces be withdrawn. The Civil War having ended, the United States could enforce the ultimatum by massing a veteran army on the border. Napoleon, who saw the point, agreed, and the French were in the process of retiring from Mexico, leaving Maximilian to his fate, which was capture by Juarez and execution in June*

1867. *Mark Twain's two letters that follow reflect the uncertainties of the military and diplomatic situation. As his own best publicity man, he capitalized on the affair to call attention to himself and to his lecture.*

MARK TWAIN MYSTIFIED
San Francisco *Golden Era,* December 9, 1866

I cannot understand the telegraphic dispatches nowadays, with their odd punctuation—I mean with so many question marks thrust in where no question is asked. The dispatches appear to me to be in the last degree mysterious. I fear we are on the eve of fearful things. Now, read this ominous telegram. I cut it out of this morning's papers, and have been studying it over most of the day, but still I don't consider that I understand it any better than I did at first:

New York, December 6. The *World's* Brownsville special says:[1]

> The city of Matamoras was surrounded [?] to Gen. Sedgwick, commanding the United States horses [?] on the Rio Grande, on the evening of the 24th ult. Col. T. G. Perkins, of the 19th U. S. Infantry, being the only artillery regiment [?] now on duty there, was stationed in command of eleven [?] men of the French [?] cavalry, who crossed over and stultified [occupied?] the city that day, but did not return until the previous [?] day on account of having to remove [remodel?] the pontoon bridge, to let his baggage train cross over, whereby he did not get back again [where?] in time to prevent it, or at least not so much as he might if he had, and certainly not otherwise if he did not or was unable, or even could not and went back on him. So Gen. Wxgrclvthrvw [?] thinks.

Come, now, this is not right, you know. I have got to lecture Monday night, and my mind ought to be in repose. It is ruinous to me to have my mind torn up in this way on the eve of a lecture. Now, just at the very time that I ought to be serene and undisturbed, comes this dreadful news about Col. T. G. Perkins and his incomprehensible (but I think, wicked) conduct, and Gen. Wxgr (insert remainder of alphabet)'s blood-curdling though unintelligible opinion of it. I wish to Heaven I knew what Perkins was trying to do, and what he wanted to do it for, and what he expected to gain by it, and whether he ever accomplished it or not.

I have studied it over patiently and carefully, and it appears that he, with his regiment of American infantry, being the only artillery there, crossed over with his French cavalry, and occupied some city or other; and then returned the day before he went over and sent his baggage train across to the other side (of course returning again at some other time not mentioned), but too late, unfortunately, to prevent it, which this Gen. Wxgr, etc., thinks he might, if he had, or otherwise if he did not or was unable; he therefore—

However, it ain't any use. The telegram is too many for *me*. Despondently,

Mark Twain

LETTER TO THE EDITOR
SAN FRANCISCO *Alta California,* DECEMBER 10, 1866

Editors *Alta*: I wish, now I hadn't advertised to lecture tonight on the "Sandwich Islands," because everything seems conspiring to discompose my mind. The telegraphic dispatches about Col. Perkins tangled me up a good deal, and now right on top of it come this dreadful correspondence between Secretary Seward and Minister Bigelow[2]— and yet, whether I get that straight in my head or not, I have got to preach.[3] Do you know what Bigelow is driving at? Do you know if Bigelow drinks?

As I understand it, Bigelow says the Mexican troops have countermanded the order conveying to Austria the power to centralize her authority in the interim, and meanwhile we are to receive the policy of the French Government as pointing to ultimate repudiation of Enclosure No. 3, and the resumption of the principles set forth in Enclosure No. 1— and this in the face of the intimation that "Gen. Almonte,[4] who was appointed to replace M. [Mike?] Hidalgo[5] at this Court, has arrived." Also, as I understand Bigelow, per Enclosure No. 2, there are some Austrian troops in question, but they are not Austrians now. They were Austrians formerly, but Austria has had no difficulty in explaining to Motley[6] that they are partly Mexicans now, because they are serving in Mexico, and partly Frenchmen, because they are fighting in the ranks of the French auxiliaries. Next she will be wanting to convince Motley that they are horses, because they live on barley, in the condition of soup. Here we have Austrian volunteers and enclosures so-and-so, and old Almonte and Mike Hidalgo all mixed up together, and as if that were not enough, it appears that Princess Carlota,[7] General Grant and Marquis de Montholon[8] have got a hand in it. And Drouyn de Lhuys[9] says he has been speaking with Bigelow, who has been spending some time at Ems! Our Minister cavorting around in this way, and such infernal questions as these to be ciphered out! I don't know who Em is, and I don't care—she is not any better than she ought to be, though, I expect—but I do know that Bigelow might be in better business.

But the most tanglesome paragraph in the whole lot is the one where Seward says to this libertine Bigelow, that he "has written to the Emperor Maximilian[10] that the Austrian volunteers being only a contingent, and not a necessary interregnum within the meaning of international law, and the violation of treaty stipulations not virtually depending upon the acceptance or dismissal of a proposition so fraught with vital consequences to both nations, whether of the Old World or the New, he does not so consider it."

I copper that document.[11] It is altogether too many for me.[12] I sort of got the hang of what Bigelow was driving at (though really I don't know, yet, what he was trying to worry through his head), but Seward is entirely too lively for me. I shall be tangled hopelessly for a week, now. But this shall be a lesson to me. I will never bother my head with diplomatic correspondence any more.

Mark Twain

1. *How much Mark Twain fiction appears in this dispatch must be left to conjecture. The news item, however, is based on the fact that there was*

action on the border. American units occasionally crossed into Mexico where they engaged in harassing forays and were not above looting.

2. *John Bigelow (1817–1911) was an American journalist, author, and diplomat. He was managing editor and co-owner of the New York Evening Post (1848–61). As United States consul in Paris during the Civil War, he prevented delivery of Confederate warships built in France. As United States minister to France (1865–66), he displayed great tact in dealing with touchy diplomatic issues provoked by the French adventure in Mexico. In Paris he discovered the long-lost autobiography of Benjamin Franklin, which he edited and published in 1868, later editing a ten-volume edition of Franklin's works (1887–88). Bigelow himself wrote a number of books, among them several on the Swedish philosopher Emanuel Sweden-borg.*

3. *Mark Twain, continually professing to be a teacher, also frequently referred to himself, ostensibly in a humorous way but more than half seriously, as a preacher, sometimes as a missionary who was an apostle of truth and morality. His concern with morals gained him the West Coast sobriquet of "Moralist of the Main."*

4. *Juan Nepomuceno Almonte was the Mexican minister in Paris who had been head of the Mexican regency before the arrival of Maximilian.*

5. *José Hidalgo was a Mexican political conservative who lived in Paris, became a close friend of the Empress Eugenie, and intrigued for the monarchist cause.*

6. *John Lothrop Motley (1814–77) was an American historian and diplomat. Having published two unsuccessful novels as a young man, he turned to European history, concentrating on the period of the Spanish wars in the Netherlands. Out of years of study abroad came* The Rise of the Dutch Republic *(1856),* The History of the United Netherlands *(1860–68), and* John of Barneveld *(1874). Twice he interrupted his work to be minister to Austria (1861–67) and minister to England (1869–70). Motley based his history on thorough research, wrote like a novelist, and gave his narratives a vivid air of dramatic immediacy.*

7. *Marie Charlotte Amélie Augustine Victoire Clémentine Léopoldine (1840–1927) was the daughter of Leopold I of Belgium and Princess Louise of Orleans. An ambitious woman, Carlota at the age of seventeen married the Austrian Archduke Maximilian, then, in 1863, went with him to Mexico where they reigned briefly as emperor and empress. In 1866, when the French seemed likely to withdraw, Carlota went to Europe to seek aid from Napoleon III and the Pope, but she was unsuccessful. Her failure, or the execution of Maximilian in 1867, or both, brought on collapse and mental derangement from which she never recovered. She spent the rest of her long life as a recluse in the Chateau of Bouchout, a moated castle in*

Belgium, living in a dream world occasionally lighted by faint glimmers of sanity. During World War I, when German armies were overrunning Belgium, the Kaiser issued strict orders that the chateau was not to be disturbed. Carlota's tragic career has been a fruitful topic for romanticists of fiction and biography.

8. The French minister to Mexico was a Bonapartist, whom Maximilian described as "a cantankerous, disagreeable character, who, with his petty intrigues, showed he had never shaken off the habits of a former consul." See Joan Haslip, The Crown of Mexico (New York, 1971), p. 281.

9. As French foreign minister, he was much involved, like all the others, in political and diplomatic maneuvering.

10. Ferdinand Maximilian Joseph (1832–67), archduke of Austria, accepted the throne of Mexico offered by a coalition of conservative Mexicans who wanted to overthrow the liberal government of Benito Juarez and of Napoleon III, who wanted to further his imperial ambitions. Maximilian, with little knowledge of the conditions he would face, was something of an idealist who intended to govern paternalistically. Without adequate grounding in politics and economics, he never fully grasped the grim realities of his situation. When the French withdrew support under pressure from the United States, his regime fell apart, he was captured by Juarez forces, and shot on June 19, 1867. As a person, Maximilian was courtly, amiable, and well-intentioned, much better suited to the formality of a European court than to the uncertainties of rule in Mexico. A philanderer of note, he had numerous brief affairs, but they never seemed serious enough to cause a rift between him and Carlota.

11. To "copper" in gambling is to bet against a card, as in faro, hence, figuratively, to distrust, to reject, or to be skeptical or suspicious of. The slang expression was common in the West.

12. The modern reader who tries to find out what occurred in Maximilian's Mexico may echo Mark Twain's sentiment. To scan the record is to become enmeshed in confusing intrigue and the maneuvering of generals, noblemen, politicos, ladies in waiting, and all sorts of others. It is a bewildering story of movements and counter-movements, espionage, adherents changing sides, and of under-cover manipulation, the pattern extending to Europe and the machinations of Bismarck and Metternich. Copious facts are there, assembled by meticulous scholarship, but they are difficult to follow.

In mid-December 1866, Mark Twain set out for New York via Panama, having arranged to be a correspondent for the San Francisco Alta California. *This story evolving from the voyage to Nicaragua, first leg of the journey, is of a Sunday morning episode aboard the* America, *commanded by Captain Edgar "Ned" Wakeman. A bluff, tattooed sea dog, he was a great favorite of Mark Twain, who said of him: "I'd rather travel with that portly, hearty, boisterous, good-natured sailor, Captain Ned Wakeman, than with any other man I ever came across."*

RATS ABANDON A SINKING SHIP
SAN FRANCISCO *Alta California*, N.D.; REPRINTED IN
YREKA CITY, CALIFORNIA, *Yreka Weekly Union*, MARCH 23, 1867

Being a little under the weather, I have intruded into the Captain's room, along with the veteran Sleet, a skipper of thirty years' standing, going home on furlough from his ship. The forenoon is waning fast. Enter Captain Waxman,[1] sweating and puffing from over-exertion, and says he has "tore up the whole ship" (he scorns grammar when his mind is seething with business), has "tore up the whole ship" to build a pulpit at the after compass and rig benches and chairs athwart the quarter-deck and fetch up the organ from below and get everything shipshape for the parson—

"And—the passengers," said he, "as soon as they found they were going to be sermonized, they've up anchors and gone to sea—clean gone and deserted—there ain't a baker's dozen left on the after deck! They're worse than the rats in Hon—here, you velvet-head! you son of Afric's sunny clime! go forrard and tell the mate to let her go a couple of points free—in Honolulu. Me and old Josephus—he was a Jew, and got rich as Creosote in San Francisco afterwards—we were going home passengers from the Sandwich Islands in a bran-new brig, on her third voyage, and our trunks were down below—he went with me—laid over one vessel to do it—because he warn't no sailor, and he liked to be conveyed by a man that was—felt safer, you understand—and the brig was sliding out between the buoys, and her headline was paying out ashore—there was a woodpile right where it was made fast on the pier—when up come

the biggest rat—as big as any ordinary cat, he was, and
darted out on that line and cantered for the shore!—and up
come another! and another! and another! and away they
galloped over that hawser, each one treading on t'other's
tail, till they were so thick you couldn't see a thread of the
cable, and there was a procession of 'em three hundred
yards long over the levee like a streak of pismires, and the
Kanakas,[2] some throwing sticks from that woodpile and
chunks of lava and coral at 'em and knocking 'em endways
every shot—but do you suppose it made any difference to
them rats?—not a particle—not a particle on earth, bless
you!—they'd smelt trouble!—they'd smelt it by their un-
earthly, supernatural instinct!—they wanted to go, and they
never let up till the last rat was ashore out of that bran-new
beautiful brig!

"I called a Kanaka, with his boat, and he hove alongside
and shinned up a rope, and stood off and on for orders, and
says I:

"Do you see that trunk down there?"

"'Ai.'"

"Well, yank it out of there and snake it ashore quicker'n
you can wink. Lively, now!"

"Solomon, the Jew—what did I say his cussed name was?
Anyhow, he says:

"'What are you doing, Captain?'"

"Doing! Why, I'm a taking my trunk ashore—that's
what I'm a doing."

"'Taking your trunk ashore? Why, bless us, what is that
for?'"

"What is it for?" says I; "do you see them rats a leaving
this ship? She's doomed, sir! she's doomed past retribution!
Burnt brandy wouldn't save her, sir.[3] She'll never finish this
voyage—she'll never be heard of again, sir."

"Solomon says, 'Boy, take that other trunk ashore, too.'"

"And don't you know, that bran-new beautiful brig
sailed out of Honolulu without a rat on board, and was
never seen again by mortal man, sir! It's so—as sure as
you're born, it's so. We shipped in an old tub that was so
rotten that you had to walk easy on her main deck to keep

from going through. The timbers overhead worked backwards and forwards eleven inches in their sockets, just for all the world like an old wicker basket, sir—and the rats were as big as greyhounds, and as lean, sir; and they bit the buttons off our coats, and chawed our toenails off while we slept; and there were so many of them that in a gale, once, they all scampered to the starboard side when we were going about, and put her down the wrong way, so that she missed stays, and come monstrous near foundering. But she went through safe, I tell you, because she had rats aboard." [After this marvelous chapter of personal history the Captain rushed out in a business frenzy, and rushed back again in the course of a couple of minutes.]

"Everything's set—the passengers are back again and stowed, and the parson's all ready to cast his anchor and get under way—everybody ready and waiting on that bloody choir that was practicing and squawking and blatting all night, and now ain't come to time when their watch is called."

[Out again, and back in something like a minute.]

"D——n that choir! They're like the fellow's sow—had to haul her ears off to get her up to the trough, and then had to pull her tail out to get her away again. But rats!—don't tell me nothing about the talent of rats! It's been noticed, sir!—notes has been taken of it, sir! and their judgment is better than a human's, sir! Didn't I hear old Ben Wilson, mate of the *Empress of the Seas*—as fine a sailor and as lovely a ship as ever rode a gale—didn't I hear him tell how seventeen years ago, when he was laying at Liverpool docks empty—empty as a jug—and a full Indiaman right alongside, full of provisions, and corn, and everything a rat might prefer, and going to sail next day—how in the middle of the night the rats all left her and crossed his decks and went ashore—every one of 'em!—every bloody one of 'em, sir!—and finally—it was moonlight—he saw a muss going on by the capstan of that other ship, and he slipped around, and there was a dozen old rats laying their heads together and chattering about something and looking down the forrard hatch every now and then, and finally they appeared to have got their minds made up, and one of 'em went aft and got a scrap of old stuns'l half a foot square, and they bored holes in the corners with their teeth, and bent on some long pieces of spun-yarn—made a sort of a little hammock of it, you understand—and then they lowered away gently for a while and stopped—and directly they begun heaving again, and up out of that forrard hatch, in full view of the mate, who was watching 'em all the time, up comes that little hammock with a poor, old, decrepit, sick rat on it, all gone in with the consumption!—and they lugged him ashore, and they all went up town to the very last rat—and that ship sailed the next day for India, or Cape o' Good Hope, or somewheres, and the mate of the *Empress* didn't sail for as much as three weeks, and up to *that* time that ship hadn't been heard from, sir! Drat that choir! I must go and start 'em out—this sort of thing won't do!"

Mark Twain

1. *Another name for Captain Ned Wakeman, who appears as Captain Hurricane Jones in "Some Rambling Notes of an Idle Excursion," as Captain Stormfield in* Captain Stormfield's Visit to Heaven, *and as Captain Ned Blakely in chapter 50 of* Roughing It. *One more probable incarnation is Uncle Mumford, a steamboat mate in* Life on the Mississippi. *The tone of his spirited monologue in chapter 28 bears a strong resemblance to the robust language of Captain Waxman-Jones-Stormfield-Blakely.*

2. *The word is from a Hawaiian word meaning "man." The term* Kanaka *was used loosely to designate not only natives of the Sandwich Islands, but also of the South Seas generally.*

3. *Probably this refers to a nautical folk custom, but the explanation has eluded search. Perhaps the burnt brandy was supposed to have the same favorable influence as ancient burnt offerings intended to propitiate the gods. Burning good brandy would seem to be a sacrifice worthy of any god's merciful consideration.*

Mark Twain, the moralist, is revealed in the next sketch. The rejection of old-fashioned virtues, solid and unostentatious, in favor of modern popular vices and qualities, showy but meretricious, is a theme he "preached" on as writer and speaker. Calling one of the main characters George L. Washington is clear evidence of the moral drift of the narrative. As he tells the story, however, it is significant that among college seniors the modern concept of a gentleman barely wins in a close contest, thus showing perhaps that, to Mark Twain, the younger generation is not completely without a sense of propriety.

THE FIRST GENTLEMAN
YREKA CITY, CALIFORNIA, *Yreka Weekly Union,* MAY 18, 1867

I had a dream last night, which had about it something of the air of a revelation. I dreamed that the year had drawn to a close, and that the graduating class of Princeton College had met together to determine which of their number should be awarded the gold medal instituted by Mr. Leonard Jerome for the graduate who should be declared by his fellows to be the first gentleman of the class.

The proceedings opened with a discussion concerning what constitutes a gentleman. It soon became apparent that there were two very distinctly marked opinions upon the subject, and that the strength of the class was nearly equally divided among them. After the debate had continued for some time without any satisfactory result, it was resolved that inasmuch as there were but two candidates proposed for the medal, testimony should be at once taken as to their worthiness[1] and then submit the final decision of the matter to a ballot. John Wagner was summoned to testify on behalf of George L. Washington, the candidate of the Old Fogy party.

Q. Do you believe George L. Washington to be the first gentleman of the graduating class? *A.* I do.

Q. Has he got money? *A.* A bare competency.

Q. Is he pious? *A.* He is.

Q. Does he gamble? *A.* No.

Q. Drink? *A.* No, except that he takes wine at dinner and in drawing rooms, and upon such occasions; but he is never overcome by it.

Q. Does he chew tobacco? *A.* No.

Q. Does he smoke? *A.* Not to excess; not more than three cigars a day.

Q. Does he play billiards? *A.* Occasionally.

Q. Does he fight, drive fast horses, raise thunder, or run all night? *A.* I am not aware that he does such things.

Q. Then what makes you think he is a gentleman?[2] *A.* Because he lives comfortably, yet not ostentatiously; dresses well, but plainly; abides by all laws, human and divine; is courteous and kindly toward all; is considerate of the feelings of others, and has charity for their weaknesses and their prejudices; it is seldom that he gets mad, and when he does, he gets mad all over—he redresses grievances then. He stands by his friend first, last, and all the time. He is always taxing his time, his patience, and his purse, to make other people's lives happy. He never does a mean thing, and has only just enough small vices to breed in him a humane and liberal spirit when sitting in judgment upon the vices of his neighbors, and keep him from being too disagreeably good for a mere man of flesh and blood.

Other witnesses corroborated the above statements, and the Old Fogies rested their case.

Thomas Williamson was called to testify on behalf of William E. Fourth, the candidate of the Modern party.

Q. What do you know of William E. Fourth?[3] *A.* I know him to be in all respects a brick.

Q. Has he got money? *A.* Rich as Croesus.

Q. Is he pious? *A.* Well—I don't hardly—well, 'taint—it ain't his strong suit, as you may say.

Q. Does he ever go to church? *A.* Well, he—he don't go as much as he used to.

Q. How often does he go? *A.* Well, you see, he don't get to church much now. He don't get up till noon on Sundays, and he thinks it puts a kind of dampener on his appetite to go to church before breakfast.

Q. You have not answered my question yet. How often does he go to church? *A.* To come down to the fine points of it, he only goes seldom. But he loves it. I have known him to go to church in the hardest kind of a rain-storm. [Cheers.]

Q.   Did he have an umbrella? A.   No, he didn't even have an umbrella. He would scorn it.

Q.   Was he away from home when he took the notion? A.   I believe he was.

Q.   Now, no trifling—no prevarications! Answer strictly. What did he go in the church for? A.   Well, he— he went there to get out of the rain.

[Cheers from the other party.]

Q.   Does the candidate gamble? A.   Him! Why, he's the envy of the public. Take him at any gentlemanly amusement you can name, from faro, for stacks of red checks, down to pitch seven-up for Limburger cheese and lager, and he is prince of them all.

Q.   Does he drink? A.   Oh, don't mention it! Why, he is the pride of the village. He can banish more champagne and Jersey lightning[4] than any man in the State, and still be the gayest of the gay.

Q.   Does he chew tobacco, or smoke? A.   He does. He don't lack any gentlemanly accomplishment.

Q.   Does he dress well? A.   Him! Why, he sports the stunningest harness in America; the tightest-legged pants and the shortest-tailed coats, and the reddest cravats on the continent, and the most of them. He gives all the powers of his mind to it, and as a woman-killer there isn't his equal anywhere.

Q.   Is he convivial? A.   He is the most companionable gentleman I know. When he turns out of a night to have a time, somebody's premises have got to suffer; he is a regular calamity to street lamps and door-bells when he gets started; and if anyone objects, why, there's trouble, you know. And his team is the fastest.

Q.   Does he play billiards? A.   He can beat the man that invented the game.

Q.   Does he pay his debts? A.   Most regular man in the world. Always gives his note, and is always affable and polite when a body wants him to renew it.

Here the original discussion broke out again, but the Moderns seemed to have the best of the argument.

The election closed with the first ballot, and in favor of the Moderns; George L. Washington, 13; William E.

Fourth, 14. Amidst the wildest enthusiasm on the part of the Modern party, William E. Fourth was declared the chosen recipient of the Jerome gold medal, as the first gentleman of the graduating class. [Sudden sensation outside; all turn toward the door.]

Enter William E. Fourth in a state of hilarious excitement. "I licked him, boys! (hic!) I don't know who he was, but I licked him, you bet!"

All—"Hooray for the gold medal boy—never fails to whip his man! I want to vote for him again! Who was the man that tackled you? Show us the man! Anyway, hooray!"

Enter a graduate in dismay, and says: "O, great Gemini, boys, it was Leonard Jerome." [Sudden and impressive silence.]

My dream ended there.

1. *The questions, illustrating popular nineteenth-century convictions on righteous behavior, also show Mark Twain's ambivalent attitude. Evidently he approves of the gentlemanly attributes of George L. Washington, a man of modest means, pious, a temperate drinker and smoker, no gambler, and only an occasional billiard player—billiards probably being suspect because allied with the murky reputation of the lowdown pool hall. Yet Mark Twain continually yearned for wealth, scorned piety, was far from a temperate drinker in Washoe, smoked constantly, and was a fanatical billiardist who could keep at it all night. Though not a gambler at cards or roulette, he certainly gambled when he risked large sums in all sorts of speculative ventures. Perhaps, while denouncing the conventional virtues, he retained some respect for them. The conflict, like that of his long-time attraction to and aversion for the Bible, may have contributed to the paradoxes that make Mark Twain a fascinating, if sometimes irritating, character.*

2. *The catalog of qualities making up Mark Twain's definition of a gentleman reveal awareness of his own shortcomings. He preferred to live ostentatiously, and did so in Hartford, New York, Vienna, and elsewhere. He longed to wear flashy clothes and managed to do so late in life, when he sported white suits summer and winter and donned the red Oxford gown on occasions suitable and unsuitable. He was not always courteous and kindly, and when he suspected that a friend had lied to him or swindled him, he could be vindictive thereafter. Like the Old Fogy candidate, he had plenty of small vices, and surely there should be unanimous agreement that Mark Twain was not "too disagreeably good for a mere man of flesh and blood."*

3. *Possibly this is an allusion to William IV, king of England, 1830–37. He was not a remarkable man, not brilliant or innovative, yet he was more attentive to duty than his predecessor, George IV. Although William was not a conspicuous example of dissolute behavior, he did have a mistress, the actress Dorothea Jordan, and in numerous youthful affairs he had fathered ten illegitimate children. Such irregularities would have been sufficient to damn him in the eyes of so stern a moralist as Mark Twain.*

4. *Jersey lightning was a powerful kind of applejack (brandy distilled from cider). The term was also loosely used as a name for whiskey.*

Renewing his acquaintance with New York, Mark Twain was not enchanted with the city. In his Alta *correspondence he called the metropolis "a splendid desert—a domed and steepled solitude, where the stranger is lonely in the midst of a million of his race." Nevertheless, he took in a variety of attractions, like the sensational theatrical extravaganza,* The Black Crook, *described as "a wilderness of girls . . . dressed with a meagerness that would make a parasol blush." He journeyed to Missouri to visit the home folks, then returned to Manhattan where he made his eastern debut as a lecturer, giving the "Sandwich Islands" at Cooper Union on May 6, 1867. The occasion was a financial failure but a critical success with an enthusiastic audience that was large only because most of the people in it had been given free tickets. He was not yet famous on the eastern seaboard, but after he signed on for the* Quaker City *excursion to Europe and the Holy Land, he was somewhat surprised to find himself cited on the passenger list as one of the celebrities. For the* Alta, *which paid his passage, he contracted to write travel letters at $20 each that later provided material for* The Innocents Abroad *(1869). This letter written to Col. John McComb of the* Alta *is an account of Mark Twain's vinous adventures shortly before the sailing of the* Quaker City.

EAT, DRINK FOR TOMORROW WE SAIL
BOSTON *Sunday Globe*, NOVEMBER 29, 1964

New York, June 8, [1867], 2 a.m.

Dear John—D——n it I have intended all along to write you the night before sailing, but here it is within 12 hours of leaving and I have not been to bed or packed my trunk yet. But I went to dinner at 3 p.m. with "Private Miles O'Riley"[1] and Jno Russell Young,[2] managing editor of the Tribune (I am going to write for that—I find the weekly has 200,000 circulation)—drank wine, dined from 6 to 9 at Jno Murphy's[3] (God made him, you know, and Mrs. M. too). Drank several breeds of wine there, naturally enough, dined again from 9 till 12 at Mr. Slote's[4] (my shipmate's) whom the same God made that made Jno Murphy—and mind you I say that such men as they are, are almighty scarce—you can shut your eyes and go forth at random in a strange land and pick out a [son of a bitch][5] a great deal easier; drank much wine there, too. So I am only just getting over it now. Mr. MacCrellish[6] and I are to take Christmas dinner at Jno Murphy's.

Now I feel good—I feel d——d good—and I could write a good correspondence—can, anyway, as soon as I get out of this most dismal town. You'll see. Got an offer to-day for 3-months course of lectures next winter—$100 a night and no bother and no expense. How's that?

John, I'll write from Paris. God be with you.

Yrs fraternally,
Mark

1. *Private Miles O'Reilly was a pseudonym of Charles Graham Halpine (1829–68), an Irish-American journalist and poet. One of the New York Bohemians, along with Walt Whitman and Fitz-James O'Brien, he had been secretary to P. T. Barnum, co-editor of the Boston* Carpet-Bag, *and secretary to Stephen A. Douglas. In the Sixty-ninth New York Regiment during the Civil War, Halpine was also on the staff of General Hunter and was brevetted brigadier general in 1865. Under the name of Miles O'Reilly, an ignorant Irish private, he wrote letters to popular journals and published* Miles O'Reilly His Book *(1864). A lively, impetuous man known as a brilliant conversationalist, he must have been a spirited drinking companion for Mark Twain.*

2. *John Russell Young (1840–99) was an American journalist who started as copy boy for the Philadelphia* Press *(1857). He became reporter and war correspondent, then managing editor of the New York* Tribune *(1866). He was sent to Europe on confidential missions for the State Department (1870–71), then moved to an editorial position on the New York* Herald. *Appointed minister to China (1882), he was a judicious diplomat who won the confidence of the Chinese. Made librarian of*

Congress (1897), he directed transfer of books from the Capitol to the new building and launched the Library of Congress on its modern career. Young was a quiet man of great charm, acknowledged to be an excellent judge of human nature.

3. *John J. Murphy was chief of the New York bureau of the San Francisco* Alta California. *He handed Mark Twain a check for $1,250, having been instructed by telegram to "ship Mark Twain in the Holy Land Excursion and pay his passage."*

4. *Dan Slote, Mark Twain's roommate on the* Quaker City *excursion, was fifteen years the elder. Mark Twain characterized him as a true man, splendidly godless, immoral, and addicted to all the right vices. On the voyage they struck up a friendship that flourished for a few years, then withered. When Slote, Woodman and Company manufactured and marketed the self-pasting scrapbook patented by Mark Twain in 1873, he accused Slote of peculation with royalties and added Dan's name to a long list of suspects he believed had swindled him in various enterprises.*

5. *The Boston* Globe *delicately omits these words, which are indicated by "... .. . ." and adds the explanation "(s.o.b.)." Probably the paper deleted the profanity in deference to Boston propriety, for Mark Twain in his private correspondence was not squeamish about giving out the word with the bark on it.*

6. *Frederick MacCrellish was the chief proprietor of the* Alta. *When he announced his intention to publish a book based on the foreign travel letters, Mark Twain had to go out to California to negotiate for their release for his own book. McComb interceded for him, and MacCrellish finally agreed, on condition that Mark Twain thank the* Alta *for its generosity. He refused, but in his preface to the* Innocents, *he did give a slight nod to the proprietors for "having waived their rights and given me the necessary permission." Thereafter, MacCrellish was in Mark Twain's growing blacklist of villains.*

After the Quaker City *excursion, Mark Twain sojourned for a few months (1867–68) in Washington, D.C., as secretary to Senator William H. Stewart of Nevada. The job was not congenial, and relations between the senator and the secretary came to be less than cordial. Yet the experience was not a total loss. It gave him firsthand knowledge of political corruption rampant in postwar Washington, an insight that would illuminate* The Gilded Age *(1873), written in collaboration with Charles Dudley Warner. Like Walt Whitman and Henry Adams, Mark Twain regarded*

the flagrant venality of public officials with abhorrence and contempt, which he expressed in acidulous comments. Instead of attending to secretarial duties, he wrote humorous and satirical pieces for New York papers and others, tossing off barbed remarks like "Whiskey is carried into committee rooms in demijohns and carried out in demagogues" and "It could probably be shown by facts and figures that there is no distinctly native American criminal class except Congress." His articles, dealing with current events as well as politicians, were not syndicated, but they nevertheless traveled around the country, turning up in papers nearby and far away.

COLONEL BURKE AND THE FENIANS

WASHINGTON *Star*, N.D.; REPRINTED IN
VIRGINIA CITY *Territorial Enterprise*, JANUARY 14, 1868

Washington, December 14.   Since Gideon's band marched forth against the "children of the East" at dead of night,[1] each man with a jug in one hand and a "horn" in the other, military history has shown no such instance of inspired originality as the foreign telegrams tell us of this morning. Colonel Burke, a Fenian patriot,[2] is a prisoner in Clerkenwell; his friends desire his liberty; other people would have bribed the jailer, tunneled to the prisoner's cell, hauled him out through a hole in the roof, petitioned Government for his pardon, sent a woman in to swap clothes and change places with the culprit. Other people, I say, would have essayed one or the other, or all of these methods. But did the Fenians? Not they. They scorned such threadbare devices. They would liberate their friend by some invention that would be worthy of the occasion—by some invention that should bear about it the sign of a creative genius—by some untried plan that should dazzle the sleepy world with its splendid originality. Wherefore they put a barrel of blasting powder under the prison and tried to blow their friend out of the hated land of England. The idea was good. It was excellent, and should have succeeded. There was powder enough to have sent Colonel Burke and his baggage to Dublin, where he would have been safe from their persecution, if it could have been put under him instead of off to one side.

The enterprise failed, but shall its lesson be lost to us? May we not use it freely, in the absence of an international copyright system?[3] In cases where a Cabinet officer refuses to resign and will not be removed, may we not put a barrel of powder under him and blast him from his position? The thing looks feasible to me. It is expeditious, unostentatious, and singularly effective. Why distress Secretary Stanton[4] with arguments and theories when he could be so suddenly and pleasantly convinced by the graceful logic of the New Fenian Persuader? I only throw out the suggestion.

A word more. I must find fault with the sagacity of the police who were awakened from their slumbers by this Clerkenwell explosion, and who arrested two men and a woman, whom they found in the vicinity, on suspicion of being the persons who fired the barrel of powder. Now, if you set a barrel of gunpowder, *would* you be ass enough to remain in the vicinity? Wouldn't you meander a quarter of a mile or such a matter?

Mark Twain

P.S. On reflection I find that my suggestion concerning Mr. Stanton may have one fault about it. It is just possible that if you blew him up you might elevate him so much above his fellow citizens as to excite envy. Envy is bad. Let the powder be placed above him, and blow him downward. It does not outrage our feelings to see people go downward.

1. *Gideon, a judge of Israel, marched against the great host of Amalekites and Midianites "in the beginning of the middle watch," and routed them with 300 men. According to Judg. 7 : 16: "And he divided the three hundred men into three companies, and he put a trumpet in every man's hand, with empty pitchers, and lamps within the pitchers." In Mark Twain's account, he probably meant the "horn" to be, not a trumpet, but Washoe bar slang for a stiff drink of whiskey or brandy.*
2. *Fenians was a popular name for the Irish Republican Brotherhood, founded in 1858. It was an Irish nationalist secret society, active in the cause of Irish freedom in Ireland, Britain, and the United States. Fenian derives from fiann or feinne, a legendary band of Irish warriors led by Finn MacCumhaill. American Fenians caused friction between the United States and Canada by staging abortive raids across the border, and in England they*

harassed the British government by disruptive episodes like that of Mark Twain's story.

3. Thus early in his career Mark Twain was aware of copyright laws, which became one of his most persistent concerns. From time to time hereafter we shall hear of his attempts to influence copyright legislation.

4. Edwin McMasters Stanton (1814–69) was appointed secretary of war by Lincoln on January 15, 1862 and remained in the cabinet under President Johnson. Mark Twain's story refers to the conflict between the president and Stanton when the latter allied himself with radical Republicans determined upon a punitive policy of Southern reconstruction. On August 5, 1867, Johnson asked for Stanton's resignation, but the secretary, invoking the Tenure of Office Act, refused to resign. Whereupon he was suspended, but resumed his post in January 1868, when the Senate did not concur in the suspension. Johnson then dismissed Stanton, an act that led to impeachment charges against the president. When impeachment failed by one vote (May 26, 1868), Stanton resigned. He died four days after being appointed to the United States Supreme Court (1869).

The subject of Mark Twain's letter which follows is George Francis Train (1829-1904), American merchant, author, and entrepreneur. A great traveler, he promoted shipping firms, railroads, and street railways at home and abroad. An ardent Unionist during the Civil War, he later espoused the cause of the Fenians, joined the French Commune, made impassioned speeches on behalf of women's rights, and supported the dashing Victoria Woodhull when she was arrested on a charge of obscenity. He wrote voluminously—books, pamphlets, leaflets—was once expelled from France, landed in jail a number of times, and in his endorsement of unpopular beliefs exemplified his own description of himself as a "champion crank." His frenzied comings and goings, startling actions, and conflicts with the constabulary made him a favorite of newsmen, who delighted to report his eccentric doings. Today, some of his ideas have long since been accepted as sensible commonplaces, but in the nineteenth century he was regarded as an entertaining, if irritating, member of the lunatic fringe. Mark Twain's letter has satirical point because Train was in jail at the time.

LETTER TO THE EDITOR
NEW YORK *Tribune*, JANUARY 22, 1868

To the Editor of the *Tribune*—Sir: If you can, I wish you would give me some information of a man by the name of George Francis Train. It is for an uncle of mine that I want it. My uncle has had a pretty hard time of it, and if any man does deserve sympathy, and if any man would appreciate that sympathy, it is he. He is in the decline of life, and wants to be quiet; but you know he tried Walrussia,[1] and the bears ousted him; and then he tried St. Thomas,[2] and the earthquakes ousted him; and so he hung up his fiddle, so to speak, and concluded he would wait and look around awhile, till Government bought some more property.[3] And while he was waiting, somebody recommended him to hunt up this gentleman, Mr. Train.

They said Mr. Train was a slow, quiet sort of a body, and had no isms or curious notions about him, and that he was going over to the old country to buy Ireland for those persons they call the Fenians. They said he was very popular with the English Government, and that if the English Government would sell to anybody, they would to Mr. Train. They said that if Mr. Train concluded to take it my uncle would have an excellent chance to buy into a quiet locality in Cork, or Tipperary, or one of those calm, religious regions there, by speaking to him early.

So my uncle went after Mr. Train, but he was building a couple of railroads out West, somewhere, and before my uncle got there he had finished those railroads and was making Democratic speeches in the East. It was a considerable disappointment, but my uncle always had a great idea of doing business with a slow, quiet man, and so he came East. But he came the last part of the journey in a canal boat (it being his nature to prefer quiet and safety to speed), and he missed that man again. Mr. Train had got the Democratic party reorganized and all straight, and he was out in the middle of the Rocky Mountains clearing off a place and driving away the buffaloes, so that he could build a metropolis there. But my uncle went in an ox wagon, and he missed that man again. Mr. Train had finished that metropolis and paved it with the Nicolson pavement,[4] and started a couple of daily newspapers, and was gone East again with another lady to lecture on female suffrage.[5]

It was a little discouraging, but my relative rested about a week and started after him again. He caught him this time, because Mr. Train had sprained his ankle, and was obliged to remain quiet until he could get the leg removed and a reliable patent wooden one put on in its place that could not sprain again. So he mentioned his business to Mr. Train, and he replied:

"You are all right, Sir. Put your trust in me. I'll buy Ireland, and you shall have as good a chance as any man. I am going to sail right away. You will hear about me as soon as I touch the Emerald shores. I shall get out some advertisements and make my presence known. I make no pretensions, but you will see pretty soon that I shall be heartily welcomed there and promptly cared for."

Since that time my uncle has not heard of Mr. Train. He has confidence in him, but he thinks that maybe he is too quiet a man to make much stir, and has not yet been heard of on that account. But have you heard anything of Mr. Train? Do you know if he got out any advertisements? And do you know if they received him heartily there, and more especially if they took care of him? This last is the main thing with my relative. If they took care of Mr. Train it is all he cares for. He has said to me repeatedly that all he is afraid of is that he has been neglected and not taken care of. If he were to hear that Mr. Train is there, in a strange land, without any place to stay, it would nearly break his heart. If you could only inform us that Mr. Train is safe, and has been received hospitably, and has a good tranquil place to board in, suitable to a quiet man like him, it would be a great comfort to the old man.

Mark Twain

1. *This word is made from* walrus *and* Russia. *It was suggested as a name for the territory known as Russian America, purchased from Russia by the United States in 1867. Other proposed names were Polario, American Siberia, Zero Islands, and Icebergia. Secretary Seward chose the name advocated by Senator Charles Sumner: Alaska, from the aboriginal word Al-ak-shak, meaning "the great country" or "the continent."*
2. *The largest of the Virgin Islands, Saint Thomas is not remarkable for earthquakes, although it is in the earthquake zone that sweeps down the West Coast of the United States and across Central America.*
3. *Secretary of State William H. Seward contracted for the purchase of Alaska from Russia in 1867, and the American flag was first raised there on October 18 of that year. Public opposition to Seward's action, however, delayed Senate confirmation and the necessary House appropriation until 1868.*
4. *Nicholson pavement was made of wood blocks laid on tarred planks, chinks filled with fine gravel, and washed with hot tar. Although the surface became slippery in wet weather, the pavement was popular until the early twentieth century, when it gave way to the more resistant brick and concrete.*
5. *In the nineteenth century, the battle over women's rights was rough for both sexes, especially for men bold enough to come out with public endorsement of female suffrage. Such advocates were likely to be the targets of masculine raillery. In a dinner speech for the Washington Correspondents' Club on January 11, 1868, Mark Twain, citing prominent women of the past and present, said, "Look at the Widow Machree! Look at Lucy Stone! Look at Elizabeth Cady Stanton! Look at George Francis Train!" The "male chauvinist" of the late twentieth century had not yet been invented, but he was nevertheless on the scene.*

To negotiate with the proprietors of the Alta *for release of his* Quaker
City *letters, Mark Twain took off for California on March 11, 1868,
arriving in San Francisco on April 2. Remaining three months, he dickered
with MacCrellish and colleagues, gave three lectures in San Francisco, made
a two-weeks' speaking tour over the route covered in 1866, and enjoyed a
sociable reunion with old acquaintances. In one frolic he and a man named
Pierson entertained six guests at a "Lick House State Banquet," the printed
menu offering "Whale, Esquimaux style," "Ham, also, Shem and
Japhet," "Broiled Missionary, with mushrooms, a la Fiji Islands,"
"Saddle of Mutton, with bridle and other harness," "Grasshoppers, Digger
style," "Pie Ute," and other unusual dishes. Before his farewell platform
appearance in San Francisco on July 2, he published an advertisement
composed of fictitious letters from friends, clergymen, benevolent societies,
newspapermen, "Citizens on Foot and Horseback," and others, all begging
him not to torment the people with another lecture. Affecting indignation, he
replied that such a request was unprecedented and that he was determined to
inflict himself upon the public just once more. Besides concocting such
foolery, he amused himself by writing squibs like the next short piece.*

"ANOTHER OLD CALIFORNIAN GONE"
SAN FRANCISCO *Daily Dramatic Chronicle,* JUNE 18, 1868

San Francisco, June 13, 1868

Editors *Chronicle*: With a promptness which can never be
over-estimated, you have delivered, three days since, a box
sent to you for me about two months ago. However, you
may have considered it slow freight.[1] It contained a dead
frog—and a very flat one. He could not have been flatter if
he had lain on some level surface a fortnight, with the
United States on top of him. It cannot be the Celebrated
Jumping Frog of Calaveras County, however, as it purports
to be, because that frog was not susceptible of flattery. The
following note accompanied the box:

San Andreas, April 18, 1868

Mark Twain: Will you be kind enough to accept from your
many friends in Calaveras county, the enclosed. You will
perceive that the evidence[s] of his last great struggle are
"fresh upon him." It was the *shot* that killed him. Hoping that
you will acknowledge the kindness of your friends in pursuing,

capturing and delivering to you the hero of your story. We are sincerely your friends and well-wishers.

Many

Gentlemen: The honored dead has arrived. Accept my cordial gratitude. I have taken the liberty of using the heading the newspapers here always use when a person of no particular consequence dies—"Another Old Californian Gone!" It always gives the deceased a sort of fictitious consequence, and prevents him going out of the world a complete and perfect nobody. It also insures him against making an unnoticed entrance into the next world. Surely no Old Californian could appear in perdition without making something of a stir, and I think maybe if one appeared in the other place, it would create a positive excitement. The daily repetition of "Another Old Californian Gone" grows monotonous, after awhile, and the reader feels that it would be a pleasing variation to have a New Californian go, now and then. Such I judge to be the case with the general reader—but as for me, give me my accustomed Old Californian Gone, for breakfast—give him to me with pathos and with an imposing flourish of his achievements on ranches and in mines and uncelebrated legislatures—and I am happy. When I get thoroughly used to a thing, I like to have it all the time.

However, let explanations pass. I simply desire to say that I value this present very highly, but chiefly on account of the sumptuous character of the box it comes in. I have succeeded in borrowing money on it at the hotel, where it now remains in the safe as security—frog and all. Send me another. Your servant and well-wisher,

Mark Twain

To "Many Friends," San Andreas, Calaveras county.

1. *The uncertainties of mail service are not unique to our times. In a dinner speech in 1901, Mark Twain said that a letter from the Associated Press had been ten days on the way and that another from Ohio had taken eleven days to reach New York. Then he remarked, "But, oh, I should like*

to know the name of the Lightning Express by which they were forwarded; for I owe a friend a dozen chickens, and I believe it will be cheaper to send eggs instead, and let them develop on the road."

In August 1869, Mark Twain, with the aid of $12,500 borrowed from his future father-in-law, Jervis Langdon, bought a third interest in the Buffalo Express, for which he became an associate editor. The steady demands of that sort of job were incompatible with his temperament, yet for a time he made a brave show of industry, spending long hours daily at the office. He modified the screaming typography of the paper to make it look less like a yellow journal, and he urged reporters to restrain the adjectives and avoid slang. He wrote a great deal—strong editorials against injustice, brief notes about "People and Things," satires, and sketches.

MARK TWAIN'S IDEA OF A GOOD LETTER
Grass Valley, California, *Daily National,* December 6, 1869

The most useful and interesting letters we get here from home are from children seven or eight years old. This is a petrified truth. Happily they have got nothing else to talk about but home, and neighbors and family—things their betters [believe] unworthy of transmission thousands of miles. They write simply and naturally and without strain for effect. They tell all they know, and stop. They seldom deal in abstractions or homilies. Consequently their epistles are brief; but, treating as they do of familiar scenes and persons, always entertaining. Now, therefore, if you would learn the art of letterwriting, let the child teach you. I have preserved a letter from a little girl eight years of age— preserved it as a curiosity, because it was the only letter I ever got from the States that had any information in it. It ran thus:

St. Louis, 1865

Uncle Mark, if you was here I could tell you about Moses in the bulrushes again. I know it better now. Mr. Sowberry has got his leg broke off a horse. He was riding it on Sunday.

Margret—that's the maid—Margret has taken all the spit-toons, and slop buckets and old jugs out of your room, because she says she don't think you are coming back any more, you have been gone too long. Sissy McElroy's mother has got another little baby. She has them all the time. It has got little blue eyes, like Mr. Swimley that boards there, and looks just like him. I have got a new doll, but Johnny Anderson pulled one of the legs out. Miss Dusenberry was here yesterday; I gave her your picture, but she said she didn't want it. My cat has got more kittens—oh! you can't think—twice as many as Lottie Belden's. And there's one—such a sweet little buff one with a short tail—and I named it for you.

All of them's got names now—General Grant, and Halleck,[1] and Moses, and Margret, and Deuteronomy, and Captain Semmes,[2] and Exodus, and Leviticus, and Horace Greeley[3]— all named but one, and I am saving it because the one I named to you's been sick all the time since, and I reckon it'll die. [It appears to be mighty rough on the short-tailed kitten for naming it for me. I wonder how the reserved victim will stand it.] Uncle Mark, I do believe Hattie Caldwell likes you, and I know she thinks you are pretty because I heard her say nothing could hurt your good looks—nothing at all—she said, even if you were to have the small-pox ever so bad, you would be just as good-looking as you were before. And ma says she's ever so smart. [Very.] So no more this time, because General Grant and Moses are fighting.

Annie

This child treads on my toes in every other sentence, with perfect looseness, but in the simplicity of her time of life she doesn't know it. I consider that a model letter—an emi-nently readable and entertaining letter, and, as I said before, it contains more matter of interest and real information than any letter I ever received from the East. I had rather hear about cats at home and their truly remarkable names, than listen to a lot of stuff about people I am not acquainted with, or read "The Evil Effects of the Intoxicating Bowl," illustrated on the back with the picture of a ragged scallawag pelting away right and left in the midst of his family circle with a junk bottle.[4]

1. *Henry Wager Halleck (1815–72) was a West Pointer (1839), who returned there to lecture on* Elements of Military Art and Science, *a textbook widely used in the Civil War. He was a staff officer in the Mexican War, helped frame a constitution for the new state of California (1849), and resigned with the rank of captain (1854). Returning to the army on the outbreak of civil war as major general of volunteers, he was given supreme command of the Department of Missouri. Remaining in Washington, he was an able administrator but a poor tactician, often a hindrance to field commanders. This deficiency persisted when he became chief of all the armies in 1862. Too far from the scene of action, he failed to grasp the military situation, which remained confused until General Grant replaced him in 1864.*

2. *Raphael Semmes (1809–77) resigned from the U.S. Navy at the outbreak of civil war and was made commander in the Confederate States Navy. Briefly skipper of the raider* Sumter, *he is best known as commander of the* Alabama, *assuming command at Liverpool in 1862. For two years the* Alabama, *roaming the seas of the world, captured or sank 126 merchant ships. When she put in at Cherbourg for refitting in June 1864, the U.S.S.* Kearsarge *appeared, inviting battle. Semmes accepted the challenge, and in the engagement the* Alabama *was sunk, Semmes being rescued by a British ship. He returned to Richmond, became a rear admiral, and assumed command of the James River squadron, which he burned when Richmond was evacuated in April 1865. Taken prisoner, he was released by presidential order. Semmes recounted the story of his adventures in* Memoirs of Service *(1869).*

3. *Greeley (1811–72) who was a newspaper editor and political leader, founded the New York* Tribune *(1841), of which he was editor thereafter. Setting high standards and engaging writers like Charles A. Dana, Margaret Fuller, George Ripley, and Bayard Taylor, Greeley made the* Tribune *a potent influence. A strong Unionist, he was also an advocate of the Free Soil movement, Fourierism, antislavery, temperance, universal suffrage, and post-Civil War amnesty. With equal vehemence he opposed liquor, tobacco, gambling, prostitution, and capital punishment. Taking part in founding the Republican party (1854–55), he later defected to become Liberal Republican presidential candidate (1872), but suffered a crushing defeat that probably hastened his death. Greeley was a quick-tempered man of uncertain judgment, but as a moral leader noted for clarity of expression and fervent convictions, he was the greatest editor of his time.*

4. *A junk bottle was a black bottle used for porter, short for porter's beer. It is a brew similar to stout, but weaker and less sweet, containing about 4 percent alcohol. To the makers of tracts on the evils of strong drink, a bottle was apparently the favorite blunt instrument of a sot assaulting his family in a drunken rage.*

Above: *An 1895 caricature in the Sydney, Australia,* Bulletin *depicts an exchange between* (left) *Mark Twain and* (right) *Sir Henry Parkes. Twain—"Alas! that I should envy you!" Parkes—"What do you henvy?—my politics, my poems, or my brains?" Twain—"Alas! neither. 'Tis your hair consumes me with envy!" (From The Mark Twain Papers.) Left: The caption on an illustration of Mark Twain in Portland's* The Sunday Oregonian *of August 11, 1895, read "A Characteristic Attitude (Caught at the Lecture)."*

Mark Twain suspended editorial duties while he made a lecture tour in 1869–70, giving "Our Fellow Savages of the Sandwich Islands" on a three-months' swing around eastern towns and cities. A memorable event of the jaunt was meeting William Dean Howells in Boston. Mark Twain startled the midwesterner—and Boston, too—by appearing in a sealskin coat with the fur outside, but that idiosyncrasy did not blight the beginning of a close friendship that endured thereafter. Mark Twain ended the tour shortly before marriage to Olivia Langdon on February 2, 1870. When the couple moved into a fine house with a mansard roof on Delaware Avenue— a wedding present from the father of the bride—he thought of himself as settled for life in Buffalo. In March when he began to write a monthly "Memoranda" section for the New York Galaxy, *the new assignment, coming in the midst of honeymoon euphoria, seemed to confirm his intention to be a proper citizen with a steady job. For the* Express *and the* Galaxy, *he followed his preferred method of writing on whatever topics struck his fancy, casually mixing fact and fiction as his habit was.*

MARK TWAIN IN NEW YORK
AUBURN, CALIFORNIA, *Stars and Stripes,* JUNE 23, 1870

I arrived in New York a few days ago, and immediately took rooms at the Astor House. To be sure I had no money to pay for them; but why think of pay if we are only good? I have always made it a rule to have the best of everything, even if I am obliged to get trusted for it. This sterling maxim was instilled into my mind by a kind father; and who shall say that that gray-haired old man is not proud of his orphan boy?

But the times are so hard just now that I find it very difficult to make both ends meet, and lay up money besides.

I had not been at the Astor more than one day, when the clerk brought me my bill.

"Is it customary," said I, "to pay by the day?"

"It is with men of your stamp," he replied.

"What kind of a stamp do you take me for?" said I.

"You look like a two-cent stamp," he replied—"mighty thin; if anybody should wet it once, you'd stick like thunder, but we don't propose to try it. You either pay this bill, or get out! Have you any money?"

"My estimable young friend," I replied, "you have

probably heard of Dr. Ben Franklin, long since deceased. That eminent physician was at one time in the proverb business, and did a very good thing. He said, among other things, that time is money. Now, I haven't got any money, but, as regards time, I am in affluent circumstances, and if you will receipt that bill, I will give you a check for as much time as you think equivalent, and throw you in a couple of hours for your trouble."

He made no reply, but from the fact of the porter's coming up immediately thereafter, removing my trunk to the sidewalk, and hustling me out after it, I inferred that I wasn't considered a financial success.

"Say, Mister," said a small boy with a very long coat and cap with considerable visor; "don't tear yourself away."

"Oh, you let him alone," said another, "his mother sent for him."

Oh, world thou art ever cruel!

I immediately called a hackman, and told him to take me to a cheap but respectable hotel. "And the cheaper it is," I added, "the more respectable I shall consider it."

He drove me to the Excelsior House, and I told him I was under a great obligation to him, and if at any time I could do him a favor, I should feel grieved if he didn't speak to me about it, for my proud spirit spurns an obligation.

"If you don't fork over that fifty cents," said he, "there'll be a funeral in your family, and it won't be your wife, nor none of your children."

"But I'm busted," said I. "If meeting houses were selling two for a cent, I could not buy the handle of a contribution box."

He swore at me awfully, and said he would have it out of my trunk—so he burst it open.

But the contents of that trunk are far from valuable, for I carry it filled with sawdust. It looks just as respectable, and in an emergency of this kind is invaluable.

I will not say this hackman looked daggers at me. He looked a whole arsenal, with a back room full of extra bayonets; and as he mounted his box and drove away, the air was fairly blue with oaths. He got off string after string without making a single mistake, and he must have had the Devil's dictionary at his tongue's end.

It fairly curdled my blood to hear him swear such awful swears. I never had my blood curdled before, so I put some in a bottle to look at.

I afterwards heard that the hackman was always very wicked, and wouldn't go to Sunday school when he was a little boy; but when his mother put on his cap with a tassel on it, and gave him a cent to put in the contribution box, he would go off with other bad boys and pitch pennies. Is it any wonder that he is a great horrid thing, and uses oaths when he swears?

As might have been expected, Mark Twain did not maintain the pose of the staid householder, departing for work every morning, and returning some hours later after a busy day at the office. That sort of conventional life was not meant for a man of his mercurial disposition. He became so bored with the Express that he ceased to pay much attention to anything about it except his own contributions, and the monthly requirements of the Galaxy came to be irksome, too. Buffalo, which he had never cared for, grew more distasteful by the week. In April 1871, he quit the Galaxy and sold his interest in the Express at a loss of some $10,000. It was the end of his career as journalist and job-holder. Thereafter he was author and free-lancer, unhampered by organizational routine and subject to no demands other than his own. Quarry Farm near Elmira was the next stop, where he made headway on his new book, Roughing It, while preparing to set up residence in Hartford.

The following nonsense is a composite version of the two sources, which differ slightly in minor details. Theriaki, a short-lived monthly published at Laporte, Indiana, called itself "A magazine devoted to the interests of opium eaters." The label implies a tongue-in-cheek spirit of misdirection that no doubt made the editors hospitable to the tall tale impulses of Mark Twain.

MARK TWAIN IN A RAILROAD CAR
JACKSON, CALIFORNIA *Amador Dispatch*, DECEMBER 30, 1871;
Theriaki, JANUARY, 1873, 164-65

I got into the cars and took a seat in juxtaposition to a female. That female's face was a perfect insurance company for her—it insured her against ever getting married to anybody except a blind man. Her mouth looked like a crack in a dried lemon, and there was no more expression in her face than there is in a cup of cold custard. She appeared as if she had been through one famine and got about two-thirds through another. She was old enough to be a great-grandmother to Mary that had the little lamb. She was chewing prize pop-corn, and carried in her hand a yellow rose, while a bandbox and a cotton umbrella nestled sweetly by her side. I couldn't guess whether she was on a mission of charity, or going West to start a saw-mill. I was full of curiosity to hear her speak, so I said:

"The exigencies of the time require great circumspection in a person who is traveling."

Says she, "What?"

Says I, "The orb of day shines resplendent in the blue vault above."

She hitched around uneasy like, then she raised her umbrella, and said, "I don't want any more of your sass—git out"; and I got out.

Then I took a seat alongside a male fellow, who looked like the ghost of Hamlet lengthened out. He was a stately cuss; and he was reading.

Said I, "Mister, did you ever see a camel-leopard?" I said a camel-leopard because it is a pious animal, and never eats any grass without getting down on its knees. He said he hadn't seen a camel-leopard.

Then said I, "Do you chew?"

He said, "No sir."

Then I said, "How sweet is all nature."

He took this for a conundrum and said he didn't know. Then he said he was deeply interested in the history of a great man. "Alas!" he exclaimed, "we are but few."

I told him I knew one; "the man that made my cooking stove was a very grate man."

Then he asked me, "would I read?"

Says I, "What have you got?"

He replied, "Watts Hymns," "Reveries by Moonlight," and "How to Spend the Sabbath."

I said, "None of them for Hannah," but if he had an unabridged Business Directory of New York City, I would take a little read.

Then he said, "Young man, look at these gray hairs."

I told him that I saw them, and when a man got as old as he was he ought to dye. Said I, "You needn't think these hairs are any sign of wisdom; it's only a sign that your system lacks iron, and I advise you to go home and swallow a crowbar."

He took this for irony, and what little *entente cordiale* there was between us was spilled. It turned out that he was chaplain of a base ball club.

When we got to Rochester I called for a bowl of bean soup. I send you the receipt for making it:

"Take a lot of water, wash it well, and broil it until it is brown on both sides; then very carefully pour one bean into it and let it simmer. When the bean begins to get restless, sweeten it with salt, then put it up in air-tight cans, hitch each can to a brick, and chuck them overboard, and the soup is done."

The above receipt originated with a man in Iowa, who got up suppers on odd occasions, for Odd Fellows. He has a receipt for oyster soup, leaving out the salt.

Speaking of Iowa reminds me of the way I got the money to pay for that fellow's supper. I bet a fellow a dollar that I could tell him how much water to a quart went under the railroad bridge over the Mississippi at Dubuque in a year. He bet, and I said two pints to a quart.

I won the bet, but after all, that supper was an awful swindle. If the city didn't settle faster than the coffee did, its old settler's club would be a failure, and the city too.

Dubuque is celebrated for its fine turnouts on the streets. While I was there a wagon upset and spilled a lot of women. I didn't see it—I looked the other way. No cards.

In August 1872, Mark Twain made his first trip to England, where he was received with great enthusiasm.[1] In a busy three months, he visited historic sites, met many famous Victorians, and was hospitably entertained by peers and commoners. In November he sailed for home aboard the Cunarder Batavia. *In mid-Atlantic the ship fell in with the British bark* Charles Ward *which had been dismasted in a gale and was in danger of foundering. The liner's lifeboat crew pulled through heavy seas to take off all the survivors clinging to the wreckage on the waterlogged bark. To gain recognition for the heroic sailors who had manned the lifeboat, a meeting of passengers on the* Batavia *appointed Mark Twain chairman of a committee to draft a communication to the Royal Humane Society. The account is undoubtedly his alone, not the report of a committee.*

PERILS OF THE SEA
New York *Times,* November 26, 1872

On Sunday night a strong west wind began to blow, and not long after midnight it increased to a gale. By 4 o'clock the sea was running very high. At 7½ our starboard bulwarks were stove in, and the water entered the main saloon. At a later hour the gangway on the port side came in with a crash, and the sea followed, flooding many of the staterooms on that side. At the same time a sea crossed the roof of the vessel, and carried away one of our boats, splintering it to pieces, and taking one of the davits with it. At 9½ the glass was down to 28.35, and the gale was blowing with a severity which the officers say is not experienced oftener than once in five or ten years. The storm continued during the day and all night, and also all day yesterday, but with moderated violence.

At 4 P.M. a dismasted vessel was sighted. A furious squall had just broken upon us, and the sea was running mountains high, to use the popular expression. Nevertheless Capt. Mouland immediately bore up for the wreck, which was making signals of distress, ordered out a life-boat, and called for volunteers. To a landsman it seemed like deliberate suicide to go out in such a storm, but our third and fourth officers and eight men answered the call with a promptness that compelled a cheer. They carried a long line with them, several life-buoys, and a lighted lantern, for the atmosphere was murky with the storm, and sunset was not far off.

The wreck, a bark, was in a pitiful condition; her mizzenmast and her bowsprit were gone, and her foremast was but a stump wreathed and cumbered with a ruin of sails and cordage from the fallen foretop and foretop-gallant masts and yards. We could see nine men clinging to the main rigging. The stern of the vessel was gone, and the sea made a clean breach over her, pouring in a cataract out of the broken stern, and spouting through the parted planks of her bows.

Our boat pulled 300 yards, and approached the wreck on the lee side. Then it had a hard fight, for the waves and the wind beat it constantly back. I do not know when anything has alternately so stirred me through and through,[2] and then disheartened me, as it did to see the boat every little while, get almost close enough, and then be hurled three lengths away again by a prodigious wave; and the darkness settling down all the time. But at last they got the line and buoy aboard, and after that we could make out nothing more. Presently we discovered the boat approaching us, and found she had saved every soul—nine men. They had had to drag these men, one at a time, through the sea to the life-boat with the line, and buoy, for of course they did not dare to touch the plunging vessel with the boat.

The peril increased now, for every time the boat got close to our lee, our ship rolled over on her and hid her from sight. But our people managed to haul the party aboard one at a time, without losing a man, though I said they would lose every single one of them. I am, therefore, but a poor success as a prophet. As the fury of the squall had not diminished, and as the sea was so heavy, it was feared we might lose some men if we tried to hoist the life-boat aboard, so she was turned adrift by the Captain's order, poor thing, after helping in such a gallant deed.

To speak by the log, and to be accurate, Capt. Mouland gave the order to change our ship's course, and bear down toward the wreck at 4:14 P.M. At 5¾ our ship was under way again with those nine poor devils on board; that is to say, this admirable thing was done in a tremendous sea, and in the face of a hurricane, in sixty minutes by the watch, and if your honorable Society could be moved to give to Capt. Mouland and his boat's crew that reward which a sailor prizes and covets above all other distinctions, the Royal Humane Society's medal,[3] the parties whose names are attached to this paper will feel as grateful as if they themselves were the recipients of this great honor.

The wrecked bark was the *Charles Ward,* Capt. Bell, bound from Quebec to Scotland, with lumber. The vessel went over on her beam ends at 9 o'clock Monday morning, and eleven men were washed overboard and lost. Capt. Bell and eight men remained, and these our boat saved. They had been in the main rigging some thirty-one hours, without food or water, and were so frozen and exhausted, that, when we got them aboard, they could hardly speak, and the minds of several of them were wandering. The wreck was out of the ordinary track of vessels, and was 1,500 miles from land. She was in the center of the Atlantic. Our lifeboat crew of volunteers consisted of the following: D. Gillies, third officer; R. Kyle, fourth officer; Nicholas Foley, quartermaster; Henry Foley, quartermaster; Nathaniel Clark, quartermaster; Thomas Henry, seaman; John Park, seaman; Richard Brennan, seaman.

After speaking of the enthusiasm of the passengers, Mark Twain continues.

As might have been anticipated, if I have been of any service toward rescuing these nine shipwrecked human beings by standing around the deck in a furious storm, without any umbrella, keeping an eye on things and seeing that they were done right, and yelling whenever a cheer seemed to be the important thing, I am glad and I am satisfied. I ask no reward. I would do it again under the same circumstances. But what I do plead for, earnestly and sincerely, is that the Royal Humane Society will remember our Captain and our lifeboat crew, and in so remembering them increase the high honor and esteem in which the Society is held all over the civilized world. In this appeal our passengers all join with hearty sincerity, and in testimony thereof will sign their names, begging that you will pardon me, a stranger, for addressing your honored Society with such confidence and such absence of ceremony, and, trusting that my motive may redeem my manner, I am, gentlemen, your obedient servant,

Mark Twain

All of the Batavia's *passengers signed the communication.*

1. *Mark Twain's hearty reception in England contrasted sharply with lack of recognition by his peers at home. Although he had won popular favor as the author of* Innocents Abroad *and as a lyceum lecturer, he was still on probation among the literati of the Atlantic seaboard. In a cultural atmosphere heavy with reverence for the New England tradition, Mark Twain was looked upon as a dubious character, a wild western upstart who was sometimes dismissed as a mere buffoon. Hence the warm British welcome generated a fondness for England that persisted thereafter, more or less, despite transitory disillusionments of later years. For a detailed account of the ups and downs of his relations with Britain, see Howard G. Baetzhold,* Mark Twain & John Bull (*Bloomington: Indiana University Press, 1970*).

2. *In a letter to the Boston* Daily Journal, *February 7, 1873, Mark Twain said: "It was worth any money to see that life-boat climb those dizzy mountains of water, in a driving mist of spume flakes, and fight its way inch by inch in the teeth of the gale. Just the mere memory of it stirs a body so that I would swing my hat and disgorge a cheer now, if I could do it without waking the baby. But if you get a baby awake once you never can get it to sleep again, and then you get in trouble with the whole family. Somehow I don't have a chance to yell the way I used to."*

3. *The Royal Humane Society gave a gold medal and a letter of thanks to Captain Mouland, silver medals to officers Gillies and Kyle, as well as monetary rewards to them and £7 to each of the six seamen who manned the lifeboat. The Cunard Line promoted Gillies and Kyle to first officers and gave £5 each to the seamen. Mark Twain said in his letter to the Boston Journal cited above: "We are a nation of forty millions, and we have some little money. Cannot we have a society like that? Why, it is the next most noblest thing to sending moral tracts to Timbuctoo. And it would cost less money, too. Not that I object to sending moral tracts to Timbuctoo; far from it; I write most of them myself, and gain the greater part of my living that way. I would grieve to see Timbuctoo redeemed, and have to lose its custom. But why not start a Humane Society besides?"*

After returning from England in November 1872, Mark Twain spent all of six months in the United States. The Redpath Lyceum Bureau made tempting proposals for a lecture series, and many other invitations to speak offered high fees—$400 to $800 a night—but he declined. Still, he did take to the platform a few times in New York and once in his newly-adopted home town of Hartford. The occasion was a benefit for the City Mission of Father Hawley, a self-appointed good Samaritan who attempted to care for the poor and helpless of the community. To stimulate interest, Mark Twain prefaced his appearance with an appeal to the public.

THE POOR OF HARTFORD AND THE SANDWICH ISLANDS
CHARACTERISTIC CARD FROM MARK TWAIN
HARTFORD *Courant,* JANUARY 29, 1873

With the present new-laid ten inches of snow for a text, one might preach a pithy sermon upon the distress this vigorous winter has brought, in Hartford, to many a fireside where there is no fire. But no doubt it is sufficient to say that Mr. Hawley knows of a great many widows and little children here who suffer from cold and hunger every day and every night, and yet the means he is able to gather up fall far short of being enough to relieve them. He has made some strong appeals for aid, through the press, and they have been responded to with considerable liberality; but still the empty mouths and the fireless hearths are so many that he is pretty well discouraged. His appeals are not in behalf of able-bodied tramps who are too lazy to work, but in behalf of women and children—women broken down by illness and lack of food, and children who are too young to help themselves. If I were to go into details and tell what Father Hawley knows about these blameless unfortunates, the purse-strings of this benevolent old city would relax with one impulse, and the trouble would be at an end.

Now several of us have conceived the idea that we might raise a thousand dollars for Father Hawley's clients through the medium of a lecture to be given at Allyn Hall next Friday night by the undersigned. I am thoroughly and cheerfully willing to lecture here for such an object, though I would have serious objections to talking in my own town for the benefit of my own pocket—we freebooters of the platform consider it more graceful to fly the black flag in strange waters and prey upon remote and friendless communities.

We desire that *all* the proceeds of the lecture shall go into Father Hawley's hands; therefore we called for volunteers to pay the expenses of hall rent, advertising, etc., and his excellency, the governor of the state, promptly offered to foot the whole bill, but as a dozen other prominent citizens demanded a chance, we let them have it, for there is nothing mean about us. When we appeal for liberality in others we are willing to be generous ourselves. One of the first merchants of Hartford,[1] one of her most capable and energetic business men, has shouldered the whole work of advertising and managing the business details of our enterprise, and it will be done well. He gives to it for nothing, time which is worth a great many dollars a day to him.

The price of our tickets will be one dollar each, all over the house—and reserved seats can be secured at Brown & Gross' without extra charge. We hear of parties who are taking from ten to fifty of them, and we receive the news with high gratification. We place the tickets at double price for several reasons.[2] One is, the lecture itself being worth nearly twenty-five cents, the ticket-purchaser would really be *giving* only about twenty-five to the charity if the tickets were fifty cents; but by making the price a dollar, the purchaser has a chance to make a good, honest, undefiled contribution of seventy-five to charity. The idea is mine— none but an old business head would have thought of an attraction like that. Another reason for high prices is, that charity is a dignified and respectworthy thing, and there is small merit about it and less grace when it don't cost anything. As a general thing, charity entertainments are the cheapest that are offered to the public—and that is paying but a poor compliment to the public. One would suppose that the idea was to get the thing down to a figure that would enable the hungry poor to attend their own entertainments and support themselves. Now that cannot be right—it cannot be either just or generous.

Lucca charges $4 a ticket,[3] and so my first idea was to put our tickets at $4, too, and run opposition. But friends said no, there was a difference—Lucca sings. I said, very well, I would sing, too. I showed them what I could do. But they still objected, and said that a mere disturbance was not singing. So I have come down to a dollar; but I do it with reluctance.

I must not deceive any one; therefore I will say, in parenthesis, as it were, that I am going to deliver a lecture that I delivered here before the Young Men's Institute two or three years ago—a lecture on the Sandwich Islands. I do this because Father Hawley's need is so pressing that I have not time to prepare a new lecture; I happen to be just fixed and primed for this Sandwich Islands talk, for the reason that I have been rubbing it up to deliver before the New York Mercantile Library some ten days hence. Now we offer these following terms: all who have not already heard the lecture can pay a dollar and come in; and all who have heard it before can commute for two dollars apiece, and remain at home if they prefer. In which case the police will be instructed not to disturb them. But if they come to the hall they must behave, and not cry over old jokes that merely made them sad when they heard them before.

We would like to have a thousand dollars in the house;[4] we point to the snow and the thermometer; we call Hartford by name, and we are not much afraid but that she will step to the front and answer for herself.

Mark Twain

Hartford, Jan. 28

1. *He was John S. Ives, "whose industry and zeal in its business management," said the* Courant, *"contributed so much to the success of the lecture."*

2. *A lecture ticket, especially in small towns, was usually fifty cents. Villagers grumbled over what they considered a high price, and if the lecturer did not give them a spectacular oratorical performance of roaring and thumping, they believed they had been swindled. A dollar was looked upon as outrageous. Mark Twain was hesitant to ask a dollar for his first San Francisco lecture in 1866, but he soon revised his attitude in favor of charging as much as he thought the traffic would bear.*

3. *Pauline Lucca (1841-1908), daughter of Italian parents, was a Viennese soprano who made her debut in Verdi's* Ernani *in 1859. A tremendous success in Berlin, London, and Saint Petersburg, she made an operatic tour of the United States (1872-74). Possessing a strong voice with a range of two and a half octaves, she was also praised for a talent rare in an operatic singer, her skill as an actress.*

4. *At the close of the lecture, a one-armed postman named Jaggers, well known in Hartford, came upon the stage carrying a huge envelope containing a card about two feet square on which was printed in large letters, "$1,500 for Father Hawley."* The Courant, *next day, said that Mark Twain's performance was "by far the best of the lecturer's efforts here. . . . We have heard nothing better upon the platform. . . . The audience appeared thoroughly interested and pleased throughout."*

On April 26, 1871, Avery D. Putnam, a New York provision merchant, was savagely assaulted as he assisted two women to leave a Broadway car at Forty-sixth Street and Seventh Avenue. The drunken attacker was William Foster, a former conductor on the Broadway line, who struck his victim with a long iron bar called a car-hook. When Putnam died four days later, Foster was indicted for first-degree murder, tried, convicted, and sentenced to hang. Then followed a series of legal delays—stay of proceedings, temporary reprieve, and so forth—that kept the case in the courts and the news for almost two years. In that time, all New York papers were deluged with a flood of letters about Foster, many of them defending him as a model citizen of exemplary character, temperate habits, and harmless impulses. Governor Dix was petitioned to commute the sentence to a life term. Mark Twain contributed his own ironic comments on Foster and on the vagaries of the law.

FOSTER'S CASE
New York *Tribune*, March 10, 1873

To the Editor of the *Tribune*

Sir: I have read the Foster petitions in Thursday's *Tribune*. The lawyers' opinions do not disturb me, because I know that those same gentlemen could make as able an argument in favor of Judas Iscariot, which is a great deal for me to say, for I never can think of Judas Iscariot without losing my temper. To my mind Judas Iscariot was nothing but a low, mean, premature Congressman. The attitude of the jury does not unsettle a body, I must admit; and it seems plain that they would have modified their verdict to murder in the second degree[1] if the Judge's charge had permitted it. But when I come to the petitions of Foster's friends and find out Foster's true character, the generous tears will flow—I cannot help it. How easy it is to get a wrong impression of a man. I perceive that from childhood up this one has been a sweet, docile thing, full of pretty ways and gentle impulses, the charm of the fireside, the admiration of society, the idol of the Sunday school. I recognize in him the divinest nature that has ever glorified any mere human being. I perceive that the sentiment with which he regarded temperance was a thing that amounted to frantic adoration. I freely confess that it was the most natural thing in the world for such an organism as this to get drunk and insult a stranger, and then beat his brains out with a car-hook because he did not seem to admire it. Such is Foster. And to think that we came so near losing him! How do we know but that he is the Second Advent? And yet, after all, if the jury had not been hampered in their choice of a verdict I think I could consent to lose him.

The humorist who invented trial by jury played a colossal practical joke upon the world, but since we have the system we ought to try to respect it. A thing which is not thoroughly easy to do, when we reflect that by command of the law a criminal juror must be an intellectual vacuum,[2] attached to a melting heart and perfectly macaronian bowels of compassion.

I have had no experience in making laws or amending them, but still I cannot understand why, when it takes twelve men to inflict the death penalty upon a person, it should take any less than twelve more to undo their work. If I were a legislature, and had just been elected, and had not had time to sell out, I would put the pardoning and commuting power into the hands of twelve able men instead of dumping so huge a burden upon the shoulders of one poor petition-persecuted individual.[3]

Mark Twain

Hartford, March 7, 1873

1. *Foster, in his own letter to the New York* Times, *June 4, 1871, denied premeditation. Admitting that he was drunk, he said he had not intended to kill Putnam and claimed that "public resentment and exasperation brought about the verdict."*

2. *Mark Twain believed that the method of selecting a jury favored ignorance and penalized intelligence. In* Roughing It, *a Virginia City jury was "composed of two desperadoes, two low beer-house politicians, three barkeepers, two ranchmen who could not read, and three dull, stupid, human donkeys! It actually came out afterward, that one of these latter thought that incest and arson were the same thing." In* The Gilded Age, *of the jurors at the trial of Laura Hawkins, "only two could read, one of whom was the foreman. . . . Low foreheads and heavy faces they all had; some had a look of animal cunning, while the most were only stupid. The entire panel formed that boasted heritage commonly described as the 'bulwark of our liberties.'"*

3. *Governor Dix did not commute the sentence, and Foster, after attempting to commit suicide, was hanged March 21, 1873.*

Mark Twain satirized pious Sunday School fiction by inventing tales in which the bad boy prospered and the good boy came to grief. With sardonic humor, he dwelt upon the irony of sentimental concern for criminals, as in his letter about Foster and his sketch "Lionizing Murderers." In the following story, the hero is the poor-but-honest thief who resembles the bank robber of today's TV thrillers, even to the extent of feeling put-upon and determined to get back at the world. There is also a suggestion of the modern syndicate boss who poses as a pillar of society while directing large criminal enterprises. The Moralist of the Main could make his points by turning the moral order upside down.

MAKING A FORTUNE
JACKSON, CALIFORNIA *Amador Dispatch,* MARCH 29, 1873

Samuel McFadden was a watchman in a bank. He was poor, but honest, and his life was without reproach. The trouble with him was that he felt he was not appreciated. His salary was only four dollars a week, and when he asked to have his salary raised, the President, Cashier and Board of Directors glared at him through their spectacles and frowned on him, and told him to go out and stop his insolence, when he knew business was dull, and the bank could not meet its expenses now, let alone lavishing one dollar on such a miserable worm as Samuel McFadden. And then Samuel McFadden felt depressed, sad, and the haughty scorn of the President and Cashier cut him to the soul. He would often go into the side yard and bow his twenty-four inch head, and weep gallons and gallons of tears over his insignificance, and pray that he might be made worthy of the Cashier's and President's attention.

One night a happy thought struck him; a gleam of light struck upon him, and gazing down the dim vista of years with his eyes all blinded with joyous tears, he saw himself rich and respected. So Samuel McFadden fooled around and got a jimmy, a monkey wrench, a crosscut saw, a cold chisel, a drill, and about a ton of gunpowder and nitro-glycerine, and those things. Then, in the dead of night, he went to the fire-proof safe, and after working at it for a long while, burst the door and brick into an immortal smash, with such a perfect success, that there was not enough of that safe left to make a carpet tack. Mr. McFadden then proceeded to load up with coupons, greenbacks, currency and specie, and to nail all the odd change that was lying anywhere, so that he pranced out of the bank with more than a million dollars on him. He then retired to an unassuming residence out of town, and then sent word to the detectives where he was.

A detective called on him the next day with a soothing note from the Cashier. McFadden treated it with lofty scorn. Detectives called on him every day with humble notes from the President, Cashier and Board of Directors. At last the bank officers got up a magnificent private supper, to which Mr. McFadden was invited. He came, and as the bank officers bowed down in the dust before him, he pondered well over the bitter past, and his soul was filled with exultation.

Before he drove away in his carriage that night, it was all fixed that Mr. McFadden was to keep half a million of that money, and to be unmolested, if he returned the other half. He fulfilled his contract like an honest man, but refused with haughty disdain the offer of the Cashier to marry his daughter.

Mac is now honored and respected. He moves in the best society, he browses around in purple and fine linen and other good clothes, and enjoys himself first rate. And often now he takes his infant son on his knee and tells him of his early life, and instills holy principles into the child's mind, and shows him how, by industry and perseverance and frugality, and nitro-glycerine, and monkey wrenches, and cross-cut saws, and familiarity with the detective system, even the poor may rise to affluence and respectability.[1]

1. *Mark Twain's story "Edward Mills and George Benton; a Tale" (1880) tells of Edward, the hard-working bank cashier, and George, the forger and thief who went after the cash in Edward's bank and murdered the cashier. Arrested and indicted, George got religion. Then he was showered with sentimental attention: "From that time forth his cell was always full of girls and women and fresh flowers; all the day long there was prayer, and hymn-singing, and thanksgiving, and homilies, and tears, with never an interruption, except an occasional five-minute intermission for refreshments." Anguished pleas on his behalf failing to move the authorities, George was hanged, sanctified and glorified to the end.*

In May 1873, Mark Twain again embarked for England, this time taking along his wife, Olivia, and infant daughter, Susy. Before sailing, he responded to a request from the New York Graphic *for a farewell message, which the paper published on page one as an enlarged facsimile of Mark Twain's handwriting.*

MARK TWAIN'S FAREWELL
New York *Daily Graphic,* April 22, 1873

Hartford, April 17, 1873

Ed. *Graphic:* Your note is received. If the following two lines which I have cut from it are your natural handwriting, then I understand you to ask me "for a farewell letter in the name of the American people." Bless you! The joy of the American people is just a little premature. I have not *gone* yet, and what is more I am not going to stay when I do go. Yes, it's too true. I'm only going to remain beyond the seas six months—that is all. I love stir and excitement, and so the moment the spring birds begin to sing, the zephyrs to sigh, the flowers to bloom, and the stagnation, the pensive melancholy, the lagging weariness of summer to threaten, I grow restless. I get the fidgets, I want to pack off somewhere, where there is something going on. But you know how that is—you must have felt that way. This very day I saw the signs in the air of the coming dullness, and I said to myself, "How glad I am that I have already chartered a steamship to tow myself and my party over on my life raft." There was absolutely nothing in the morning papers. You can see for yourself what the telegraphic headings were:

BY TELEGRAPH

A Colored Congressman in Trouble
EXCITEMENT IN ALBANY

Five Years Imprisonment

WALL STREET PANICKY
Two Failures and Money at 150 per cent

TWO CRIMINAL CASES
Arrested for Highway Robbery
THE ASSAULT ON THE GAS COLLECTOR
A Striker Held for Murder in the Second Degree

The Murderer King Dangerously Sick
LUSIGNANI, THE WIFE MURDERER, TO BE HUNG
TWO WOULD BE MURDERERS TO BE HUNG

INCENDIARISM IN A BAPTIST FLOCK

A FATAL MISTAKE

WASHING AWAY OF A RAILROAD

Ku Klux Murders

A SHOCKING DISASTER
A Chimney Falls and Buries Five Children
Two of Them Already Dead

THE MODOC MASSACRE

Riddle's Warning

A FATHER KILLED BY HIS SON
A Bloody Fight in Kentucky
AN EIGHT YEAR-OLD MURDERER

A GRAVE-YARD FLOATING OFF

A Louisiana Massacre
A COURT HOUSE FIRED AND NEGROES
THEREIN SHOT WHILE ESCAPING
TWO TO THREE HUNDRED MEN ROASTED ALIVE

A LIVELY SKIRMISH IN INDIANA
A TOWN IN A STATE OF GENERAL RIOT
A PARTY OF MINERS BESIEGED IN A BOARDING HOUSE
Troops and Police From Indianapolis Asked For
BLOODY WORK EXPECTED
FURIOUS AMAZON LEADERS

A HORRIBLE STORY
A NEGRO OUTRAGE
A Suffering and Murdered Woman Terribly Avenged
A MAN IS 24 HOURS BURNING, AND CARVED PIECE-MEAL

The items under the headlines all bear date *of* yesterday, April 10, (refer to your own paper) and I give you my word of honor that that string of common-place stuff was everything there was in the telegraphic columns that a body could call news. Well, said I to myself, this is getting pretty dull; this is getting pretty dry; there don't appear to be anything going on anywhere; has this progressive nation gone to sleep? Have I got to stand another month of this torpidity before I can begin to browse among the lively capitals of Europe? But never mind—things may revive while I'm away.

During the last two months my next-door neighbor, Charles Dudley Warner,[1] has dropped his "Back-Log Studies," and he and I have written a bulky novel in partnership.[2] He has worked up the fiction and I have hurled in the facts. I consider it one of the most astonishing novels that ever was written. Night after night I sit up reading it over and over again and crying. It will be published early in the fall, with plenty of pictures. Do you consider this an advertisement?—and if so, do you charge for such things, when a man is your friend and is an orphan?

Drooping, now, under the solemn peacefulness, the general stagnation, the profound lethargy that broods over the land, I am

Yours truly,
Sam'l L. Clemens (Mark Twain)

1. *Warner (1829-1900) gave up a law practice in Chicago and turned to journalism on the staff of the Hartford* Evening Press *(1860). He remained there when the paper consolidated with the* Courant *(1867), later becoming a contributing editor of* Harper's Magazine *(1884-98). He is best known as an essayist, by such collections as* My Summer in a Garden *(1871),* Backlog Studies *(1873),* On Horseback *(1888), and others. Urbane and good-natured, he wrote in the manner of the* Sketch Book, *following a fashion that was becoming alien to the nervous materialism of late nineteenth-century America. Yet Warner was sufficiently aware of the current of his times to collaborate with Mark Twain on a novel,* The Gilded Age *(1873), the title of which defines a society remote from the world of Washington Irving.*

2. *In import,* The Gilded Age *is not as bulky as it might have been, considering the scandalous evidence, political and financial, the authors had at hand. Yet the book is noteworthy for satirical characterization, as of the corrupt Senator Dilworthy, modeled after Senator Samuel C. Pomeroy of Kansas. Another entertaining character is Colonel Sellers, the cheerful dreamer and failure, continually making imaginary fortunes out of vast projected enterprises, always broke, but constantly reiterating his favorite remark, "There's millions in it." Sellers is supposedly drawn from a distant Clemens cousin, James Lampton, but as critics have pointed out, his get-rich-quick fantasies are similar to the rosy dreams of Mark Twain himself. When made into a play in 1874,* The Gilded Age *was the most successful of Mark Twain's several efforts as a dramatist.*

In England, Mark Twain was at once caught up in a social swirl like that of the year before, enjoying the hospitality of metropolitan clubs, meeting famous Englishmen, attending banquets, making after-dinner speeches. In June, he covered the visit of the Shah of Persia for the New York Herald, *writing a half dozen or more dispatches that were a familiar blend of fact, fiction, and editorializing. He told of going over to Ostend to meet the royal party; noting the customs of the Flounders (Flemish people); boarding the escort ship, HMS* Lively; *sailing back across the Channel with other correspondents and plentiful champagne; viewing the grand naval parade; and observing the glittering London pageantry of florid uniforms, brassy bands, and marching regiments, of princes and peers weighted down with plumed hats, medals, and orders. He referred to the shah as "the long expected millennium" and "this splendid barbarian," so bejeweled that "he shone like a window with the westering sun on it." The* Herald *matched his lese majesty by flippantly headlining the monarch as "O'Shah." This fragment is an excerpt from one of Mark Twain's accounts.*

THE SHAH CALLS UPON THE QUEEN
New York *Herald,* n.d.; Reprinted in Cleveland *Herald,* July 12, 1873

After a day's rest the Shah went to Windsor Castle and called on the Queen. What that suggests to the reader's mind is this: That the Shah took a hand satchel and an umbrella, called a cab and said he wanted to get to the

Paddington station; that when he arrived there the driver charged him sixpence too much, and he paid it rather than have trouble; that he tried now to buy a ticket, and was answered by a ticket seller as surly as a hotel clerk that he was not selling tickets for that train yet; that he finally got his ticket, and was beguiled of his satchel by a railway porter at once, who put it in a first-class carriage and got a sixpence, which the company forbade him to receive; that presently when the guard (or conductor) of the train came along the Shah slipped a shilling into his hand and said he wanted to smoke, and straightway the guard signified that it was all right; that when the Shah arrived at Windsor Castle he rung the bell, and when the girl came to the door asked her if the Queen was at home; and she left him standing in the hall and went to see; that by and by she returned and said would he please sit down in the front room and Mrs. Guelph[1] would be down directly; that he hung up his hat on the hat rack, stood his umbrella up in a corner, entered the front room and sat down on a hair cloth chair; that he waited and waited and got tired; that he got up and examined the old piano, the depressing lithographs on the walls and the album of photographs of faded country relatives on the center table, and was just about to fall back on the family Bible when the Queen entered briskly and begged him to sit down, and apologized for keeping him waiting, but she had just got a new girl and everything was upside down, and so forth and so on; but how are the family and when did he arrive, and how long should he stay and why didn't he bring his wife.

I knew that that was the picture that would spring up in the American reader's mind when it was said that the Shah went to visit the Queen, because that was the picture which the announcement suggested to my own mind. But it was far from the facts, very far. Nothing could be further. In truth, these people made as much of a to do over a mere friendly call as anybody else would over a conflagration. There were special railway trains for the occasion; there was a general muster of princes and dukes to go along, each one occupying room forty; there were regiments of cavalry to clear the way, railway stations were turned into flower gardens, sheltered with flags and all manner of gaudy splendor; there were multitudes of people to look on over the heads of interminable ranks of policemen standing shoulder to shoulder and facing front; there was blaring of music and booming of cannon. All that fuss, in sober truth, over a mere off-hand friendly call. Imagine what it would have been if he had brought another shirt and was going to stay a month.

1. *In Germany, the House of Welf was a dynasty of nobles and rulers who were contenders for power in central Europe and also in Italy, where the Guelphs and the Ghibellines were the two great parties of medieval politics. In the eighteenth century, Hanoverian Welfs (or Guelphs) became rulers of Great Britain upon the accession of George I as King of England (1714).*

In October, Mark Twain took to the lecture platform, giving the "Sandwich Islands" for a week in the Queen's Concert Rooms, Hanover Square. The auditorium was too small, he thought, but the audiences, which belonged literally to the carriage trade, were appreciative if at times puzzled by western American humor. After two appearances at Liverpool late in the month, he had to shepherd his family back home because Olivia was weary of the constant social grind. Having installed his charges in Hartford, he immediately set out for England once more; and by December 1, he was again billed for a week of the "Sandwich Islands," then shifted to "Roughing It on the Silver Frontier" for another ten days. Toward the end of the brief series, when he knew he had won the cordial regard of the British people, he made the following audacious publicity gesture. Perhaps he half-seriously hoped that his frivolous bid for attention might induce some member of the royal family or a prominent nobleman to attend one of his lectures. None did. Possibly a few minor barons came and miscellaneous Sir Somebodies, but no belted earls.

LETTER TO THE EDITOR
London *Morning Post*, c. December 12, 1873

Sir: Now that my lecturing engagement is drawing to a close, I feel that there is one attraction which I forgot to provide, and that is, the attendance of some great member of the Government to give distinction to my entertainment.

Strictly speaking I did not really forget this or underrate its importance, but the truth was, I was afraid of it. I was afraid of it for the reason that those great personages have so many calls upon their time that they cannot well spare the time to sit out an entertainment, and I knew that if one of them were to leave his box and retire while I was lecturing it would seriously embarrass me.

I find, however, that many people think I ought not to allow this lack to exist longer; therefore, I feel compelled to reveal a thing which I had intended to keep a secret. I early applied to a party at the East-end who is in the same line of business as Madame Tussaud,[1] and he agreed to lend me a couple of Kings and some nobility, and he said that they would sit out my lecture, and not only sit it out, but that they wouldn't even leave the place when it was done, but would just stay where they were, perfectly infatuated, and wait for more. So I made a bargain with him at once, and was going to ask the newspapers to mention, in the usual column, that on such-and-such an evening his Majesty King Henry VIII would honour my entertainment with his presence, and that on such-and-such an evening his Majesty William the Conqueror would be present; and that on the succeeding evening Moses and Aaron would be there, and so on. I felt encouraged now, an attendance like that would make my entertainment all that could be desired, and besides, I would not be embarrassed by their going away before my lecture was over.

But now a misfortune came. In attempting to move Henry VIII to my lecture hall, the porter fell downstairs and utterly smashed him all to pieces; in the course of moving William the Conqueror, something let go, and all the sawdust burst out of him, and he collapsed and withered away to nothing before my eyes. Then we collared some dukes, but they were so seedy and decayed that nobody would ever have believed in their rank; and so I gave them up, with almost a broken heart. In my trouble I had nothing in the world left to depend on now but just Moses and Aaron, and I confess to you that it was all I could do to keep the tears back when I came to examine those two images and found that that man, in his unapproachable ignorance, had been exhibiting in Whitechapel for Moses and Aaron what any educated person could see at a glance, by the ligature, were only the Siamese Twins.

You see now, sir, that I have done all that a man could do to supply a complained of lack, and if I have failed I think I ought to be pitied, not blamed. I wish I could get a king somewhere, just only for a little while, and I would take good care of him, and send him home, and pay the cab myself.

Mark Twain

London, Dec. 10

1. *Marie Tussaud (1761-1850), having learned the art of wax modeling, established her exhibit of wax figures, historical and topical, on Baker Street, London, in the early nineteenth century. Notorious characters and crimes were in a special section that* Punch *dubbed the "Chamber of Horrors." Some of her original models—of Voltaire, Franklin, Nelson, Walter Scott—are said to be extant. The story goes that Mark Twain, standing before some striking figure in Madame Tussaud's, was suddenly poked by a lady with an umbrella. When he jumped, she exclaimed, "Oh, lor' it's alive!" and fled.*

Back home by January 1874, Mark Twain remained in the United States for several years this time. The family moved into the elaborate new house of three stories, nineteen large rooms, and five baths—an unconventional structure of Gothic angles with a balcony that resembled a pilot house and a long porch like the deck of a steamboat. Before long the place became a way station for a steady stream of visitors, who were lavishly entertained. Mark Twain led a crowded life as host to numerous guests, as lecturer once in a while, as founder and patron of the Saturday Morning Club for young women of Hartford, and as entrepreneur conjuring imaginary fortunes out of inventions he invested in. As an author, he was working on The Adventures of Tom Sawyer *and writing occasional pieces like the following.*

SOCIABLE JIMMY
NEW YORK *Times*, NOVEMBER 29, 1874

[I sent the following home in a private letter some time ago from a certain little village. It was in the days when I was a public lecturer. I did it because I wished to preserve the memory of the most artless, sociable, and exhaustless talker I ever came across. He did not tell me a single remarkable thing, or one that was worth remembering; and yet he was himself so interested in his small marvels, and they flowed so naturally and comfortably from his lips that his talk got the upper hand of my interest, too, and I listened as one who receives a revelation. I took down what he had to say,[1] just as he said it—without altering a word or adding one.]

I had my supper in my room this evening (as usual), and they sent up a bright, simple, guileless little darky boy to wait on me—ten years old—a wide-eyed, observant little chap. I said:

"What is your name, my boy?"

"Dey calls me Jimmy, sah, but my right name's James, sah."

I said, "Sit down there, Jimmy—I'll not want you just yet."

He sat down in a big arm chair, hung both his legs over one of the arms, and looked comfortable and conversational. I said:

"Did you have a pleasant Christmas, Jimmy?"

"No, sah—not zackly. I was kind o' sick den. But de res' o' de people *dey* had a good time—mos' all uv 'em had a good time. Dey all got drunk. Dey all gits drunk heah, every Christmas, and carries on and has awful good times."

"So you were sick and lost it all. But unless you were *very* sick I should think that if you had asked the doctor he might have let you get—get—a *little* drunk—and—"

"Oh, no, sah—I don' never git drunk—it's de *white* folks—dem's de ones I mean. Pa used to git drunk, but dat was befo' I was big—but he's done quit. He don' git drunk no mo' now. Jis' takes one sip in de mawnin', now, cuz his stomach riles up, he sleeps so soun'. Jis' one sip—over to de s'loon—every mawnin'. He's powerful sickly—powerful—sometimes he can't hardly git aroun', he can't. He goes to de doctor every week—over to Ragtown. An' one time he tuck some stuff, you know, an' it mighty near *fetched* him. Ain't it dish yer blue vittles dat's pison?—ain't dat it?—truck what you pisons cats wid?"

"Yes, blue vittles [vitriol] is a very convincing article with a cat."

"Well, den, dat was it. De ole man, he tuck de bottle and shuck it, and shuck it—he seed it was blue, and he didn't know but it was blue mass, which he tuck mos' always—blue mass pills—but den he 'spected maybe dish yer truck might be some other kin' o' blue stuff, and so he sot de bottle down, and drat it if it wa'n't blue vittles, sho' nuff, when de doctor come. An' de doctor he say if he'd a tuck dat blue vittles it would a highsted him, *sho*. People can't be too particlar 'bout sich things. Yes, *indeedy.*

"We ain't got no cats heah, 'bout dis hotel. Bill he don't like 'em. He can't stan' a cat no way. Ef he was to ketch one he'd slam it outen de winder in a minute. Yes he would. Bill's down on cats. So is de gals—waiter gals. When dey ketches a cat bummin' aroun' heah, dey jis' *scoops* him—'deed dey do. Dey snake him into de cistern—dey's been cats drownded in dat water dat's in yo' pitcher. I seed a cat in dere yistiddy—all swelled up like a pudd'n. I bet you dem gals done dat. Ma says if dey was to drownd a cat for *her*, de fust one of 'em she ketched she'd jam her into de cistern 'long wid de cat. Ma wouldn't *do* dat, I don't reckon, but 'deed an' double, she *said* she would. I can't kill a chicken— well, I kin wring its neck off, cuz dat don't make 'em no sufferin' scacely; but I can't take and chop dey heads off, like some people kin. It makes me feel so—so—well, I kin see dat chicken nights so's I can't sleep. Mr. Dunlap, he's de richest man in dis town. Some people says dey's fo' thousan' people in dis town—dis city. But Bill says dey ain't but 'bout thirty-three hund'd. And Bill he knows, cuz he's lived heah all his life, do' dey *do* say he won't never set de river on fire. I don't know how dey fin' out—*I* wouldn't like to count all dem people. Some folks says dis town would be considerable bigger if it wa'n't on accounts of so much lan' all roun' it dat ain't got no houses on it." [This in perfect seriousness—dense simplicity—no idea of a joke.] "I reckon you seed dat church as you come along up street. Dat's an awful big church—awful high steeple. An' it's all solid stone, excep' jes de top part—de steeple, I means—dat's wood. It falls off when de win' blows pooty hard, an' one time it stuck in a cow's back and busted de cow all to de mischief. It's gwine to kill somebody yit, dat steeple is. A man—big man, he was—bigger'n what Bill is—he tuck it up dere and fixed it again—an' he didn't look no bigger'n a boy, he was so high up. Dat steeple's awful high. If you look out de winder you kin see it." [I looked out, and was speechless with awe and admiration—which gratified Jimmy beyond expression. The wonderful steeple was some sixty or seventy feet high, and had a clock-face on it.]

"You see dat arrer on top o' dat steeple? Well, sah, dat arrer is pooty nigh as big as dis do' [door]. I seed it when dey pulled it outen de cow. It mus' be awful to stan' in dat steeple when de clock is strikin'—dey say it is. Booms and jars so's you think the world's a comin' to an end. *I* wouldn't like to be up dere when de clock's a strikin'. Dat clock ain't just a striker, like dese common clocks. It's a *bell*—jist a reglar *bell*—and it's a buster. You can hear dat bell all over dis city. You ought to hear it boom, boom, boom, when dey's a fire. My sakes! Dey ain't got no bell like dat in Ragtown. *I* ben to Ragtown, and I ben mos' halfway to Dockery [thirty miles]. De bell in Ragtown's got so old now she don't make no soun' scacely."

[Enter the landlord—a kindly man, verging toward fifty. My small friend, without changing position, says]:

"Bill, didn't you say dat dey was only thirty-three hund'd people in dis city?"

"Yes, about thirty-three hundred is the population now."

"Well, some folks says dey's fo' thousan'."

"Yes, I know they do; but it isn't correct."

"Bill, I don't think this gen'lman kin eat a whole prairie-chicken, but de *tole* me to fetch it all up."

"Yes, that's right—he ordered it."

[Exit "Bill," leaving me comfortable; for I had been perishing to know who "Bill" was.]

"Bill, he's de oldest. And he's de bes', too. Dey's fo'teen in dis fam'ly—all boys an' gals. Bill he suppo'ts 'em all—an' he don' never complain—he's *real* good, Bill is. All dem brothers an' sisters o' his'n ain't no 'count—all ceptin' dat little teeny one dat fetched in dat milk. Dat's Kit, sah. She ain't only nine year ole. But she's de mos' lady-like one in de whole bilin'. You don't never see Kit a-rairin' an' a-chargin' aroun' an' kickin' up her heels like de res' o' de gals in dis fam'ly does gen'ally. Dat was Nan dat you hearn a cuttin' dem shines on de pi-anah while ago. An' sometimes ef she don't rastle dat pi-anah when she gits started! *Tab* can't hole a candle to *her*, but Tab kin *sing* like de very nation. She's de only one in dis fam'ly dat can sing. You don't never hear a yelp outen Nan. Nan can't sing for shucks. I'd jes lieves hear a tom-cat dat's got scalded. Dey's fo'teen in dis fam'ly 'sides de ole man and de ole 'ooman—all brothers an' sisters. But some of 'em don't live heah—do' Bill he suppo'ts 'em—lends 'em money, an' pays dey debts an' he'ps 'em along. I tell you Bill he's *real* good. Dey all gits drunk—all 'cep Bill. De ole man he gits drunk, too, same as de res' uv 'em. Bob, he don't git drunk much—jes' sloshes roun' de s'loons some, an' takes a dram sometimes. Bob he's next to Bill—'bout forty year old. Dey's all married—all de fam'ly's married—cep' some of de gals.

Dere's fo'teen. It's de biggest fam'ly in dese parts, dey say. Dere's Bill—Bill Nubbles—Nubbles is de name; Bill, an' Grig, an' Duke, an' Bob, an' Nan, an' Tab, an' Kit, an' Sol, an' Si, an' Phil, an' Puss, an' Jake, an' Sal—Sal she's married an' got chil'en as big as I is—an' Hoss Nubbles, he's de las'. Hoss is what dey mos' always calls him, but he's got another name dat I somehow disremember, it's so kind o' hard to git de hang of it." [Then, observing that I had been taking down the extraordinary list of nicknames for adults, he said]: "But in de mawnin' I can ask Bill what's Hoss's other name, an' den I'll come up an' tell you when I fetches yo' breakfast. An' maybe I done got some o' dem names mixed up, but Bill, he kin tell me. Dey's fo'teen."

By this time he was starting off with the waiter (and a pecuniary consideration for his sociability), and, as he went out, he paused a moment and said:

"Dad fetch it, somehow dat other name don't come. But, anyways, you jes read dem names over and see if dey's fo'teen." [I read the list from the flyleaf of Longfellow's *New England Tragedies*.] "Dat's right, sah. Dey's all down. I'll fetch up Hoss's other name in the mawnin', sah. Don't you be oneasy."

[Exit whistling "Listen to the Mocking Bird."]

---

1. *Mark Twain may have been attuning his ear to the variations of Negro dialect and attempting to get it down credibly on paper. As Arthur G. Pettit observes in* Mark Twain & the South *(1974), the notebooks of the 1880s and 1890s are full of dialect fragments, as well as folk expressions, as if Mark Twain were testing accuracy by the sound and experimenting with spelling to make print convey the sound correctly. In* Huckleberry Finn, *he explains, there are seven varieties of dialect, black and white. Furthermore, "The shadings have not been done in a haphazard fashion, or by guesswork; but painstakingly, and with the trustworthy guidance and support of personal familiarity with these several forms of speech." Perhaps Mark Twain wrote "Sociable Jimmy" partly as an exercise in vernacular language.*

In the Shakespeare vs. Bacon controversy that flared up briskly in the latter half of the nineteenth century, Mark Twain eventually allied himself with the Baconians, taking a stand toward the end of his life in his long article, or short book, "Is Shakespeare Dead?" (1909). Still, he was familiar with the great plays, which he quoted from as often as he invoked the Bible, and he appreciated the poetry despite any doubts about who wrote it. Hence, though not a Bardolater, he could support, with good grace, an international movement to build a Shakespeare Memorial Theatre in Stratford.

PROPOSED SHAKESPEAREAN MEMORIAL
NEW YORK *Times*, APRIL 29, 1875

To the Editor of the New York *Times:* I have just received a letter from an English friend of mine, whose hospitality I enjoyed some days at his house, in Stratford-on-Avon, and I feel sure that the matter he writes about will interest Americans. He incloses a circular, which I will insert in this place:

A preliminary committee was recently formed for the purpose of ascertaining the possibility of carrying out the project of a Shakespeare Memorial Theatre[1] in Stratford-on-Avon, the old theatre in the town having been purchased and pulled down by Mr. J. O. Halliwell-Phillips[2] for the purpose of restoring the site to New Place[3] and completing those gardens. A meeting was held at the Town Hall on Monday to receive the committee's report. Sir Robert N. C. Hamilton, Bart., K.C.B., was in the chair. The honorable Secretary, Mr. C. E. Flower, stated that the proposal had been most favorably received, and the committee recommended that the theatre should be erected by subscription and any sum raised beyond the amount required for the building, and any profit realized by the rental on ordinary occasions to be applied, after defraying the necessary expenses of the establishment, to the celebration of the anniversary of the poet's birthday and to the promotion and improvement of legitimate acting, by the establishment of prizes for essays upon the subject, lectures and ultimately a dramatic training school or college. The building to be erected upon a site which has been given for the purpose, the surrounding ground, from which beautiful views of the church and the river can be obtained, to be laid out as ornamental gardens. Connected with the theatre the committee also recommended that a library and saloon or gallery, intended to receive pictures and statuary of Shakespearean subjects, (several of which have been already promised), should be provided. Donors of £100 and upward to be Governors and managers of the property. The Governors to meet annually and vote personally, or by proxy, for the election of the Executive Council and frame rules for the general management of the memorial property and funds. For convenience of administration the association to be incorporated under section 23 of the Companies act (1867) for associations formed not for profit but for the promotion of science, art, etc. The report was unanimously adopted, a list of promised donations to the amount of £2,563 10s. was read, and generous offers from managers and members of the theatrical profession of free performances were announced. Subscriptions of the smallest amount will be received, and it is hoped that a truly appropriate memorial to Shakespeare in his native town will receive the support of many in all parts of the world who have received instruction and pleasure from his works.

By another circular I perceive that this project, young as it is, is already becoming popular, for no less than twenty-two lovers of Shakespeare have come forward with their £100 apiece, and assumed the dignity of Governors of the Memorial Theatre. In this list I find the following: Creswick, the actor; F. B. Chatterton,[4] of the Drury Lane, London; Benjamin Webster,[5] of the Adelphi, London; Buckston,[6] the comedian, and Mr. Sothern.[7]

I now come to my point, which will be found in this extract from my English friend's letter:

You may possibly remember some timber wharves on the Avon above my garden. These I have bought and given for a site for a Memorial Theatre. I think it possible that some Americans who have visited Stratford might be able and feel inclined to become Governors, (that is, £100 shareholders), in the Memorial Theatre and grounds, and that others not so well off might like to contribute smaller sums to help beautify it.

Therefore he asks me to make the suggestion in point here, and I very gladly do it. I think the mere suggestion is all that is necessary. We are not likely to be backward when called upon to do honor to Shakespeare. One of the circulars says:

Subscriptions can be paid to the Shakespeare Memorial Fund at the Old Bank, Stratford-upon-Avon, and will be invested in the names of Sir R. N. C. Hamilton, Bart., and C. E. Flower, Esq., who have consented to act as Trustees until the registration is completed.

Will you, Sir, undertake to receive and forward the American subscriptions? Or if not, will you kindly name some responsible person who will do it?

I believe that Americans of every walk in life will cheerfully subscribe to this Shakespeare memorial; I think that some of our prominent actors (I could almost name them) will come forward and enroll themselves as Governors; I think our commercial millionaires and literary people will not be slow to take governorships, or at least come as near it as they feel able; and I think it altogether likely that many of our theatres, like those of England, will give it a benefit.

Americans have already subscribed $1,000 for an American memorial window to be put in the Shakespeare Church at Avon. About three-fourths of the visitors to Shakespeare's tomb are Americans. If you will show me any American who has visited England and has not seen that tomb, Barnum shall be on his track next week.[8] It was an American who roused into its present vigorous life, England's dead interest in her Shakespearean remains. Think of that! Imagine the house that Shakespeare was born in being brought bodily over here and set up on American soil! That came within an ace of being done once. A reputable gentleman of Stratford told me so. The old building was going to wreck and ruin. Nobody felt quite reverence enough for the dead dramatist to repair and take care of his house; so an American came along ever so quietly and bought it. The deeds were actually drawn and ready for the signatures. Then the thing got wind and there was a fine stir in England! The sale was stopped. Public-spirited Englishmen headed a revival of reverence for the poet,[9] and from that day to this every relic of Shakespeare in Stratford has been sacred, and zealously cared for accordingly. Can you name the American who once owned Shakespeare's birthplace for twenty-four hours? There is but one who could ever have conceived of such an unique and ingenious enterprise, and he is the man I refer to—P. T. Barnum.

We had to lose the house; but let us not lose the present opportunity to help him build the Memorial Theatre.

Mark Twain

Hartford, Monday, April 26, 1875

1. *The memorial was proposed by Charles Edward Flower, a wealthy brewer of Stratford, who donated the site, took an active part in soliciting funds, and contributed generously himself. He was undoubtedly the man Mark Twain referred to as "an English friend of mine." The theatre was opened on April 23, 1879. A structure of modern Gothic with odd gables and Elizabethan half-timbering, it was both derided as pinchbeck medievalism and praised as a beautiful building. Attached were a library and picture gallery. The theatre burned in 1926, but a new one was completed in 1932, Americans having contributed almost half the £316,000 needed for construction. It is now known as the Royal Shakespeare Theatre.*

2. *James Orchard Halliwell-Phillips (1820-89), a distinguished Shakespearean scholar, published* Life of Shakespeare *(1848), which rejected romantic legends in favor of verifiable fact. His copiously annotated foliosize edition of Shakespeare's works (1853-65) is rich in antiquarian illustration. He also published* Shakespeare Forgeries at Bridgewater House *(1853) and* Dictionary of Old English Plays *(1860).*

3. *In Shakespeare's day, it was either the largest or the second-largest house in Stratford. In 1597, Shakespeare bought it for £60, one of a number of real estate investments he made during the next few years in Stratford and London. He returned to New Place when he retired from London, conjecturally in 1611. The house was pulled down in the nineteenth century.*

4. *He was one of several unsuccessful managers of the Drury Lane Theatre at a time when its fortunes were on the wane. "Shakespeare spells ruin," he said, "and Byron bankruptcy." He meant Henry James Byron (1834–84), prolific writer of farcical comedies:* Our Boys, Uncle Dick's Darling, *and others.*

5. *Benjamin Nottingham Webster (1797-1882), actor, manager, and playwright, was long-time lessee of the Haymarket, then took over the*

Adelphi (1844), where he was associated with Mme. Celeste and Dion Boucicault. In 1859 Webster opened the New Adelphi, where he remained until retirement in 1874.

6. *John Baldwin Buckstone (1802-79) was educated for the law, but turned to the stage, making a provincial reputation in low comedy roles, then appearing in London theaters. His voice, a mixture of chuckle and drawl, set audiences laughing and made him a popular London comedian for fifty years. As manager of the Haymarket, he staged many of his own plays in which he also acted:* Married Life, Single Life, The Flowers of the Forest, *and others.*

7. *Edward Askew Sothern (1826-81) was a British actor who built a great reputation on the strength of one role, that of Lord Dundreary, a bumbling Colonel Blimp or Wodehouse variety of peer in* Our American Cousin, *which was a huge success in New York and London. The luxuriant side-whiskers of the character became known as dundrearies.*

8. *Phineas Taylor Barnum (1810-91) was a superlative showman who operated on the premise that people are gullible. Opening the American Museum in New York (1842), he exhibited such marvels as Niagara Falls, the Feejee Mermaid, General Tom Thumb, the bearded lady, the elephant Jumbo, and the Egress. He managed the American tour of Jenny Lind, the Swedish Nightingale (1850-51), organized a circus, "The Greatest Show on Earth" (1871), and traveled the lyceum circuit lecturing on "The Science of Money Making and the Philosophy of Humbug." The story of his buying Shakespeare's birthplace, however, though entirely in character, is apparently fiction.*

9. *As noted earlier, Mark Twain's reverence for Shakespeare swung around, thirty-five years later, to a belief that Bacon wrote the plays. Like many another Baconian, he was convinced, or deluded, by the shopworn claims of cryptographic signatures, as presented in William Stone Booth's* Some Characteristic Signatures of Francis Bacon *(1909). Mark Twain accepted the supposed evidence without question.*

The experience Mark Twain tells about in the following letter may have suggested or given impetus to his paper, "The Facts Concerning the Recent Carnival of Crime in Connecticut," which he read to the Monday Evening Club of Hartford on January 24, 1876. It is a fantasy that concerns the vexing problem of a citizen's duty: whether to feed tramps, turn them away, or hand them over to the police. Harassed by his nagging conscience, embodied as a disagreeable misshapen dwarf, the narrator is made to feel that

no matter what course of action he chooses, it is the wrong one. Finally he succeeds in killing the dwarf. Then, no longer badgered by a conscience, he sharply increases mortality among tramps in Connecticut. In his letter to the Courant, Mark Twain deals seriously with the sort of problem presented facetiously in "Carnival of Crime."

A PERSISTENT BEGGAR

HARTFORD *Courant,* N.D.; REPRINTED IN NEW YORK *Times,*
OCTOBER 1, 1875

To the Editor of the *Courant*

Sir: I have been unjust to a stranger to-day, or unfaithful to my duty as a citizen, I cannot yet determine which. I wish now to right that stranger if I have wronged him, and I wish also to retrieve my citizenship.

Here are the facts in the case: Yesterday evening while I was at dinner a card was brought to me bearing the inscription, "Prof. A— B—." I said, "I do not know the Professor; ask him to excuse me; and if he should chance to call again, tell him to drop me a line through the Post Office and state his business." [Experience has taught me that strangers never call upon a man with any other desire than to sell him a lightning-rod; and experience has also taught me that if you suggest the post to these parties, they respect your sagacity and do not trouble you any more.] But the Professor called again this morning at 10 o'clock, and sent up a couple of documents—documents so conspicuously dirty that it would be only fair and right to tax them as real estate. One of these papers was a petition for aid to establish a school in a Southern State, the petitioner justifying his appeal upon the ground that he had suffered for his Union sentiments in that State during the war. The supplication was signed, "A— B—, late candidate for the Legislature of" (said State). It seemed to me that of all the mild honors I had ever heard of men claiming, that of defeated candidate for legislative distinction was certainly the mildest.

Peering into the dirt of this paper, I perceived through the rich gloom a string of names, with "$10," "$25," "$50," "$100," and other sums, set opposite them. Several were well-known Hartford names, others were familiar New York names. A few seemed to be autograph signatures, the rest not. "Hon." Peter Cooper[1] was down for a generous sum; so also was "Hon." W. C. Bryant[2]—both in a foreign hand. Just think of the idea of trying to add dignity to the old poet's name by sticking that paltry "Hon." to it!

I turned to the late candidate's other soiled document. It was a letter-sheet with half a dozen grimy "notices" from village newspapers pasted on it. These were all highly complimentary to "Hon." A— B—, "the great English elocutionist and reader." [There was also gratuitous mention of the smallness of one of the audiences he had enchanted—a remark which might as well have been left out.]

I said to myself: Last night this person was "Prof." A— B—; in his petition he is "late candidate" for a Legislature; when he travels as the great English elocutionist he is "Hon." A— B—; what he is Professor of does not appear; he does not account for his title of "Hon.," for merely running for that dazzling legislative position does not confer the title; he could not have brought it from England, for only certain officials and the younger sons of noblemen are permitted to use it there, and if he belonged to either of those lists he is not the person to forget to mention it. About this time my cold in the head gave my temper a wrench and I said: "Go and tell the Professor I don't wish to invest in his educational stock."

Now, there is where I acted precipitately, and failed of my duty either as a citizen or toward this stranger. I ought to have looked into his case a little. By jumping to the conclusion that he was a fraud, I may possibly have wronged him. If he is a fraud I ought to have proved it on him and exposed him, that being the plain duty of a citizen in such cases.

Very well. Having committed this error I now wish to retrieve it; so I make the following proposition to Mr. A— B—, to wit: That he send me that list of names again, so that I can write to the parties and inquire if they ever gave those sums, and if they did, what proofs they had of A—

B—'s worthiness; that he refer me to reputable persons in that Southern State, to the end that I may inquire of them concerning his history there, (not that I wish to inquire into his "late candidacy," for I think that when a man has unsuccessfully aspired to be a legislator, and is capable of mentioning it where people could not otherwise find it out, he is manifestly telling the petrified truth); that he refer me to a trustworthy authority who can inform me how he got the title of "Professor"; how he got the title of "Hon.," and what the name of his English birthplace is, so that I can have this parish register examined. These data being furnished me, and I finding by means of them that A— B— is not an imposter, I will take stock in his school, and also furnish him a certificate of character which shall be signed by some of the best men of Hartford—a certificate which shall far out-value his present lame documents.

But if A— B—'s references shall fail to establish his worthiness, I will publish him and also try to procure his arrest as a vagrant.

I will assist A— B— all I can, by inclosing copies of his article to Mr. Austin Dunham,[3] Mr. William E. Dodge,[4] Mr. Bryant, Mr. Peter Cooper, Messrs. Arnold, Constable & Co., and other parties in his list, (including the officials of the Southern city he mentions), to the end that they may quickly testify in his favor if they can. [I remember, now, that A— B— called on me just a year ago, and that he was then adding to his name the imperishable glory of "late candidate," etc.]

Mark Twain

1. *Cooper (1791–1883), manufacturer, inventor, and philanthropist, began his rise to fortune by running a New York glue factory, which acquired almost a monopoly of the glue business. Then he branched out, eventually controlling iron works, foundries, blast furnaces, iron mines, rolling mills, and other enterprises. He was a capitalist of enlightened outlook and humanitarian impulses. On the New York City Board of Aldermen, he advocated public schools, paid police and firemen, and pure water. He is best remembered as the founder of Cooper Union (1857-59) for the advancement of science and art, an institution offering free courses in*

Left: *Mark Twain about 1906. (From the Franklin J. Meine collection.)* Below: *This caricature of Mark Twain by Albert Scott Cox was the author's favorite of himself. (Appeared in the New York* Times *on September 2, 1906, and May 1, 1910.)*

the arts and technology. Mark Twain gave his first New York lecture in Cooper Union on May 6, 1867.

2. *William Cullen Bryant (1794–1878), a precocious youth, was writing poetry by the age of thirteen. By his early twenties, he was recognized as one of the leading American poets. Briefly a lawyer, he turned to journalism and in 1826 joined the staff of the New York* Evening Post, *of which he became chief editor in 1828. For half a century he held the position with distinction, publishing volumes of verse as well as others like* Letters of a Traveler *(1852),* Letters from the East *(1869), and translations of the* Iliad *and the* Odyssey.

3. *Dunham (18?–1917), a prominent Hartford businessman, was president of the Hartford Electric Light Company and a member of the Monday Evening Club.*

4. *William Earl Dodge (1805–83), a native of Hartford, was a dry goods merchant in New York, then extended his range to iron and copper mining and railroads, out of which he amassed a fortune. A strong antislavery advocate, he espoused postwar religious and philanthropic causes, fostering the Y.M.C.A. and temperance reforms as president of the National Temperance Society (1865–83). Among friends and acquaintances, he was known as a man of fine presence and winning manner.*

In subject and tone, the following trifle resembles a casual product of Mark Twain's or Sam Clemens's Washoe days, emerging long afterwards like an old prospector who shambles into town after pegging away for years and years far out in the hills somewhere. If it is really an Enterprise *refugee, it is fitting that it should have shown up in a western paper.*

MARK TWAIN'S HOTEL
Downieville, California, *Mountain Messenger,* July 28, 1877

Having lately opened a hashery, I send you these, my rules and regulations:

This house will be considered strictly intemperate.

None but the brave deserve the fare.

Persons owing bills for board will be bored for bills.

Boarders who do not wish to pay in advance, are requested to advance and pay.

Boarders are requested to wait on colored cooks—for meals.

Sheets will be nightly changed, once in six months, or more if necessary.

Double boarders can have two beds with a room in it, or two rooms with a bed in it, as they choose.

Boarders are requested to pull off their boots if they can conveniently. do so.

Beds with or without bugs.

All monies and other valuables are to be left in the care of the proprietor. This is to be insisted upon, as he will be responsible for no other losses.

Inside matter will not be furnished editors under any consideration.

Relatives coming to make a six months' visit will be welcomed; but when they bring half their household furniture, virtue will cease to be a forbearance.

Single men and their families will not be boarded.

Dreams will be charged for by the dozen. Nightmares hired out at reasonable rates.

Stone vaults will be hired to snoring boarders, and the proprietor will in no wise be responsible for the broken tympanums of others.

In the spring of 1877 Mark Twain spent about six weeks in Bermuda with his good friend, the Rev. Joe Twichell.[1] They enjoyed the clean white towns, mild climate, and the casual ways of the unhurried inhabitants, all duly remarked upon in Mark Twain's sketch, "Some Rambling Notes of an Idle Excursion." On the return voyage aboard the Bermuda, *the ship bespoke a drifting schooner, the* Jonas Smith, *flying signals of distress. In a letter to the Hartford* Courant, *Mark Twain wrote about this wanderer, which seemed fated, like the* Flying Dutchman, *never to make port.*

A TRAMP OF THE SEA
HARTFORD *Courant*, SEPTEMBER 20, 1877

New York, Sept 18. A Wilmington, N. C., dispatch says that the schooner Jonas Smith, with a black crew of thirteen and only one white man, was spoken by Pilot Joe Burris, twenty miles south of Cape Fear, last Friday. They claimed to be from Boston to Savannah, out three weeks and had lost their bearings. Burris gave them the bearings, and the vessel squared away for the south. As it did so and the backs of the black crew turned from him, the white man made signals for Burris to return. On Saturday the cutter Colfax sailed in search of the schooner, but returned on Monday, and will not give any account of her trip. A schooner named the Jonas Smith, was reported off Faulkner's Island, August 18, with her foreboom patched and mainsail torn, since when nothing has been heard of her.

To the Editor of the *Courant:* The above appeared in the telegraphic columns of our evening papers yesterday. The *Courant's* telegram from Wilmington and some particulars, this morning:

Some of her sails had been blown entirely away, while others hung in shreds from the masts, only a few being at all serviceable. Near the water line weeds and grass a foot long were growing from the hull, evidencing that she had been a long time out of port.

The affair has caused considerable discussion here, and there are many surmises as to the character of this vessel and her ultimate destination, but the opinion most generally received is that the crew of negroes are mutineers, and that the white man seen on board was retained by the crew when they mastered the vessel for the purpose of navigating her.

It sounds like a dreadful mystery, but I can throw some light upon it which may dispel some of the darker features. These poor fellows are not mutineers. I know them to be men of good character. Four months and a half ago I was at sea, with Rev. Joseph H. Twichell of Hartford, in the steamship Bermuda, Captain Angrove. We had sailed from Hamilton, Bermuda, on the Queen's birthday, May 24. At 4 p.m., May 25, twenty-four hours out, our position was 250 miles northwest from Bermuda. When I read the above telegrams, I said, "Here is something I have been watching the papers for during a great many weeks." I hunted up my old note-book of our Bermuda voyage and turned to the date May 25. There I found a rude pencil sketch of a disabled vessel, and this note concerning it:

Friday, 25. Jonas Smith, ten days out from Bermuda, 250 miles. Signal of distress flying (flag in the main rigging with the Union down). Went out of our course to see her. Heavy ground swell on the sea, but no wind. They launched their boat, stern first, from the deck amidships (of course it filled with water at once), and then a man took hold of a rope that was rove through a block at the starboard end of the foreyard arm, and swung himself off over the sea like a spider at the end of his thread. The vessel's deck stood up as high as a house, she was so empty. Naturally, she rolled fearfully in the ground swell. That man would swing far out over the waves and then go rushing back again like a pendulum and slam against the ship's side. The boat never was there when he arrived. However, he made his trip at last, and began to bail out. Two others followed him in the same precarious spider fashion. They pulled off to our ship, and proved to be two colored men and a Portuguese, who was blacker than both of them put together. They said they had sailed from Bermuda for New York ten days before, with five days' provisions! They were about out of everything now—had a little bread left and a cask and a half of water. The vessel had an absurdly large crew—we could see as many as a dozen colored men lying around taking it easy on her deck. We loaded four barrels of potatoes into their boat, together with some 300 pounds of salt junk and a great quantity of sea biscuit, but no water, for it was stowed where we could not well get at it. We saw the sun go down on the rolling and tumbling hulk, and later caught a final glimpse of her, black and ragged in the broad track of the moon. Shall we ever hear of those negroes again?

One of the three men who came to us in the boat was the captain and owner of the hulk. We questioned him freely, and all that he said was confirmed afterwards by three of our passengers who knew all about the matter. The poor old tub had been condemned officially in Bermuda and sold at auction, and, queerly enough, not as a whole, but piece-meal, as one may say. For instance, one man bought the topmasts and all the sails, I think; another had bought an anchor; another such odds and ends as sky-lights and such things; and this colored man had bought what was left, viz:the empty hulk and its stumps of the fore and main-masts. He paid £42 for his bargain. Then he bought three old rags, and made one do duty as a spencer on the mainmast, another as a jib, and the third as a sort of flying jib or jib stay-sail, whichever you please to call it. These had become rags indeed, when we saw them, and poetically appropriate to the wandering food-soliciting ocean tramp which the poor old outcast has been all these months that have since dragged by. One of our passengers said that the new owner of this solemn property was offered a sufficiency of ballast for his purposes, for $25, but he was not able to afford it, and so went to sea in all his perilous emptiness. His idea was to take the creature to New York and sell her at a profit, either as a coaster or to be broken up.

We did not hear of any white man being on board, but of course there may have been one. (I don't mean that Portu-guese.) But there were fifteen colored men at first, if I remember rightly. I asked Captain Angrove how he could account for that extraordinary crew when five men would have been more than enough. He said it was easily ex-plained; it was a great thing for those colored islanders to go abroad and see the world—that is to say, New York; that without doubt their only pay was their pleasure excur-sion.

So this four months' horror is a Pleasure Excursion— imagine that!

I said I should think that unless the winds were very favorable those rags would not enable the hulk to overcome the ocean currents; that when she struck the Gulf Sream she might be carried south; that the provisions would soon run out again, and so, taking all things into consideration, that crew might be looked upon as doomed, perhaps. But Captain Angrove said that their main trouble would be their danger of getting out of the track of vessels; if they could manage to keep in that, they could borrow food and water and extend their excursion indefinitely.

Your telegram says: "Near the water line, weeds and grass a foot long were growing from the hull, evidencing that she had been a long time out of port." One easily perceives from this that when Captain Burris thought the hulk's skipper said he was from Boston (where he hadn't been at all), the real word was "Bermuda"; and that when the skipper seemed to say he was "three weeks" out, he really said three months. You know how the winds distort a message at sea when the speaker can afford no better speaking trumpet than his cylindered hands. I remember that the colored skipper used no trumpet when he spoke us. I wonder he didn't tell Captain Burris he was three years out instead of three weeks; it must have seemed about that long.

What that poor fellow probably said, was that he was from Bermuda and was trying to make Savannah—or he had found out that he wasn't going to make New York and was very anxious to get to the nearest port he could find.

What an excursion it is! Four months ago the hulk was ten days out and was 250 miles northwest of Bermuda; a week ago she was 250 miles south of that position, and when Captain Burris spoke her she was 500 miles from Bermuda and directly west of it! She was then four months and one week out from port.

I have heard of a good many dismal pleasure trips, but this one heads the list. It is monumental. The hulk was spoken just a month ago, off Faulkner's Island. If we could overhaul the log books of the mercantile marine, we should doubtless find that she has been spoken and relieved with provisions a dozen times during her strange voyage. It is a great pity the cutter Colfax did not continue to chase her up till she found her. That hulk can't run; she can only drift her lubberly and unmanageable way down the Gulf Stream. There can be small difficulty about finding her. And if ever the tired old tramp is found, I should like to be there to see him in his sorrowful rage and his venerable beard of grass and sea weed, and hear those ancient mariners tell the story of their mysterious wanderings through the solemn solitudes of the ocean.

Mark Twain

Hartford, September 3

1. *Joseph Hopkins Twichell (1838–1918) was Civil War chaplain of the Seventy-first New York Volunteers (1861–64) and in 1865 became pastor of the Asylum Hill Congregational Church of Hartford, where he remained thereafter. A good-humored man of broad sympathies, he was well qualified to share with Howells the privilege of being the most intimate friend of Mark Twain. Although Twichell was a better talker than writer, he published* John Winthrop *(1891),* Some Old Puritan Love-Letters *(1893), and "Mark Twain" in* Harper's Magazine *(May 1896).*

The New England Society of New York staged annual banquets with much éclat. Mark Twain, who enjoyed gaudy full-dress affairs sparkling with wit and champagne, was undoubtedly sincerely regretful in declining an invitation to speak at the society's seventy-second annual celebration. A selection of letters of regret, especially those from well-known people, was generally read by the dinner chairman during the evening. Mark Twain's letter was assuredly among those read to the assembled banqueters.

LETTER OF REGRET
Seventy-Second Anniversary Celebration of the
New England Society in the City of New York at
Delmonico's December 22, 1877

Farmington Avenue, Hartford, Dec. 5, 1877

D. F. Appleton, Esq.[1]

Dear Sir: Remembering Mr. Curtis's great speech,[2] and other great and enjoyable features of the New England Society's last annual banquet,[3] it is with very real regret that I am obliged to deny myself the privilege of being present at this year's dinner; but I have an offensive business engagement for that day in Hartford. Most people would shirk this, under the temptation which your invitation offers, but I have young George Washington's disease (which is much rarer now than Bright's), and my word is the one unfractionable thing about me. [I do not know what Bright's disease *is,* but anyway, I do not feel bright enough this morning to be afraid I have got it.]

Still, I shall not be without my share in the pleasures of the occasion for my private telephone will be connected with your banqueting hall, if my plans and purposes succeed. It has an improvement of my own invention which I call the *Olfactorium,* and I shall sit by my own fireside, with a few friends whom I have taken the liberty to invite to your celebration, and we will smoke our pipes and sip our lemonade, applaud your speeches judiciously, and refresh ourselves with a fragrant sniff of each of your courses as it comes on your table. We shall also have one privilege which will be denied to your (otherwise) more fortunate guests: for if an orator ventures to spread himself out over the edge of the regulation ten minutes, he must be proportionally interesting, or we will *shut down the lid on him* and wait for the next speaker. Since we shall necessarily not be in the list of your guests appointed to respond to toasts, we shall sorrow to be unable to contribute a sentiment or two to the general entertainment, but there is a new song here which you may not have heard, and if you care for music, we shall be very glad indeed to sing it for you by telephone. I am not right sure of the name of it, but I think it is called "In the Sweet Bye-And-Bye."

Again thanking the Committee for the compliment of their invitation, I am, with great respect,

Mark Twain

1. *Probably Daniel Appleton (1852-1929), a publisher who was the grandson of the founder of the publishing firm of D. Appleton and Company (1871).*

2. *George William Curtis (1824-92) was an American writer and editor. Getting a job with Harper and Brothers in 1852, he became editor of the "Easy Chair" of* Harper's Magazine *in 1859 and remained there the rest of his life. Well known on the lyceum circuit as an antislavery advocate and defender of women's rights, he was also a prolific writer whose best-known books are* Potiphar Papers *(1853) and* Prue and I *(1875). A public-spirited man, he was often asked to accept governmental positions but resolutely refused to become involved in politics.*

3. *At the seventy-first annual dinner, given at Delmonico's on December 22, 1876, the hall was decorated with flags and bouquets, and the president's table was adorned with a floral design representing Plymouth Rock. In the distinguished gathering of several hundred gentlemen were political honorables, legal lights, professors, reverends, and representatives of other societies: Saint George's, Saint Andrew's, Saint Patrick's. The New York* Times *reported next day that the affair was "one of the most brilliant celebrations of its kind that has ever been held in this City." Among the speakers were Curtis, Mayor Wickham, Edward Everett Hale, Joseph H. Choate, and Mark Twain, who responded to the toast, "The Oldest Inhabitant—the Weather of New England."*

In April 1878, the entire family embarked for Europe, accompanied by Clara Spaulding, an Elmira friend; Rosina Hay, governess and tutor for six-year-old Susy; and George Griffin, Hartford butler and general handyman. Mark Twain told reporters at dockside: "I am going to the most out-of-the-way place that I can find, fifty miles away from any railroad, where I can sleep more than half the time. . . . I am going to do some writing. I have been contemplating it for a long time, and now I'm in for it." Over there they did not live in seclusion, but roamed around from Heidelberg to Berlin, Munich, Venice, Florence, and elsewhere. Mark Twain's travels, including a so-called walking tour with Twichell, provided material for his next book, A Tramp Abroad, but he worked on it only desultorily in the course of rambling from town to town, none of them satisfactory for steady writing. The spring of 1879 found the travelers in France, raw weather not modifying Mark Twain's long-standing distaste for the French way of life. Interviewed by the Paris correspondent of the New York World, he talked about his experiences and impressions. These comments on England illustrate his perennial interest in the people and customs of Britain.

MARK TWAIN ON ENGLAND
New York *World*, N.D.; Reprinted in Hartford *Courant*,
May 14, 1879

Reporter: Why have you never written a book about England?

I have spent a good deal of time in England (your question is not a new one to me) and I made a world of notes, but it was of no use, I couldn't get any fun out of England. It is too grave a country. And its gravity soaks into the stranger and makes him as serious as everybody else. When I was there I couldn't seem to think of anything but deep problems of government, taxes, free trade, finance—and every night I went to bed drunk with statistics. I could have written a million books, but my publisher would have hired the common hangman to burn them. One is bound to respect England—she is one of the three great republics of the world—in some respects she is the most real republic of the three, too, and in other respects she isn't, but she is not a good text for hilarious literature. No, there wasn't anything to satirize—what I mean is, you couldn't satirize any given thing in England in any but a half-hearted way, because your conscience told you to look nearer home and you would find that very thing at your own door. A man with a hump-backed uncle mustn't make fun of another man's cross-eyed aunt.

Reporter: The English love for the lord, for instance? I don't mean the Lord of the prayer-book, but the lord of the peerage.

I couldn't gird at the English love for titles while our own love for titles was still more open to sarcasm.[1] Take our "Hon.," for instance. Unless my memory has gone wholly astray, no man in America has any right to stick that word before his name; to do it is a sham, and a very poor sham at that. At the beginning of this century members of the two houses of Congress were referred to simply as "Mr." So-and-So. But this sham "Hon." has since crept in, and now it is unlawfully conferred upon members of state legislatures and even upon the mayor and city councillors of the paltriest back settlements. Follow the thing a little further. In England temporary titles are dropped when their time is up. The Lord Mayor of London is addressed as "My Lord" all through his year of office, but the moment he is out he becomes plain "Mr." again. But with us, once "Hon." always "Hon.;" once "Governor," always "Governor." I know men who were members of legislatures, or mayors of villages, twenty years ago, and they are always mentioned in the papers as "the Hon." to this day. I knew people who were lieutenant-governors years ago and they are called "Governor" to this day—yet the highest title they have ever had any right to, in office or out of it, was plain "Mr." You see, yourself, it wouldn't quite answer for me to poke fun at title-loving Englishmen—I should hear somebody squeal behind me and find I had stepped on the tail of some ex-official monkey of our own.

I couldn't satirize the English civil service; it was excellent and ours wasn't; it was open to everybody, rich or poor, conspicuous or obscure, whereas ours was only open to scrubs who would do political dirty work for public enemies like Mr. Conkling[2]—"Hon." Mr. Conkling, to use the obsequious illegal phrase of the day. I couldn't venture to be sarcastic about the horrible corruption of English officials, for how could I know but that something of the same kind, in a minor degree, might be discovered among our own officials at any moment? I could not poke fun at the "court column" which daily sets forth the walking and driving and dining achievements of kings and queens and dukes, while our own papers have a still longer court column of "personals" wherein the movements of half a dozen Permanent Celebrities, a dozen Evanescents and two dozen Next-to-Nobodies are duly and daily recorded. I couldn't satirize English justice, for it was exactly like our own and every other country's. That is to say, there didn't appear to be any particular rule in the matter of penalties. In New York I have known an Irishman to be sentenced to a month's confinement for nearly killing his wife, and another man to be jailed for a dreary long term for stealing a blanket. Now here is some English justice—these two paragraphs from yesterday's London *Standard*:

Hanley

A strange case of cruelty came before the stipendiary magistrate this morning. An elderly woman was charged with assaulting her niece. The allegations were that *the child had been beaten with undue severity until she was much bruised, and she was then washed in turpentine and salt, causing great agony.* The defense was a denial, and that the child was incorrigible. The bench, commenting on the undue severity of the punishment, imposed a fine of 1s. *and costs.*

Northampton

At the police court to-day John Old was summoned by the Society for the Prevention of Cruelty to Animals for gross cruelty to a dog. The evidence showed that the prisoner had brutally ill-treated the animal. He was seen to dash it against the stones, and sick it repeatedly in the streets. He afterwards severely wounded it by striking it with a shovel. He was about to bury it while still alive, but was prevented. The animal died soon after from the effects of prisoner's ill-usage. Old was sentenced to *a month's hard labor without the option of a fine.*

The italics are mine. You see, if you treat a dog inhumanly you can't get off with a fine; you must go to prison for a month at hard labor. But if you treat a little girl inhumanly you catch a scathing lecture from the bench, and you have to pay a fine of twenty-five cents besides and stand the costs on top of that. No, I whittled my opportunities down to this: One could fling criticisms at the ill-matched colors of English ladies' dresses, he could poke fun at the peddling of sermons and reversions of "livings," and say sarcastic things about various other trifles, but after his book was finished there wouldn't be fun enough in it to keep the reader from dying of melancholy. No, I looked the ground all over; there's nothing funny in England.

Reporter: Why, there's the English humorous papers.

They are not funny; they are pathetic.

Reporter: You could have written about the manners and customs?

Yes, but only to a certain extent. For instance, I could have written freely about public manners and customs and given instances. I could have said that the innocent and ignorant backswoodsman of the unvisited remoteness of America is the twin brother of innumerable well-dressed Londoners in one respect—the disposition to glare and stare into a lady's face in the street and to follow her up, shoulder to shoulder, and crane his head around, and still eagerly glare and stare until the poor victim is ready to cry with mortification and fear. I could have written as much as I pleased about public manners and customs and been free to applaud or to blame—but there an end. The real interest would lie in private and domestic manners and customs, and I had no right to print anything about those, either praisefully or otherwise. I was a guest in many English homes, but when a man takes you into his house he tacitly takes you into his confidence, and it would be a graceless thing to abuse it.

Reporter: Mr. Dickens was not so particular with America?[3]

No, he wasn't; but he recognized later that he had not done a thing to be proud of, but just the reverse. When he came to America the second time he apologized. But that is neither here nor there. Private matters are private matters, and it is not right to meddle with them. We all have our superstitions, and that is one of mine.

1. *During the following decade Mark Twain, with characteristic inconsistency, girded at English love for titles in several dinner speeches and in sharp notebook comments, his satire culminating in* A Connecticut Yankee in King Arthur's Court *(1889). But he also took ironical note of American love for foreign titles and of American heiresses scrambling to marry European counts and barons, however dubious their claim to nobility.*

2. *Roscoe Conkling (1829–88) was a congressman and senator from New York for several terms. He was a radical Republican who advocated stringent postwar military control in southern states. A pompous, arrogant man, he was a divisive force in the Republican party, opposing civil service reforms of President Hayes and refusing to endorse his renomination. When Garfield was elected (1880), Conkling resigned. Henry Adams characterized him as an "aggressively egoistic" stage exaggeration, possessed of extreme dogmatism that "became Shakespearian and* bouffe . . . *like Malvolio," and as one of those politicians who "could not be burlesqued; they were more grotesque than ridicule could make them." Mark Twain would probably have concurred in that estimate, and he might have added another reason for disfavor: that Conkling was an abstemious man who neither smoked nor drank.*

3. *After his first American tour in 1842, Dickens published* American Notes *(1842) and* Martin Chuzzlewit *(1844), both of which contained ridicule of Americans as greedy, boastful, and ill-bred. Some modern critics maintain, however, that there are more compliments than complaints in those books, and that slavery was the only institution Dickens attacked with severity. Be that as it may, on his second American tour (1867–68), he was received as enthusiastically as he had been the first time. At a grand dinner tendered by New York journalists at Delmonico's before his final performance, he made amends for having offended. George William Curtis, who was there, reported in* Harper's *"Easy Chair" (February 1868): "In his speech, with great delicacy and feeling, Dickens alluded to some possible misunderstanding, now forever vanished, between him and his hosts, and declared his purpose of publicly recognizing that fact in future editions of his works." A few days later he made his last American appearance in Steinway Hall. Mark Twain attended in the company of a lady who was, conjecturally, Olivia Langdon, his future wife.*

Mark Twain was not a political activist, although he was not backward about expressing his opinions, generally unfavorable, of politicians. In the presidential campaign year of 1876, taking a public stand for the first time, he had endorsed the Republican ticket of Hayes and Wheeler. The announcement of his own candidacy may have been written that year, but the precise date is of no consequence.

MARK TWAIN
AS A PRESIDENTIAL CANDIDATE
New York *Evening Post,* June 9, 1879

I have pretty much made up my mind to run for President. What the country wants is a candidate who cannot be injured by investigation of his past history, so that the enemies of the party will be unable to rake up anything against him that nobody ever heard of before. If you know the worst about a candidate, to begin with, every attempt to spring things on him will be checkmated. Now I am going to enter the field with an open record. I am going to own up in advance to all the wickedness I have done, and if any Congressional committee is disposed to prowl around my biography in the hope of discovering any dark and deadly deed that I have secreted, why—let it prowl.

In the first place, I admit that I treed a rheumatic grandfather of mine in the winter of 1850. He was old and inexpert in climbing trees, but with the heartless brutality that is characteristic of me I ran him out of the front door in his nightshirt at the point of a shotgun, and caused him to bowl up a maple tree, where he remained all night, while I emptied shot into his legs. I will do it again if I ever have another grandfather. I am as inhuman now as I was in 1850. I candidly acknowledge that I ran away at the battle of Gettysburg. My friends have tried to smooth over this fact by asserting that I did so for the purpose of imitating Washington, who went into the woods at Valley Forge for the purpose of saying his prayers. It was a miserable subterfuge. I struck out in a straight line for the Tropic of Cancer because I was scared. I wanted my country saved, but I preferred to have somebody else save it. I entertain that preference yet. If the bubble reputation can be obtained only at the cannon's mouth, I am willing to go there for it, provided the cannon is empty. If it is loaded my immortal and inflexible purpose is to get over the fence and go home. My invariable practice in war has been to bring out of every fight two-thirds more men than when I went in. This seems to me Napoleonic in its grandeur.

My financial views are of the most decided character, but they are not likely, perhaps, to increase my popularity with the advocates of inflation. I do not insist upon the special supremacy of rag money or hard money. The great fundamental principle of my life is to take any kind I can get.

The rumor that I buried a dead aunt under my grapevine was correct. The vine needed fertilizing, my aunt had to be buried, and I dedicated her to this high purpose. Does that unfit me for the Presidency? The Constitution of this country does not say so. No other citizen was ever considered unworthy of this office because he enriched his grapevines with his dead relatives. Why should I be selected as the first victim of an absurd prejudice?

I admit also that I am not a friend of the poor man. I regard the poor man, in his present condition, as so much wasted raw material. Cut up and properly canned, he might be made useful to fatten the natives of the cannibal islands and to improve our export trade in that region. I shall recommend legislation upon the subject in my first message. My campaign cry will be: "Desiccate the poor working-man; stuff him into sausages."

These are about the worst parts of my record. On them I come before the country. If my country don't want me, I will go back again. But I recommend myself as a safe man— a man who starts from the basis of total depravity and proposes to be fiendish to the last.

After about seventeen months abroad, Mark Twain sailed for home aboard the Cunard liner Gallia, *accompanied by Olivia, twelve trunks, and twenty-two cumbersome boxes of furniture and objets d'art collected on his European travels. At Quarantine on September 2, 1879, reporters swarmed aboard and crowded around him in the main saloon. They observed that he had aged somewhat, his hair having become gray, but that the drawl was unchanged. The* Sun *man attempted to illustrate the slow speech when he told how Mark Twain delegated to his brother-in-law the job of looking after the mountainous pile of baggage: "I shall le-t hi-m ta-ke ca-re of my luggage and fi-ght it ou-t with the custom house offi-cers." Newsmen fired many questions, although Mark Twain, as usual in his encounters with the press, did not need much priming to keep him talking. This interview is a composite of versions in the New York* Times *and* Sun.

MARK TWAIN HOME AGAIN
New York *Times*, September 3, 1879; New York *Sun*, September 3, 1879

I've had a good time during the seventeen months I've been abroad. You remember I went out on a Dutch steamer—the same one that Bayard Taylor went on.[1] He got out at Plymouth, and I never saw him again. While he was at Berlin I corresponded with him, and we made an appointment to meet in the fall. His death was a great surprise to me.

Oh, no, I did not lend Mr. Halstead any clothes.[2] He could not get into mine; and, besides, I didn't have any more than I wanted for myself.

Reporter: How far have you got in "Ollendorf"?[3]

Oh, I don't speak German. It's enough that I've endured the agony of learning to read it. I made two or three speeches in German at Heidelberg—in my peculiar German. I stayed at Heidelberg four months. I could have written my book in German; but then, you see, I want the book read.[4] So I wrote it in English. English is about the cleverest language I ever handled. I like English.

Yes, I stayed a long while in Heidelberg and in Dresden and Munich and Venice and Paris, and about four weeks in London. Wherever I stayed a month I went to work on my book. It's finished, and will be published in November. I don't know what the name of it is, but I know what it's about. It's about this trip I've taken. No, it isn't fiction—it's about my journey, like the *Innocents Abroad,* all serious—all facts and wisdom.

I say it's finished, but it isn't. The first half is done, but I've got to go through the last half and throw whole rafts of it away. After that I may run through the first half and throw away lots of that; then it will be ready for the printer. This new book of mine is different from any book I ever wrote. Before, I revised the manuscript as I went along, and knew pretty well at the end of each week how much of the week's work I should use, and how much I should throw away. But this one has been written pretty much all in a lump, and I hardly know how much of it I will use or how much will have to be torn up. When I start at it I tear up pretty fast, but I think the first half will stand pretty much as it is. I am not quite sure that there is enough yet prepared, but I am still at work on it. They want me to stay in New York and revise it, but I cannot possibly do that. I am going to start tomorrow morning for Elmira, where we will stay for some time.

I suppose New York's changed. I want a ride on one of the elevated railroads.[5] I've never been on one of them yet. I used to be afraid of them, but it is no use. Death stares us in the face everywhere, and we may as well take it in the elevated form. I used to go up a block or two above the Gilsey House to see the men work on the elevated railroads—to see how fast they slung the iron together.

Before I went away Dan Slote and I parted one afternoon, and next day Dan told me that he wanted to hurry up town, so he started for the elevated railroad—the one in Greenwich Street was running then. Well, he got to thinking, and he thought that it was risky for a man with a family and a good business to trust to one of those roads. So he turned on his heel, and walked away to get a bus. Well, there was a woman washing windows near the top of a four-story house, and down she came, so close to Dan that her heels took the buttons off his coat and her head grazed his shoulder. She was killed, of course, and Dan had a narrow escape. It's no use; there are women washing windows everywhere, and we may as well fall as be fallen upon. The moral of that is, in my opinion, that a man who is looking out for his life might as well trust to his first impulses.

When I sailed in the *Batavia*,[6] I had a different opinion of the Cunard line from that which I now entertain. I objected to the prunes. I suppose you know that when the Cunarders changed from sailing to steam power, they maintained some of their old sailing ideas on the new steam propelled ships. Prunes was one of those old ideas. Why, they had regular days for things—"duff day" was Thursday, and Sunday was a duff day too—that was when they served out puddings, the same as they do to sailors aboard a sailing ship. Then there was Tuesday beans, and Saturday beans, and prunes twenty-one times a week for dessert. They hunted the world for cooks and got the worst there were. Why, you could make up your bill of fare a week ahead—yes, for the return trip—but that's all done now.

We are fed like princes aboard here, and have made a comfortable voyage. We have been in some seas that would have made the old *Quaker City* turn somersaults, but the ship kept steady through it all. We could leave a mirror lying on the washstand and it would not fall off. If we stood a goblet loose on the shelf at night, it would be there in the morning.

A Times *reporter asked whether a cocktail left standing on the shelf at night would be there in the morning. Mark Twain replied that the ship was hardly steady enough for that.*

Oh, yes, Lord Dunraven and several other lords and many New Yorkers are on board, and we had a good time. I never express any opinions about people, but Lord Dunraven is an uncommonly clever fellow—nothing stuck up about him. He has brushed up against ordinary clay in his lifetime, and he is very talented besides.

1. *James Bayard Taylor (1825–78) was a journalist, poet, scholar, and traveler. Acquainted with Europe, India, China, and Africa, and observer of such American events as the California gold rush, he was a prolific writer of*

poetry, drama, and travel books: Views Afoot *(1846)*, Rhymes of Travel *(1848)*, Eldorado *(1850)*, Poems of the Orient *(1855)*, *a translation of Goethe's* Faust *(1870–71)*, The Masque of the Gods *(1872)*, *and others. Wit, raconteur, and brilliant parodist, he was well known on the lyceum circuit and a popular dinner speaker. His appointment as United States envoy extraordinary and minister plenipotentiary to Germany (1878) occasioned pleased surprise that the State Department had for once chosen a man who knew the language of the country he was going to. Taylor died about a month after assuming his duties in Berlin. Mark Twain admired him as a writer and enjoyed his society as a companionable man.*

2. *Murat Halstead (1829–1908), a veteran journalist, was associated with the Cincinnati* Commercial *and Brooklyn* Standard-Union. *He reported the John Brown episode, the Civil War as a field correspondent, the Franco-Prussian War as an observer with German armies, the Spanish-American War, and other major events at home and abroad. In more than twenty books on American and world affairs*—Full Official History of the War With Spain *(1899)*, The World on Fire *(1902)*, *and others*—*he revealed himself as a vigorous reporter of independent mind, but as an historian naive and garrulous. Mark Twain's comment about lending clothes refers to the outbound voyage on the* Holsatia *in the spring of 1878. Halstead, after a late party with Taylor and others, had come aboard barely in time, but without having been able to pack properly.*

3. *Ollendorf's System, devised by Heinrich Gottfried Ollendorf (1803–65), was a method of learning languages without a teacher. His manuals, stressing mastery of conversational diction and familiar idioms, minimized grammatical rules. Mark Twain strove to learn the German rules, but like many another student of that language, he came to grief on the multiple forms required by its three genders and four cases. For the story of his linguistic struggles, see his entertaining essay, "The Awful German Language."*

4. A Tramp Abroad *was the book. Writing it had been such an uphill job that he had tried to think of an excuse for abandoning it. When the book was published in 1880, however, it was received more favorably than he had expected. Some of the most engaging episodes concern the alleged walking tour of six weeks with Twichell.*

5. *The first elevated in New York, operated by steam power, opened in 1871. The first electrically-powered elevated line in the United States opened in Chicago in 1895.*

6. *In the essay "About All Kinds of Ships" (1892), Mark Twain commented on the primitive conditions of sea travel in the 1870s: "In the steamer* Batavia, *twenty years ago, one candle, set in the bulkhead between*

two staterooms, was there to light both rooms, but did not light either of
them. It was extinguished at eleven at night, and so were all the saloon
lamps except one or two, which were left burning to help the passenger see
how to break his neck trying to get around in the dark. The passengers sat at
table on long benches made of the hardest kind of wood," and so on, further
comments remarking upon dismal furnishings, grimy smoking room, and wet
decks—all contrasting with the luxurious accommodations of the liner of the
1890s.

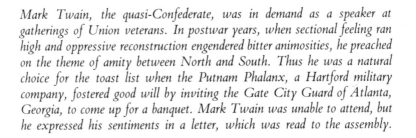

Mark Twain, the quasi-Confederate, was in demand as a speaker at
gatherings of Union veterans. In postwar years, when sectional feeling ran
high and oppressive reconstruction engendered bitter animosities, he preached
on the theme of amity between North and South. Thus he was a natural
choice for the toast list when the Putnam Phalanx, a Hartford military
company, fostered good will by inviting the Gate City Guard of Atlanta,
Georgia, to come up for a banquet. Mark Twain was unable to attend, but
he expressed his sentiments in a letter, which was read to the assembly.

LETTER OF REGRET
NEW YORK *Times,* OCTOBER 19, 1879

Elmira, Oct. 14 [1879]

D. D. Poltier, Esq.

Dear Sir: Please receive my best thanks for the invitation
to meet the Atlanta soldiers and the Putnams. I was on the
point of starting when a committee requested me to remain
here and introduce Gen. Joseph R. Hawley[1] to a political
mass-meeting. This was a great surprise to me, for I had
supposed the man was comparatively well known. I shall
remain, of course, and shall do what I can to blow the fog
from around his fame. Meantime will you kindly see that
the portion of your banquet which I should be allowed to
consume if I were present is equitably distributed among
the public charities of our several States and Territories; I
would not that any partiality be shown on account of
political creed or geographical position, but would beg that

all the crates be of the same heft. I am glad to add my voice to yours in welcoming the Georgians to Hartford. Personal contact and communion of Northerners and Southerners over the friendly board will do more toward obliterating sectional lines and restoring mutual respect and esteem than any other thing that can be devised. We cannot meet thus too often; for whereas we meet as Northerners and Southerners we grow in breadth and stature meantime, and part as Americans. There is not any name among the world's nationalities that can oversize that one. Sincerely hoping that our guests will receive a welcome at our town's hands which will cause them to forget the length of their journey and make them willing to come again, I am truly yours,

S. L. Clemens

1. *Joseph Roswell Hawley (1826–1905) was the first man in Connecticut to enlist in the Union Army. He ended the war as brevet major general of volunteers. He was governor of Connecticut (1866), then became co-editor, with Warner, of the Hartford* Courant *(1867) and chairman of the Republican National Convention (1868). He served three terms as congressman, as president of the Centennial Commission (1876), and as United States senator from Connecticut (1881–1905).*

In 1879 when the Nashville American *maintained that Artemus Ward[1] was the greatest American humorist and wit, the Knoxville* Tribune *countered with an article that claimed first place for Mark Twain. When the editor of the* Tribune *sent the paper containing his argument to Hartford, Mark Twain wrote a diplomatic reply tinctured with irony.*

MARK TWAIN ON ARTEMUS WARD
KNOXVILLE *Tribune*, N.D.; REPRINTED IN NEW YORK *Times*, JANUARY 2, 1880

Hartford, Dec. 18 [1879]

Frank H. Earnest, Esq.

Dear Sir: I thank you very much for that pleasant article. Of course, it is not for me to judge between Artemus and myself or trade merits, but when it comes to speaking of matters personal, I am a good witness, Artemus was one of the kindest and gentlest men in the world, and the hold which he took on the Londoners surpasses imagination. To this day one of the first questions which a Londoner asks me is if I knew Artemus Ward. The answer, "yes," makes that man my friend on the spot. Artemus seems to have been on the warmest terms with thousands of those people. Well, he seems never to have written a harsh thing against anybody—neither have I, for that matter—at least nothing harsh enough for a body to fret about—and I think he never felt bitter toward people. There may have been three or four other people like that in the world at one time or another, but they probably died a good while ago. I think his lecture on the "Babes in the Wood" was the funniest thing I ever listened to. Artemus once said to me gravely, almost sadly, "Clemens, I have done too much fooling, too much trifling; I am going to write something that will live."

"Well, what, for instance?"

In the same grave way, he said:

"A lie."

It was an admirable surprise. I was just getting ready to cry, he was becoming so pathetic. This has never been in print—you should give it to your friend of the *American*, for I judge by what he writes on Artemus that he will appreciate it. I think it's mighty bright—as well for its quiet sarcasm as for its happy suddenness and unexpectedness.

Yours, truly,
S. L. Clemens

1. *This was the pen name of Charles Farrar Browne (1834–67). Posing as a showman of "wax figgers," he wrote humorous sketches about his travels, current events, politics, and well-known people. These pieces, marked by garbled syntax and strange spelling, were printed and reprinted, like his "goaks," in papers all over the country. He was a favorite of Lincoln, who once scandalized his cabinet by reading a Ward story before presenting the Emancipation Proclamation. Ward was a great success as a comic lecturer at home and in London, his conviviality winning a host of admirers everywhere and enhancing a reputation that flourished for years after his death. Meeting him in Virginia City in 1863, Mark Twain became well acquainted during a crowded week of sight-seeing, dinners, and vinous hilarity. He studied the showman's platform technique, observing his solemn demeanor, assumed distress, irrelevancies, anticlimaxes, and non sequiturs, all of which Mark Twain adopted and improved upon in his own speaking career.*

When Boston philanthropists organized a fair in aid of abused children, Mark Twain was asked for an endorsement that could be used as publicity. In his response, he assumed the role of the harassed parent bedeviled by offspring, adopting a put-upon manner somewhat like that of the sufferer in his early sketch, "Those Blasted Children."

MARK TWAIN'S BABY
Nevada City, California, *Daily Transcript,* January 12, 1881

Dear Editors: I do it with pleasure . . . but I also do it with pain because I am not in sympathy with this movement. Why should I want a "Society for the prevention of cruelty to Children" to prosper, when I have a baby down stairs that kept me awake several hours last night with no pretext but a desire to make trouble?[1] This occurs every night, and it embitters me, because I see now how useless it was to put in the other burglar alarm, a costly, complicated contrivance, which cannot be depended upon, because it's always getting out of order and won't "go," whereas, although the baby is always getting out of order, too, it can nevertheless be depended upon, for the reason that the more it gets out of order the more it does go.

Yes, I am bitter against your society, for I think the idea of it is all wrong; but if you will start a society for the Prevention of Cruelty to Fathers, I will write you a whole book.

Yours, with emotion,
Mark Twain

1. *At this time Mark Twain's youngest daughter, Jean, was about six months old. It is unlikely, however, that in a large house well staffed with servants and with a solicitous mother at hand, he was ever bothered much by a crying baby or ever obliged to perform infant chores. In his speech on "The Babies" for the reunion of veterans of the Army of the Tennessee at Chicago in 1879, he left the impression that he was familiar with such duties as soothing a fretful baby by cradling it in his arms as he walked up and down at dead of night singing "Rock-a-bye, baby," warming milk for the bottle, and so on. But it was all probably a Mark Twain stretcher.*

Several correspondents in Australia were under the impression that Mark Twain had visited that country, and hearing that the well-known humorist had died, one of them wrote to inquire whether the report was true. In his reply, Mark Twain blamed imposters who had dogged his steps for the past ten or twelve years and who were responsible for all sorts of misinformation, sometimes damaging, about his movements and behavior.

AUTHORITATIVE CONTRADICTION
Adelaide, Australia, *Observer,* October 15, 1881; Reprinted in
New York *Times,* December 8, 1881

During the present year I have received letters from three gentlemen in Australia who had in past times known people who had known me "in Australia"; but I have never been in any part of Australia in my life. By these letters it appears that the persons who knew me there knew me intimately—not for a day, but for weeks and even months. And apparently I was not confined to one place, but was scattered all around over the country. Also, apparently, I was very respectable; at least I suppose so, from the character of the company I seem to have kept—Government officials, ladies of good position, editors of newspapers, etc.

It is very plain, then, that someone has been in Australia who did me the honor to impersonate me and call himself by my name.[1] Now, if this man paid his debts and conducted himself in an orderly and respectable way, I suppose I have no very great cause of complaint against him; and yet I am not able to believe that a man can falsely assume another man's name, and at the same time be in other respects a decent and worthy person. I suspect that, specious as this stranger seems to have been, he was at bottom a rascal, and a pretty shabby sort of rascal at that.

That is all I wanted to say about the matter. There are signs that I have an audience among the people of Australia. I want their good opinion; therefore I thought I would speak up, and say that if that adventurer was guilty of any misconduct there, I hope the resulting obloquy will be reserved for him, and not leveled at me, since I am not to blame.

Today's mail brings a letter to a member of my family from an old English friend of ours, dated "Government House, Sydney, May 29," in which the writer is shocked to hear of my "sudden death." Now, that suggests that that aforementioned imposter has even gone the length of dying for me. This generosity disarms me. He has done a thing for me which I wouldn't even have done for myself. If he will only stay dead now I will call the account square, and drop the grudge I bear him.

Mark Twain

Hartford, United States of America, July 24, 1881.

1. *In his first lecture on the eastern circuit, at Cleveland in 1868, he started out by talking about his double, who had spoken in various places under the name of Mark Twain, then departed without paying his hotel bills. The double, he said, "advertised Itself to lecture and didn't; It got supernaturally drunk at other people's expense; It continued Its relentless war upon helpless and unoffending boarding-houses." Of his visit to Australia in 1895, he told of watching an elaborate funeral procession in Sydney. Inquiring the name of the honored dead, he was told that the deceased was Mark Twain. Whereupon he joined the mourners to be the first man ever to attend his own funeral. The story may be a Twain fabrication, but the imposters were genuine.*

To protect his forthcoming book The Prince and the Pauper, *which was being published in London and Canada, Mark Twain went to Montreal in late November 1881 to acquire Canadian copyright. His two weeks' sojourn was a social success, culminating in a banquet tendered in his honor by literary and professional men, but his application for copyright was denied. When the Springfield* Republican *criticized his procedure and implied that he had damaged the cause of copyright in general, Mark Twain wrote a long reply.*

MARK TWAIN EXPLAINS
SPRINGFIELD *Republican*, N.D.; REPRINTED IN NEW YORK *Times*, DECEMBER 25, 1881

To the Editor of the Springfield (Mass.) *Republican:* If you will glance at the first article in your second editorial column of today's issue you may find two things forcibly illustrated there: that the less a man knows about his subject the more glibly he can reel off his paragraph, and that the difference between the ordinary court and the high court of journalism is, that the former requires facts upon which to base an injurious judgment against a man, the other requires suspicions only. You have not caught me in any divergence from the truth, nor in any incompatibility. But a truce to that; under pretext of rising to defend myself, I have really risen for a more respectable purpose. Your remarks have, of course, disseminated the impression that in my humble person a greater was defeated in Canada and got its quietus, viz., Copyright; now, I think the fact is of public and general importance—and, therefore, worth printing—that the exact opposite was the case.

I applied formally for Canadian copyright and failed to get it.[1] But that did not cripple my case, because by being in Canada (and submitting to certain legal forms) when my book issued in London I acquired both imperial and Canadian copyright.[2] I did know several hours before I left Montreal—as heretofore stated in my name—that my application for legal copyright had been refused, but I also knew that my Canadian copyright was perfect without it, and that it would not have been (absolutely) perfect if I had not sojourned in Canada while the book was published in England and printed and published in Canada. Curious as it seems to seem to you, I did leave in Canada perfected arrangements for the prosecution of any who might pirate the book, although I had hardly the ghost of a fear that any attempt would be made to pirate it. Please do not laugh at me any more for this, for the act was not ridiculous. I was not protecting myself against an expectation, but only against a possibility. Perhaps you do not catch the idea. I will put it in another form; if you were going to stop over night with me I should not expect you to set fire to the place; still, I would step down and get the house insured just the same.

Have you ever read the Dominion copyright laws? And if so, do you think you understand them? Undeceive yourself; it is ten thousand to one that you are mistaken. I went to Canada armed to the teeth with both Canadian and American legal opinions.[3] They were the result of a couple of months of industry and correspondence between trained Canadian and American lawyers. These men agreed upon but one thing—that a perfect imperial and provincial copyright was obtainable through a brief sojourn in Canada and the observance of certain specified forms.

They were pretty uncertain (under one form of procedure) as to the possibility of acquiring a copyright from the Dominion Government itself; well, as before remarked, I tried that form; it failed, but no harm was done. Some little good was done, however; the experiment established the fact, as far as it can be established without the decision of a court, that "elective domicile" is not sufficient in a copyright matter.[4] There was one other mode of procedure which promised considerably better—in fact, I was told that it had been tried already by a couple of American clergymen, and with success. This is, to kind of sort of let on, in a general way, in your written declaration to the Dominion Government, that you haven't come to Canada merely to sojourn, but to stay. My friend, there are reputations that can stand a strain like that; but you know,

Above: Harper's Weekly of July 13, 1907, captioned this photo "The 'Innocent Abroad' Again." The legend read, "Mark Twain, enroute for Oxford to receive the degree of Doctor of Letters, besieged by reporters on his steamship in England." Left: On July 20, Harper's followed the fortunes of the "Innocent": "Mark Twain, wearing the scarlet, gray-hooded robe of a Doctor of Letters, leaving the Sheldonian Theatre after receiving his degree."

yourself, that it would not answer for you or me to take any such risk. I declined to try that mode.

Mark Twain

Hartford, Conn., Sunday, Dec. 18, 1881.

1. *Books were registered with the Canadian Ministry of Agriculture. Mark Twain's friend Thomas Nash drew a cartoon showing Mark Twain with his book under his arm and holding a spray of syringas in his hand. Surrounding him are sacks labeled "small potatoes," "(dead) beets," "(some) punkins," "lily white flour," and "(We) cabbage (all we can from the Yankees)."*

2. *The New York* Times *maintained, December 29, 1881, that imperial copyright protected him "against any Canadian reprint being made of his work, but does not save him, per se, from the importation into Canada of foreign reprints, having paid 12½ percent royalty at entering. Whereas, a Canadian copyright would have secured him from the introduction into Canada of any such foreign reprints. Mr. Clemens has fallen into error in supposing that he secures the same protection in the Dominion from an imperial copyright as he would from a copyright issued in Canada."*

3. *Mark Twain had no great faith in the lawyers' opinions. He once said that not even God could make sense out of any copyright law in the world.*

4. *According to the* Times *of December 29, 1881, Mark Twain submitted an application for an interim copyright, stating that he was domiciled in Canada. This application was approved. Then, in a subsequent application for full copyright, he said that his domicile was elective. This application was rejected. "It is held," said the* Times, *"that a person is domiciled in a country who resides in said country . . . while in law an elective domicile is an address or place where it has been agreed that delivery will be accepted, although it does not follow that the person so electing his domicile there shall ever visit it."*

Besides writers, other creative people were also concerned with copyright protection, among them composers of musical works. When the editor of the Boston Musical Record *asked Mark Twain for an opinion on an international copyright law, he readily complied.*

MARK TWAIN ON COPYRIGHT LAW
New York *Times,* November 11, 1883

I am 47 years old, and therefore shall not live long enough to see international copyright established; neither will my children live long enough; yet, for the sake of my (possible) remote descendants, I feel a languid interest in the subject.[1] Yes—to answer your question squarely—I am in favor of an international copyright law.[2] So was my great grandfather—it was in 1847 that he made his struggle in this great work—and it is my hope and prayer that as long as my stock shall last the transmitted voice of that old man will still go ringing down the centuries, stirring the international heart in the interest of the eternal cause[3] for which he struggled and died. I favor the treaty which was proposed four or five years ago and is still being considered by our State department. I also favor engraving it on brass. It is on paper now. There is no lasting quality about paper.

1. *The irony camouflages an interest more militant than languid. He was a vigorous crusader for copyright, his arguments always revolving around one theme: ideas are property, of which the owner deserves permanent control, instead of the forty-two years allowed by copyright law. In 1875, he had prepared a sardonic petition to both houses of Congress, whereasing that the right of property in real estate was perpetual, that the right in literary property was limited, and that forty-two years seemed just and righteous for the retention of any property. Therefore, he concluded, "Your petitioner, having the good of his country solely at heart, humbly prays that 'equal rights' and fair and equal treatment be meted out to all citizens, by the restriction of rights in all property, real estate included, to the beneficent term of forty-two years. Then shall all men bless your honorable body and be happy. And for this shall your petitioner ever pray." See* Sketches New and Old *(1903).*
2. *According to the Copyright Office of the Library of Congress, there is no international copyright that automatically protects an author anywhere in*

the world. The Berne Convention of 1886, several times revised, extends protection to nationals of any nation on the one condition that publication occurs in a country belonging to the Berne Union. Some sixty nations, not including the United States, are members of the union. The United States is one of fifty-eight countries that are parties to the Universal Copyright Convention of 1955, its chief purpose being to minimize formalities for securing copyright in member nations. In the Western Hemisphere, a Buenos Aires Convention of 1910, ratified by the United States and seventeen Latin-American countries, specifies that an author who has secured copyright in his own country shall enjoy the same rights in other contracting countries. In short: most nations offer protection to foreign works, but some provide little or none under any circumstances. In 1877, Mark Twain said that if Adam, inventor of sin, had taken out an international copyright on it, then copyright could easily have been established.

3. He would probably have approved of a new copyright law enacted by Congress in 1976, the first revision in sixty-seven years. It stipulates that copyright shall exist for the life of the author and for fifty years after his death, precisely the provisions advocated by Mark Twain. The new law also extends existing copyrights to seventy-five years, a change he did not argue for but would surely favor.

Painters and writers were asked to contribute sketches and letters to be raffled at the Bartholdi Pedestal Fund Art Loan Exhibition, the proceeds to be applied to the project of building a pedestal for the Statue of Liberty.[1] Mark Twain responded with a letter chiefly about one of his favorite topics, his distant relative, Adam. In 1879 he, along with Thomas K. Beecher and others, had prepared a petition asking Congress to authorize a monument to Adam, and designating the site as Elmira, New York. Congressman Hawley of Hartford had agreed to present the petition but then, fearing ridicule, had backed out in 1881. Thus the effort came to naught, but from time to time Mark Twain returned to Adam.

MARK TWAIN AGGRIEVED
New York *Times,* December 4, 1883

You know my weakness for Adam, and you know how I have struggled to get him a monument and failed. Now, it seems to me, here is my chance. What do we care for a statue of liberty when we've got the thing itself in its wildest sublimity? What you want of a monument is to keep you in mind of something you haven't got—something you've lost. Very well; we haven't lost liberty; we've lost Adam.

Another thing: What has liberty done for us? Nothing in particular that I know of. What have we done for her? Everything. We've given her a home, and a good home, too. And if she knows anything, she knows it's the first time she ever struck that novelty. She knows that when we took her in she had been a mere tramp for 6,000 years, Biblical measure. Yes, and we not only ended her troubles and made things soft for her permanently, but we made her respectable—and that she hadn't ever been before. And now, after we've poured out these Atlantics of benefits upon this aged outcast, lo! and behold you, we are asked to come forward and set up a monument to her! Go to. Let her set up a monument to us if she wants to do the clean thing.

But suppose your statue represented her old, bent, clothed in rags, downcast, shame-faced, with the insults and humiliation of 6,000 years, imploring a crust and an hour's rest for God's sake at our back door?—come, now you're shouting! That's the aspect of her which we need to be reminded of, lest we forget it—not this proposed one, where she's hearty and well-fed, and holds up her head and flourishes her hospitable schooner of flame, and appears to be inviting all the rest of the tramps to come over. O, go to—this is the very insolence of prosperity.

But, on the other hand—look at Adam. What have we done for Adam? Nothing. What has Adam done for us? Everything. He gave us life, he gave us death, he gave us heaven, he gave us hell. These are inestimable privileges— and remember, not one of them should we have had without Adam. Well, then, he ought to have a monument—for Evolution is steadily and surely abolishing him; and we must get up a monument, and be quick about it, or our children's children will grow up ignorant that there ever was an Adam. With trifling alterations, this present statue will answer very well for Adam. You can turn that blanket into an ulster without any trouble; part the hair on one side, or conceal the sex of his head with a fire helmet, and at once he's a man; put a harp and a halo and a palm branch in the left hand to symbolize a part of what Adam did for us, and leave the fire basket just where it is, to symbolize the rest. My friend, the father of life and death and taxes, has been neglected long enough. Shall this infamy be allowed to go on or shall it stop right here?

Is it but a question of finance? Behold the inclosed (paid bank) checks. Use them as freely as they are freely contrib- uted. Heaven knows I would there were a ton of them; I would send them all to you, for my heart is in the sublime work!

S. L. C.

1. *Created by Frederic-Auguste Bartholdi and paid for by contributions from the people of France, the statue was shipped in sections to New York in 1885. It was dedicated by President Cleveland on October 28, 1886.*

In 1884–85, Mark Twain and George W. Cable[1] made a long speaking tour together, appearing on programs in which they read alternately, each from his own works. A number of Mark Twain's readings were from his new book, Huckleberry Finn. *For four months they traveled through the East, the Middle West, and Canada, speaking six nights a week, in addition to occasional matinees. For a temperamental man like Mark Twain, a collaboration was a risky venture, yet at the end of the first month the partnership seemed to be working out reasonably well. In Baltimore when a reporter found him backstage at the Academy of Music, Mark Twain was, as usual, willing to talk.*

INTERVIEW
BALTIMORE *American,* NOVEMBER 29, 1884

Yes, we have stood the test very well. To be sure, whenever we would arrive in a town there would be processions and torchlight parades,[2] whether on our account or not I can't say, but they would be there. Yet the political excitement has not hurt us in regard to audiences. We were in places, too, where there was much excitement, and even after the thing was settled the people did not seem to know what to do with their old campaign trumpery, and would get up parades for picnics and socials, just to use it; but the crowd would come to us, nevertheless.

It has been seventeen years since I last appeared on the platform in this city. It was in a long hall. I can fully remember it, for I see the people sitting far down in front of me. I have been here since. Once I felt tired and like I wanted a rest. I came here. I got it. I stopped at a hotel—I have forgotten the name—but I stayed in my room all the time and in bed. There, tucked under the covers, I had my rest. I had terrapin, oysters, canvas back ducks, and lived. No one saw me; no one knew I was here, except George Alfred Townsend.[3] He was rooming about here, and I fell upon him. No, he stumbled upon me, for he found me in bed. Resting? Yes, resting.

I don't like traveling. I would, mind, if I could take my family with me; but there are those blessed darlings—the children—and what a trouble children are when they travel! And the average American child when he travels generally makes himself known. Therefore, this is my last appearance on the platform.

Yes; I mean it. I was forty-nine years of age yesterday; and if I remain off the platform seventeen years, put that to forty-nine, and by that time nobody will want to hear me. I love the platform, and I would like to live on it but I cannot be traveling about all the time. There is my family at home doing the lonesome. If I could settle down in New York, they could come in and stay there while I talked. Why, look how long a play runs in New York. I don't want such a big hall. I could talk in a small one, and I am sure there would be one man in it to hear me.

Why have I got Mr. Cable with me? Well, I don't feel like taking the responsibility of giving the entire show. I want someone to help me. It is a great burden, this awful thought that you alone have to carry everything. Then I want company. Mr. Cable is company, good company.[4] We need not talk all the time. You can be company with each other and not say a word. Sweethearts sometimes sit together a long time and don't say a word. Yet they are company for each other.

Yes, the platform has a great fascination. In regard to the way the audiences take the jokes. They say English people are slow to perceive a joke; but you get a large audience before you—why, they catch on to the joke before you have half told it. Yet, you talk to four or five Englishmen and tell them a funny story. When you get through they'll never smile. But next day they'll laugh. Fact. What is the difference between the crowd and the select party? Oh, I think it is a sort of sympathy with the crowd. One laughs, the others laugh with him, not with the fear they have to digest the fun. I was sitting one night in the Savage Club in London with Tom Hood,[5] editor of *Fun,* and one or two others. I told them a funny story, and not one laughed. Next day I met Hood in the club, and he came up to me and said, "Twain, tell that funny story you told last night to my friends here." I told it. Hood laughed loud and long. The other men never smiled. Will you believe it, I told Hood that story five times, and each time he laughed heartier than the preceding time, and the last time I thought he would die. Yet those who heard it for the first time never smiled. They wanted it to soak in.

How will F. C. Burnand,[6] the editor of *Punch,* do here on his lecture tour? If I put on a bright flaming red scarf and went out on the platform everybody would look at that scarf. They would have their thoughts distracted by it. They would forget to look at me.

Mr. Burnand speaks very broad English. How they can call it good solid English I can't understand. I once heard him give a reading, when he described a yachting party, giving imitations of the ladies and their efforts to eat off the swinging table. It was very funny, and I enjoyed it, but his pronunciation was so pronounced to me that I noticed it all the time. When Toole[7] came over to me he asked me about it. I told him plainly that I did not think his broad English pronunciation would suit the American people. If he would do the red scarf act and come before the American people, I do not think he would succeed. We shall see in regard to Mr. Burnand.

One day I was talking to George Augustus Sala[8] in London; in fact, he was having a heated discussion in regard to Americans with a friend. I spoke up and defended my countrymen. He quoted as examples the words "cow" and "now," as spoken in one part of the United States with a broad sound. I told him that that pronunciation was only common in one part of our country, and that because it was originally settled by Englishmen. What they are pleased to call Americanisms originally came from England, and it is unjust to us to lay all the vulgar, coarse things at our door. To prove to Mr. Sala that I was right, I said, now I'll call your attention in a few minutes to yourself, for you will use the very pronunciation of the words "cow" and "now" that you attribute to Americans. I was right, for I stopped him when he was saying "now," exactly as had said the Americans used the word.

1. *George Washington Cable (1844–1925) was a Confederate cavalryman, then reporter for the New Orleans* Picayune *(1865–79). He made a*

reputation as local colorist in Old Creole Days *(1879),* The Grandissimes *(1880),* Dr. Sevier *(1885), and others. His humanitarian concern with justice for the Negro, as shown in* The Silent South *(1885) and* The Negro Question *(1890), alienated him from the postwar South. Like Mark Twain, another displaced southerner, Cable settled in New England.*

2. *The Twain-Cable tour began the day after election day. Hence, the torchlight parades of the campaign were all over and done with, although the traveling speakers may have run into a few postelection celebrations.*

3. *Townsend (1841–1914), a journalist and author, began his career with the* New York Herald *(1861) and became a Civil War correspondent for the* New York World, *later publishing his dispatches as* Campaigns of a Non-Combatant *(1866). Settling in Washington (1867), he was one of the first syndicated writers, his articles about politics and major events being published in about a hundred papers. He traveled widely at home and abroad and wrote many books, the best of which is* The Entailed Hat *(1884), a novel about the kidnaping of free Negroes in border states.*

4. *Generally he was good company, their manager, Major Pond, sometimes making a jovial third. Yet Mark Twain was irked by Cable's Sabbatarianism, his refusal to travel on Sunday and idiosyncrasies like leaving a late Saturday party before midnight to avoid breaking the Sabbath. Mark Twain also came to feel that Cable took more platform time than he deserved. Hence, the partnership was not always happy. For a detailed account of the relationship, see Guy A. Cardwell,* Twins of Genius *(East Lansing: Michigan State College Press, 1953).*

5. *Hood (1835–74) was a British writer who became editor of the London* Fun *(1865) and began issuing* Tom Hood's Comic Annual *(1867), a series that continued after his death. He was the author of* Pen and Pencil Pictures *(1857), the posthumous* Favourite Poems *(1877), and others. A bon vivant, he was witty and congenial.*

6. *Francis Cowly Burnand (1836–1917) was a graduate of Eton and Trinity College, Cambridge. He began contributing to* Punch *in 1863, joined the staff, and became editor (1880–1906). Closely connected with the theater, he wrote over a hundred plays, chiefly burlesques and adaptations of French farce. He was known as a great wit and as an inveterate punster.*

7. *John Laurence Toole (1830–1906), a London actor and theater manager who was a good friend of Henry Irving, played a number of comic roles and managed the Charing Cross Theatre and others until ill health forced retirement in 1895. His one New York appearance at Wallack's (1874) was only moderately successful. Toole was a kind and genial man, highly respected in the profession, and an actor who was always on good terms with his audience.*

8. *George Augustus Henry Sala (1828–96), a British journalist, was*

editor of Chat *(1848) and contributor to* Household Words *(1851–56). Joining the staff of the London* Telegraph *in 1857, he was thereafter a special correspondent, reporting on the American Civil War, then from Spain, Venice, Paris, Russia, and Australia. Among his books are* America in the Midst of War *(1864) and* Life and Adventures *(1895). He was a facile writer, but critics complained that he wrote too much and too fast.*

By the late 1880s the author of Roughing It, Tom Sawyer, Life on the Mississippi, *and* Huckleberry Finn *had become tremendously popular with the general public, but among fastidious critics his status was still doubtful. The genteel tradition and the supremacy of the New England Brahmins made him, in some quarters, a questionable figure regarded as a vulgar fellow who was essentially a joker unworthy of literary rank. He resented that label, but, paradoxically, he worked hard as writer, lecturer, and dinner speaker to make people laugh. Professing to have no aim other than to please the man in the street, he was nevertheless gratified by the critical approval of William Dean Howells, the New Englander by transplant, and by publication in the blue-blooded* Atlantic Monthly. *Yet despite signs of an advance toward literary dignity, the former wild humorist of the Pacific slope was not in good standing with the cognoscenti. As Henry James might have put it, Mark Twain had the fatal handicap of not being in tune with the rhythm of Newport. Irked by his long probation, he was proud to receive from Yale his first honorary degree, expressing his thanks in a letter compact and pointed.*

MARK TWAIN ACCEPTS
HONORARY DEGREE
Hartford *Courant*, June 29, 1888

New York, June 26, '88

My Dear Mr. President:[1] To be made a master of arts by your venerable college is an event of large size to me, and a distinction which gratifies me quite as much as if I deserved it. To be noticed in this way by the university would be pleasing to me at any time, but it is peculiarly so at this juncture. The late Matthew Arnold[2] rather sharply rebuked the guild of American "funny men" in his latest literary delivery,[3] and therefore your honorable recognition of us is peculiarly forcible and timely.

A friendly word was needed in our defense, and you have said it, and it is sufficient. It could not become us—we being in some ways, and at other intervals, modest, like other folk—to remind the world that ours is a useful trade, a worthy calling; that with all its lightness and frivolity it has one serious purpose, one aim, one specialty, and it is constant to it—the deriding of shams, the exposure of pretentious falsities, the laughing of stupid superstitions out of existence; and that whoso is by instinct engaged in this sort of warfare is the natural enemy of royalties, nobilities, privileges and all kindred swindles, and the natural friend of human rights and human liberties. We might with propriety say these things, and so hint that in some degree our calling is entitled to respect, but since you have rehabilitated us it is not necessary. I offer my best thanks to the corporation of Yale University for the high honor which they have conferred upon me, and am very sorry that my circumstances deny me the privilege of saying my thanks by word of mouth at the dinner tomorrow night. With great respect,

I am truly yours,
S. L. Clemens

1. *Timothy Dwight (1828-1916), a Congregational clergyman, was president of Yale (1886-98). Reconstructing and coordinating various schools within the college, he transformed it into a university. Needing funds, he turned back his own salary to the Yale treasury, eventually contributing over $100,000. Dwight was a practical man, genial and modest, with a good sense of humor that no doubt allowed him to appreciate Mark Twain.*

2. *Arnold (1822–88), a British poet, essayist, and critic, was the author of* The Strayed Reveler and Other Poems *(1849),* New Poems *(1867), other volumes of verse, and* Essays in Criticism *(1865, 1888).* Culture and Anarchy *(1869), his best known book, argues for "sweetness and light" as opposed to a mechanized civilization devoid of cultural aspirations. Arnold divides British society into the Barbarians, or aristocrats; the Populace, or lower classes; and the Philistines, or middle class, which he vigorously attacks for materialism and complacency.*

3. *After two lecture tours in the United States (1883–84, 1886), Arnold published* Civilisation in the United States *(1888), in which he reprimands Americans for boasting, reckless journalism; lack of self-criticism; ugly place names like Briggsville; and glorification of the average man. Everything, says Arnold, "is against distinction in America, and against the sense of elevation to be gained through admiring and respecting it. . . . The addiction to the 'funny man,' who is a national misfortune there, is against it. Above all, the newspapers are against it." His censure of America as an example of Philistia had point, which he might have made more acceptable if he had been less toplofty. During his American visits editors and hostesses remarked upon his stiff reserve, which seemed like a blend of coldness and arrogance that made him a difficult guest. The* Detroit News *said that such austerity generated a strong desire to poke him in the ribs and say, "Hello, Matt! Won't you have suthin'?" See* Literary Anecdotes, *ed. James Sutherland (1975), pp. 258–59.*

An authors' reading was a performance for the benefit of a worthy cause, at which authors read from their own works. Well-known writers gladly gave their services, and neophytes, happy to make themselves known to the public, made the most of their brief appearance in the limelight. Mark Twain was a willing performer, but he grumbled that the long program always dragged on wearisomely because readers would not rigidly restrict themselves to the stipulated ten or fifteen minutes each. In 1889, Seth Low presided at an authors' reading at the Brooklyn Academy of Music for the benefit of a fund to secure passage of a law on international copyright. Among the readers were Edward Eggleston, Richard Watson Gilder, F. Hopkinson Smith, and Theodore Roosevelt. Although copyright was of vital interest to Mark Twain, he declined to be present, for reasons he explained in a letter that was read by Chairman Low.

AUTHORS' READINGS
NEW YORK *Times*, DECEMBER 17, 1889

Gentlemen: I have worked for copyright in all the ways that its friends have suggested ever since 1872, seventeen or eighteen years, and I am cordially willing to continue to work for it all the rest of my life in all those ways but one— but I want to draw the line there—the platform.

We can point to an aggregate of about twelve Authors'

readings now since the first attempt, but we cannot point to a single one of them and say it was rationally conducted. Conducting a show is a trade. To do it well it must be done by a master, not novices and apprentices. There is no master with grit enough for the place. You cannot find him; he has not been born yet. Consider what is required of him. He must say to the small fry: "You are allowed ten minutes platform time; if you overpass it two minutes, I shall bring down the gavel, and shut you off." To the very greatest poet he must say: "For your own sake you are allowed but fifteen minutes;[1] you must test your pieces at home and time it by a friend's watch, and allow for the difference between platform time and parlor time, which is three minutes. If it overpasses twelve minutes at home, you must cut it down to twelve. If you try to ring in an extra piece you'll hear the gavel." He must say to the audience: "The performance will close at 10 o'clock whether this programme is finished or not," and then keep his word. He must find obscurities who are willing to take the tail places on the plain condition that they may possibly never be called up, or notorieties who will promise that they will not answer to their names after 10 o'clock, and will honorably keep that promise.

There is no such man alive, unless it might be Gen. Sherman,[2] author of the brisk and delightful memoirs. And even then you would have to appoint me to police him, and whisper from time to time; "General, your time is up." For—possibly you have noticed it—in no instance in history has the Chairman of an Authors' reading failed to add an hour to the already intolerably long bill.

No. An Authors' reading conducted in the customary way turns what ought to be the pleasantest of entertainments into an experience to be forever remembered with bitterness by the audience. Remember Washington.[3] There are now living but four persons who paid to get into that house. It is also a fact, however privately it has been kept, that twenty-two died on the premises and eighty-one on their way home. I am miserable when I think of my share in that wanton, that unprovoked massacre.

Tell me any other way that I can help the cause and I will do my very level best.

Sincerely yours,
S. L. Clemens

1. *On the Brooklyn program, following Chairman Low's opening remarks, Eggleston told several humorous stories, then read "Bud Mean's Wooing" from* The Hoosier Schoolmaster. *Gilder made a speech on copyright, then read three poems. William Hamilton Gibson read an entire article, "A Midnight Ramble," from* Scribner's. *Theodore Roosevelt, a talkative man, told of his latest encounter with a grizzly bear. And so on, each of the eight scheduled authors probably taking a few minutes more than his share. Adding time for introducing the speakers makes clear why Mark Twain complained of programs that extended what was supposed to be a two-hour performance to three or more. He was scrupulous about his own timing, rehearsing orally to make sure, if allotted ten minutes, that he spoke for ten minutes, no more.*

2. *William Tecumseh Sherman (1820–91), eschewing the arts of war, was well known in the social and professional life of New York City. He was a charter member of the Players Club, a friend of writers, actors, and painters, and generally among those present at banquets in honor of prominent citizens. He attended veterans' reunions, published his* Memoirs *(1875), and steadfastly rejected the lure of politics. Practically assured of the Republican presidential nomination in 1884, he announced that he would not run if nominated and would not serve if elected.*

3. *In March 1888, a matinee authors' reading dragged on, as usual, for too many hours. The readers had been invited to the White House, but they got there too late to meet President and Mrs. Cleveland, who had left for a dinner engagement. For entertaining comments on the devastating effects of the afternoon performance, see* Mark Twain's Autobiography, *ed. Albert B. Paine, 2 vols., (New York: Harper and Bros., 1924), 2:147–51.*

When Mark Twain's publishing company went bankrupt in the 1890s and the Paige typesetter had to be given up as a costly failure, his financial affairs were in such a dismal state that Henry H. Rogers, Standard Oil magnate, undertook to disentangle them. As the right-hand man of John D. Rockefeller, Rogers was a tycoon who qualified as a Wall Street pirate and robber baron, but he was a good friend to Mark Twain, setting him once

again on the road to prosperity and firmly restraining the Twainian urge to invest in gold brick schemes that yielded only fool's gold. Hence, Mark Twain gladly agreed to speak in Fairhaven, Massachusetts, at the dedication of the town hall, which was the gift of Mrs. Rogers. He made the trip in fine style with a number of dignitaries, Rogers having provided a private car and plenty of champagne. While in Fairhaven, Mark Twain visited the Millicent Library, named for Millicent Gifford Rogers, and wrote a letter of appreciation.

LETTER TO THE MILLICENT LIBRARY
Mark Twain and Fairhaven, N.D.

Fairhaven, Feb. 22, 1894

To the Officers of the Millicent Library: I am glad to have seen it. It is the ideal library, I think. Books are the liberated spirits of men, and should be bestowed in a heaven of light and grace and harmonious color and sumptuous comfort, like this, instead of in the customary kind of public library, with its depressing austerities and severities of form and furniture and decoration. A public library is the most enduring of memorials, the trustiest monument for the preservation of an event or a name or an affection; for it, and it only, is respected by wars and revolutions, and survives them.

Creed and opinion change with time, and their symbols perish; but Literature and its temples are sacred to all creeds, and inviolate.

All other things which I have seen today must pass away and be forgotten; but there will still be a Millicent Library when by the mutations of language the books that are in it now will speak in a lost tongue to your posterity.

Truly yours,
Mark Twain

The Lotos Club, founded in New York in 1870, was an organization of men in the arts and professions, the name connoting the peace and harmony of Tennyson's lotos eaters. Mark Twain was made a life member in 1895. He was not the stereotyped clubman who drowses in a well-padded chair overlooking Fifth Avenue, but he enjoyed club functions, particularly elaborate banquets, whether in New York or London, where he had been an honored guest of the Savage Club and the Whitefriars. Unable to attend the twenty-fifth anniversary dinner of the Lotos, however, he sent a letter of regret.

MARK TWAIN
A LIFE MEMBER OF THE LOTOS
New York *Tribune,* April 25, 1895

I have been wandering the highways for a week, hence the trouble your welcome letter has had in finding me. Welcome is the right word, for nothing could be welcomer than the compliment it brings me. It is an honor to be a member of the Lotos Club,[1] and this honor I have held and prized for a good two-thirds of a generation; in promoting me to a life membership the directors have augmented this honor and added to it the quality of distinction. There is not a veteran of us all who could be prouder of this token of approval and good-fellowship than I am, or more touched by it—a mutual good-fellowship which began when my head was brown and has lasted till it is gray; began when I "came unto a land where it seemed always afternoon," and continues now when I have reached a land where it is always afternoon—and but little left of that.

I wish I could be with you the night of the 30th and say my thanks with my mouth, and help the brethren go back in reminiscent pilgrimage past the twenty-five milestones and make certain of our dead live again—Oh, John Brougham,[2] what a vacancy you made when you went out from us! But I shall be on the ocean then; my sailing is imperative and unavoidable. Still, I can be with you in spirit and shall be; and at 11 that night, New York time, I will drink health and love to you all, and hope that you will do the like for me.

1. *Mark Twain became a member of the Lotos Club about 1880. He was said to have remarked in one of his early dinner speeches there that he really did not care to belong to a club that admitted congressmen.*

2. *Brougham (1810–80), an Irish-born American actor and dramatist, made his first appearance in London (1832) and in 1842 went to New York, where he became well known in most of the Broadway theaters. As a theatrical manager in London and New York, he was not a success, but as an actor he was a great favorite, at his best as the traditional stage Irishman playing such roles as Sir Lucius O'Trigger, Dennis Brulgruddery, and Captain Cuttle. He was also a prolific writer of farces, burlesques, and adaptations. A jovial man with a robust sense of humor, he was a congenial companion and a yarn-spinner able to hold his own with Mark Twain.*

To pay off his creditors, Mark Twain, in debt for some $200,000, contracted for a lecture tour around the world. In the early summer of 1895 he started out, accompanied by Olivia and his daughter, Clara, making his first stop at Cleveland on a sweltering night in July. Then they headed west by the northern route, pausing for appearances in Duluth, Minneapolis, Winnipeg, Butte, Spokane, Portland, and other towns on a leisurely journey to Seattle. Feeling the onset of age and afflicted with chronic bronchitis and a painful carbuncle, Mark Twain was still the hardy trouper, fulfilling all his platform engagements, meeting reporters everywhere, and giving speeches at dinners or late suppers that feted him at almost every stop.

In Helena, Montana, a reporter said that the famous visitor did not look like a humorist. "On the contrary," he wrote, "he appeared to be a gentleman of great gravity, a statesman or a man of vast business interests. The dark blue eyes are as clear as crystal and the keenest of glances shoots from them whenever he speaks. . . . the kindly smile that lights up his face and the general appearance of happy abandon proclaim the author who is no bookworm. He talks easily and quietly, yet with marked deliberation."

MARK TWAIN IS HERE
Helena, Montana, *Daily Herald,* August 3, 1895

Yes, this is my first visit to Montana, and I like the country and the people very well. Though I have lived East for many years, my heart often turns to the high mountains and broad plains of the West, for I was a frontiersman once myself.

I am on a long trip now; a regular world beater. It will

take a year and perhaps more. After making the United
States circuit we will go to the Sandwich Islands;[1] next we
will round up the coast cities of Australia, New Zealand,
Tasmania, Ceylon, then up the east coast of India, across to
Bombay, down to South Africa, and last of all to England. I
can't say how long I may stay in Europe, but when I come
back I am going to settle down in my Hartford home and
enjoy life in a quiet way.[2]

I have the same programme of readings for all my dates
in America that I will render at Ming's tonight. Perhaps I
may add another programme before I sail for the East, but
in Australia I shall give two or three programmes.

*Reporter: Is your daughter Clara, who is with you, the one who was
recently quoted as saying that she had never read your works?*

I didn't know that such a report had been sent out. All my
daughters ought to be pretty familiar with my works,
seeing that they have edited my manuscript since they were
seven years old. They always sided with me whenever Mrs.
Clemens thought I had used some sentence or word that was
a little too strong. But we never stood on that because
Madame was always in the majority anyway. For a long
time I used to have Mr. Howells edit all my copy. Ah, but
isn't he a charming writer? I believe that Howells is the best
we have in America today.

But, about that report you mentioned. I think that I can,
perhaps, guess how in the course of years it was evolved.
Long years ago, when Effie Ellsler,[3] then only nine years
old, had surprised the world with her precocious acting, she
dined at my house one day. My youngest daughter, Jean,
who was of the same age, sat at the table, too. But in the
learned conversation in which the young actress took her
part and acquitted herself as well as her elders, poor Jean
understood not a word. She sat there and listened to the
conversation of the little actress, every word going over her
head, filled with admiration, and, perhaps, envy. At last
someone mentioned "Tom Sawyer." There was a theme
that Jean knew something about. Speaking up, she said: "I
know who wrote Tom Sawyer; Mrs. Harriet Beecher
Stowe did."

1. *Honolulu was on the lecture itinerary, but though the ship anchored in the roadstead there, an outbreak of cholera barred passengers from going ashore. It was great disappointment to Mark Twain, who had dreamed of returning to the romantic islands he had visited in 1866, but all he could do was to stand at the rail and gaze at the paradise he could not enter. In* Following the Equator *(1897), he says: "We lay in luminous blue water; shoreward the water was green—green and brilliant; at the shore itself it broke in a long white riffle, and with no crash, no sound that we could hear. The town was buried under a mat of foliage that looked like a cushion of moss. The silky mountains were clothed in soft, rich splendors of melting color, and some of the cliffs were veiled in slanting mists. I recognized it all. It was just as I had seen it long before, with nothing of its beauty lost, nothing of its charm wanting."*

2. *After the Clemens family gave up the Hartford house and departed for Europe as an economy move in 1891, they never again lived in Hartford. As for settling down to "enjoy life in a quiet way," Mark Twain was not equipped for that sort of existence. His life was seldom quiet, in Hartford or anywhere else.*

3. *Probably Elsie Leslie, a talented child actress, who played the dual roles of Prince Edward and Tom Canty in the Broadway production of Mark Twain's* Prince and the Pauper *in 1890. Her winsome charm and long golden ringlets were largely responsible for the moderate success of the play. Elsie became a favorite of the whole Clemens family. Mark Twain, in collaboration with the actor William Gillette, embroidered a pair of slippers for her, then told the story of that laborious achievement in an engaging letter to* St. Nicholas *(December, 1889). His association with her was not, as he said, "long years ago," but only about six years before, yet a time sufficiently remote to scramble the facts in his erratic memory.*

At Adelaide, South Australia, a reporter described Mark Twain as "a quiet, composed, elderly gentleman," who had "a striking, masterful head and face, not the sort that one would sketch mentally for the presentment of the most original jester of the age, but quite suggestive of a character." They chatted in a hotel parlor, Mark Twain, said the newsman, "extending himself upon a sofa with an air of languor, for his journey had been a wearisome one, and his carbuncle bothered him." Nevertheless, he talked at some length.

MARK TWAIN PUT TO THE QUESTION
ADELAIDE *South Australian Register*, OCTOBER 14, 1895

The reporter asked how had he managed to smuggle his carbuncle past customs officers.

It sits on me like the nation; it keeps quiet a while, but at times it gathers itself together and gives an almighty hard twist. It's pretty vigorous. I think interviewing as an institution is good enough where the man under torture has something to confess, and the torturer knows how to worry it out of him. Now I haven't got much to reveal.

Reporter: There is a lot of rubbish forced upon a long-suffering public through the competition in the interview business?

Just so. It often happens that the interviewed has nothing to say, and the interviewer does not know how to make him say it. Sometimes in despair they write up a lot the man never said, never intended to say, and couldn't say it if he thought of it; but an accurate interview is a good thing. The interviewer has his interests to serve, and he feels he must get something somehow. It may be that he is no better equipped with material than the man he wants to get the column out of. I don't think I ever interviewed anyone.

Reporter: It is an American invention?

Yes; there is a lot of nonsense talked about American reporters sticking a celebrity up, not taking a note nor exchanging half a dozen words, and then working up a column of imaginative matter. It has been done and it may be done, but there are all sorts and conditions of newspapers.

If you make anything and you stick it on a height it

becomes conspicuous, and the more conspicuous it is the more notice is taken of it. Hence if a prominent politician or a paper does or says something out of the ordinary there is an unusual fuss about it, and people who haven't anything to think with stamp the whole nation or the whole Press with the character of the individual, which is just about as senseless as it could well be. It is like the silly superstition that Americans habitually carry revolvers and shoot them off promiscuously for pastime, particularly in the southern States. Now, Americans don't know the truth about themselves—a good many of them believe this revolver business. The Northerner believes that the Southerner goes around "revolvering," shooting and killing considerable. I tell you it is not a fact. The Southern communities are just as peaceful and religious as the Northern. The Southerner may be more highly cultured, and anything he does is naturally conspicuous. Carrying a revolver is a fad, just a fad or a fashion; but the revolvers are mighty harmless. Of course there are desperadoes on the frontier, but that is the only part of the world they live in. Their deeds give a false character to their district. I have carried a revolver; lots of us do, but they are the most innocent things in the world.

Reporter: What about the racial feeling in America?

Well, that's a big question. Much of the talk is exaggerated by windy agitators and stump orators, and does not represent the real feeling. Away back there was talk of deporting the negroes to Africa, and of disfranchising a large number, but you do not hear much of it now. I expect agitators are much the same breed all over the world. Chinamen, the yellow agony; well, most of my acquaintance with them is amongst the washerman class on the Pacific slope; and as for the Japs, those I have met have been highly cultured gentlemen educated in our colleges. The Jap is a superior person, and wears his English clothes of the latest cut with all the ease of an Englishman born to them. I never was disposed to make fun of the Chinaman; I always looked upon him as a pathetic object; a poor, hardworking, industrious, friendless heathen, far from home, amongst a strange people, who treated him none too well. He has a hard life, and is always busy and always sober, therefore I never could see anything to make fun of in the Chinaman. No, he is not wanted in America. The feeling is that he ought to go, but America is a place for all people, it seems.

The reporter mentioned Smiley, hero of the jumping frog story.

He was a real character, and his name was Greeley. The way he got the name of Smiley was this—I wrote the story for the New York *Saturday Gazette*,[1] a perishing weekly so-called literary newspaper—a home of poverty; it was the last number—the jumping frog killed it. They had not enough "G's," and so they changed Greeley's name to "Smiley." That's a fact. Yes, I am going to write a book on this trip around the world. It is such a touch-and-go kind of thing—nothing but a glimpse, but I get material. After doing Australia we are going to Ceylon, India, and South Africa.

The reporter mentioned Mark Twain's recent harsh comments about Bret Harte.[2]

Let that drop; it was one of those hasty things I had no business to have said, and it should never have appeared. If one criticises a man one should do it thoroughly. I let Max O'Rell[3] drop, too.

1. *"Jim Smiley and the Jumping Frog" appeared in the New York* Saturday Press *in November 1865.*
2. *The Sydney* Argus *of September 17, 1895, reported Mark Twain as saying of Harte: "I detest him, because I think his work is 'shoddy.' His forte is pathos, but there should be no pathos which does not come out of a man's heart. He has no heart, except his name, and I consider he has produced nothing that is genuine. He is artificial." These remarks stirred up controversy and indignant retorts from Harte partisans.*
3. *This was the pen name of Leon Paul Blouet (1848-1903). A French humorist employed as a journalist in England, he wrote* John Bull and His Island *(1883), which was so popular that he turned to comic writing. Lecture tours in the United States (1887, 1890) produced* Jonathan and His Continent *(1889) and* A Frenchman in America *(1891). Mark Twain considered him an unoriginal humorist who borrowed the good things of others, then palmed them off as his own.*

Ater a short visit to Tasmania, a round of appearances in New Zealand, and return engagements in Australia, Mark Twain and party sailed for Ceylon, enjoying a long slow voyage across the Indian Ocean. In mid-January 1896, they arrived in Bombay, Mark Twain afflicted with a nagging cold that kept him out of circulation for several days. Nevertheless, in a long interview with a reporter for the Bombay Gazette at Watson's Hotel, he did not act the part of an invalid. Seldom still, he strode about nervously, sat down briefly, filled his pipe, then jumped up again to pace restlessly, talking all the while in a soft voice as if thinking aloud. The reporter noted "his long untidy hair, and ferocious moustache; and the grey eyes that are not ferocious, but kind, and gentle, and pathetic; and the deep furrows falling outwards from the thin beaked nose to the sides of the mouth, which are the external and visible signs of the nasal drawl that characterises the very thoughts of the man before he has given utterance to them."

MARK TWAIN ON HIS METHODS OF WORK
BOMBAY *Gazette*, JANUARY 23, 1896

It would have served me right to be left alone as I was for twelve hours, and then to be drowned as an idiot![1] I have seen nothing of Bombay all the time I have been here, excepting these trees, which sadly need dusting, two or three cabs, and those towers. Yes, I am decidedly better than I was, and might even venture out now, but I shall not do so; neither shall I leave my room to-morrow, as I don't want a recurrence of this cough, and want to make sure of being all right on Friday.

The talk turned to Mark Twain's contemplated book, for which his tour of the southern hemisphere would provide material.

I have what would be called pretty lazy methods in the matter of preparation for my books. It is a troublesome thing for a lazy man to take notes, and so I used to try in my young days to pack my impressions in my head. But that can't be done satisfactorily, and so I went from that to another stage—that of making notes in a note-book. But I jotted them down in so skeleton a form that they did not bring back to me what it was I wanted them to furnish. Having discovered that defect, I have mended my ways a good deal in this respect, but still my notes are inadequate.

However, there may be some advantage to the reader in this, since in the absence of notes imagination has often to supply the place of facts.

I said just now I was lazy in preparation, but I won't admit that I am lazy in writing. No, I don't write rapidly, for when I did that I found it did not pay. I used to spend so much time next day correcting the manuscript, that it went to the printer a veritable forest of erasures, interlineations, emendations, abolitions, annihilations, and revisions. I found I should save time by writing slowly and carefully, and now my manuscript gives the printer no cause to blaspheme.

You ask me how it is I have not written more largely. Well, the fact of it is that for many years while at home, in America, I have written little or nothing on account of social calls upon my time. There is too much social life in my city for a literary man, and so for twenty years I gave up the attempt to do anything during nine months of the twelve I am at home. It has only been during the three months that I have annually been on vacation, and have been supposed to be holiday-making that I have written anything. It has been the same during the five years that I have been away from America. I have done little or no work. I wish now that I had done differently and had persisted in writing when at home. I could easily have done it, although I thought I could not. I seemed to think then that I was never going to grow old, but I know better than that now. In my vacation I have steadily done four or five hours' work every day at a stretch; and if they would only let me alone, I would have done seven hours a time without getting up from my chair.

The reporter asked about quantity written during vacation periods. Mark Twain paused to work out, half aloud, a problem in mental arithemtic.

Well, my average would be from ten thousand to twelve thousand words a week. But I have numerous interruptions, and so, instead of turning out from forty-five to fifty magazine pages per month, I do not do more than thirty. Yes, I am very fond of literary work, and nothing would please me better than to be allowed to be kept at a book for six months. You ask me what my opinions are with regard to the respective merits of my books. Well, I could easily point out which are the worst, but I am not going to do that. I cannot say on which book I have spent the most time simply because my methods have been very erratic. For instance, in writing *Tom Sawyer* I got up to the middle of the book and then did not touch it for a year or two, and it was the same with *Prince and the Pauper.* It has been like this for many years, owing to my stupid notion that I could do no work at home.

Reporter: It has been said that the reason you have not published more is, that you did not desire to tire your public. How far is that correct?

Well, I have always kept that in mind, but I like literary work for its own sake, and I am sorry that I did not take time to write, and not to publish. I should like to have half a dozen works in manuscript just for the pleasure of writing them.

1. *Mark Twain thus passed judgment on himself because he believed he had caught the severe cold by lying asleep on shipboard in an exposed place.*

Completing his round-the-world tour, Mark Twain looked forward to platform appearances in Britain and the United States, but tentative plans were cancelled by the death of his eldest daughter, Susy, in August 1896. For the next four years the family lived in England and on the continent, remaining in seclusion a year or so, then emerging to be caught up in a busy life in Vienna. Mark Twain was the social lion of the Austrian capital, sought after, cultivated, and known to everybody from the emperor to the man in the street. When Americans in Germany gathered for an annual Fourth of July celebration in Leipsic, Mark Twain sent regrets from Kaltenleutgeben, a hydropathic health resort near Vienna, where the family spent the summer of 1898.

MARK TWAIN WRITES A LETTER ON ANGLO-AMERICAN UNITY
New York *Times*, July 24, 1898

Kaltenleutgeben, Near Vienna, June 28, 1898

Brainard Warner, Jr., Esq., United States Consul, Leipsic

Dear Sir: I have waited to see if I could defeat my obstructions and come to Leipsic, but have failed. I cannot venture away from my desk lest I fail to finish work in hand and soon due.[1] It costs me a pang to lose this Fourth in solitude when the fortunate may get on their feet and shout. Ordinarily I should not care, but I care this time, for this is not an ordinary Fourth.[2] On the contrary, it is a memorable one—the most memorable which the flag has known in thirty-three years—and there have been but two before it which may claim to rank with it as happy epoch posts in the history of the Republic—1865 and 1776. This one marks the burial of the estrangement which has existed so long and so perniciously between England and America,[3] a welcome condition of things, which, if wisely nursed and made permanent, can be of inestimable value to both nations and incidentally to the world.

In reverence for liberty, in humanitarian and civilizing impulses, and in other great things of the heart and spirit the two nations are kindred as well as in blood,[4] and friendly relations between them mean the forward march of the human race. That old animosity is buried. Let us hope it will stay buried, and also hope that for centuries to come this august funeral will still continue to be celebrated at our Fourth, and that meantime any man who tries to dig up that corpse will promptly be put in condition to take its place.

Truly yours,
Mark Twain

1. *His travel book,* Following the Equator, *had been published in 1897. Then, driven by desperation induced by the disasters that had overtaken him—the death of Susy, the epilepsy of Jean, and his business failures—he wrote compulsively for several years, beginning scores of manuscripts, only a few of which ever saw print. He told Howells that he sometimes kept at it eight and nine hours at a stretch, but despite his incredible labor he did not finish, or was unable to finish, most of the great mass of material he began. This furious and frustrating writing was perhaps the "work in hand." See Bernard De Voto, "The Symbols of Despair," in* Mark Twain: A Profile, *ed. Justin Kaplan (New York: Hill and Wang, 1967).*

2. *An allusion to American intervention in Cuba, a move that Mark Twain and others interpreted as a gesture to free an oppressed people from tyranny. A further cause for celebration would be the destruction of Admiral Cervera's Spanish fleet by the North Atlantic Squadron off Santiago on July 3, 1898.*

3. *During the Civil War, relations between the United States and England had been strained because the British government had favored and attempted to assist the southern Confederacy. During the Spanish-American War the British were on our side, the government acting as an unofficial watchdog to prevent hostile behavior by European powers.*

4. *A few years later Mark Twain, incensed by what he considered American aggression in the Philippines, carried the relationship a step further. Introducing Winston Churchill to a New York audience in 1900, he linked the Boer War and the American adventure in the Far East as examples of imperialism, saying that England and America were not only kin in blood, ideals, and representative government, but also kin in sin.*

After a sojourn of twenty months in Vienna, Mark Twain and family left for England. The New York Times *said, June 11, 1899: "No other town has ever seen him depart with more regret. . . . Wherever there was a festivity or something interesting to be seen or heard the famous humorist was to be found." A final episode was a private audience with the Emperor Francis Joseph. For the occasion, Mark Twain prepared a short speech in German, then, in the imperial presence, forgot the whole thing. But there was a long and amiable conversation, he said, in which he extolled Vienna as a delightful city where he had felt entirely at home, and the emperor praised the prowess of the American army and navy as recently demonstrated in the war with Spain. For the press, Mark Twain issued a brief report.*

TWAIN'S FAREWELL TO VIENNA
NEW YORK *Times,* JUNE 11, 1899

The New York papers have asked me about my audience, and I have telegraphed the following which I consider quite nice, because it is dignified and does not give any information: "It was only a pleasant unconstrained private conversation on matters unconnected with international policy. I very much wanted to explain my plan, now in the hands of the Secretary of State in Washington, for insuring universal peace, but I feared that his Majesty would laugh, or else consider it too radical."

Now, all the newspapers in America will telegraph to the Secretary of State to know what my plan is, and then they will learn that I have discovered a method of suddenly depriving the air of its vital principle, and thus of killing off the whole human race in four minutes.

Arriving in New York by the middle of October 1900, after years of wandering over the world, Mark Twain was immediately involved in events that showered him with attention. Honored guest at dinners and receptions tendered by clubs and societies and speaker on behalf of causes charitable and social, he was trailed by reporters for comments on the universe in general or anything in particular. When hazing at West Point got so far out of hand

that it became a public scandal and a military board of inquiry was accused of a coverup, a Congressional committee investigated, calling up generals and cadets for testimony that was front page news.[1] Mark Twain, of course, was consulted for his views on the subject.

MARK TWAIN ON HAZING
NEW YORK *Times*, JANUARY 20, 1901

Why, the fourth class man who is compelled to fight a man from the first class hasn't a show in the world, and it is not intended that he should. I have read the rules provided to prevent such practices, and they are wholly deficient, because one provision is omitted. I would make it the duty of a cadet to report to the authorities any case of hazing which came to his notice; make such reports a part of the vaunted West Point "code of honor" and the beating of young boys by upper class men will be stopped.

I am not opposed to fights among boys as a general thing. If they are conducted in a spirit of fairness, I think it makes boys manly, but I do oppose compelling a little fellow to fight some man big enough to whip two of him. When I was a boy, going to school down in the Mississippi Valley, we used to have our fights, and I remember one occasion on which I got soundly trounced, but we always matched boys as nearly of a size as possible, and there was none of the cowardly methods that seem to prevail at West Point.

---

1. *According to the* Times, *one of the most sadistic West Point hazers was the cadet president of the Y.M.C.A. As a result of the uproar in the press and in Congress, the heads of the four classes unanimously agreed to abolish hazing, but whether the reform was genuine or only theoretical must be left to conjecture.*

The attention Mark Twain received was not entirely favorable. As an outspoken critic of American policy in the Philippines, he incurred the disapproval of editors and the wrath of patriotic citizens. Charitable readers, puzzled and dismayed by his forthright anti-imperialism, made excuses by saying that vitriolic comments about the government and the president were only a peculiar form of his well-known humor. That was an error because he was never more in earnest, yet he paid the penalty of the perennial humorist whose most serious words are likely not to be taken seriously. When he wrote a short letter to a newspaper versifier about a patriotic poem, he ran afoul of the Army and Navy Journal. The poem has eluded search, but it apparently praised the idealism of recruits who enlisted to free Cuba from Spanish oppression. Mark Twain went on from there.

SLANDER'S MASK OF HUMOR
Army and Navy Journal, N.D.; REPRINTED IN
NEW YORK *Times*, MARCH 24, 1901

Dear Lampton:[1] Will you allow me to say that I like those poems of yours very much? Especially the one which so vividly pictures the response of our young fellows when they were summoned to strike down an oppressor and set his victim free. Write a companion to it and show us how the young fellows respond when invited by the Government to go out to the Philippines on a land-stealing and liberty-crucifying crusade. I notice that they swarm to the recruiting office at the rate of 800 a month,[2] out of an enthusiastic population of 75,000,000 free men; and that no American-born person can pronounce their names without damage to his jaw, nor spell them without a foreign education.[3]

Sincerely yours,
Mark Twain

1. *William James Lampton (d. 1917) was a newspaperman who had been a reporter for the Steubenville* Herald, Cincinnati Times, Louisville Courier Journal, Detroit Free Press, *and others, and he published verse in New York papers. His best-known lines are from his poem, "To Old Kentucky," a state "Where the golden age is regnant, / And each succeeding morn / Finds the corn is full of kernels, / And the Colonels full of corn."*
2. *The* Army and Navy Journal *said that applications at recruiting*

*offices for China and the Philippines were about fifteen times 800 a month.
"[Mark Twain's] statement . . . has 5 per cent of truth in it, which is,
perhaps, as large a proportion as we could expect of an author who has . . .
been accustomed to contribute to the good nature of the world by statements
so exaggerated and grotesque that we never . . . mistake them for anything
but humorous extravagances."*

    3. The Journal *said that over 88 percent of recruits were native-born and
that the remainder, foreign-born, were either citizens or had announced their
intention of becoming citizens. Then the military critic concluded with a
reprimand: "It is unfortunate for the reputation of Mark Twain that he
should go out of his way to slander these men because they believe in the
right and duty of our Government to enforce its authority over all of the
territory belonging to the United States. . . . It is melancholy to find the
genial Mark, in descending into the arena of partisan falsification, giving up
to party what was meant for mankind."*

*The fiction which follows was probably written in London in 1900 and may
have been one of the half dozen or more manuscripts Mark Twain had told
the Bombay reporter he liked to keep going at the same time. Turning to
lighthearted narrative, he momentarily held at bay the bitterness engendered
by disasters that had struck him and checked the savage disgust aroused by
recurrent idiocies of "the damned human race." There is mild irony about
human foibles, and gentle satire, but nothing abrasive.*

TWO LITTLE TALES
Century Magazine, November 1901

First Story:
The Man With a Message for the Director-General

Some days ago, in this second month of 1900, a friend
made an afternoon call upon me here in London. We are of
that age when men who are smoking away their time in
chat do not talk quite so much about the pleasantnesses of
life as about its exasperations. By and by this friend began
to abuse the War Office. It appeared that he had a friend
who had been inventing something which could be made
very useful to the soldiers in South Africa.[1] It was a light

and very cheap and durable boot, which would remain dry in wet weather, and keep its shape and firmness. The inventor wanted to get the government's attention called to it, but he was an unknown man and knew the great officials would pay no heed to a message from him.

"This shows that he was an ass—like the rest of us," I said, interrupting. "Go on."

"But why have you said that? The man spoke the truth."

"The man spoke a lie. Go on."

"I will *prove* that he—"

"You can't prove anything of the kind. I am very old and very wise. You must not argue with me; it is irreverent and offensive. Go on."

"Very well. But you will presently see. I am not unknown, yet even *I* was not able to get the man's message to the Director-General of the Shoe-Leather Department."

"This is another lie. Pray go on."

"But I assure you on my honor that I failed."

"Oh, certainly. I knew *that*. You didn't need to tell me."

"Then where is the lie?"

"It is in your intimation that you were not *able* to get the Director-General's immediate attention to the man's message. It is a lie, because you *could* have gotten his immediate attention to it."

"I tell you I couldn't. In three months I haven't accomplished it."

"Certainly. Of course. I could know that without your telling me. You *could* have gotten his immediate attention if you had gone at it in a sane way; and so could the other man."

"I *did* go at it in a sane way."

"You didn't."

"How do *you* know? What do you know about the circumstances?"

"Nothing at all. But you didn't go at it in a sane way. That much I know to a certainty."

"How can you know it, when you don't know what method I used?"

"I know by the result. The result is perfect proof. You

went at it in an insane way. I am very old and very w—"

"Oh, yes, I know. But will you let me tell you *how* I proceeded? I think that will settle whether it was insanity or not."

"No; that has already been settled. But go on, since you so desire to expose yourself. I am very o—"

"Certainly, certainly. I sat down and wrote a courteous letter to the Director-General of the Shoe-Leather Department, explai—"

"Do you know him personally?"

"No."

"You have scored one for my side. You began insanely. Go on."

"In the letter I made the great value and inexpensiveness of the invention clear, and offered to—"

"Call and see him? Of course you did. Score two against yourself. I am v—"

"He didn't answer for three days."

"Necessarily. Proceed."

"Sent me three gruff lines thanking me for my trouble and proposing—"

"Nothing."

"That's it—proposing nothing. Then I wrote him more elaborately and—"

"Score three—"

"—and got no answer. At the end of a week I wrote and asked, with some touch of asperity, for an answer to that letter."

"Four. Go on."

"An answer came back saying the letter had not been received, and asking for a copy. I traced the letter through the post-office, and found that it *had* been received; but I sent a copy and said nothing. Two weeks passed without further notice of me. In the meantime I gradually got myself cooled down to a polite-letter temperature. Then I wrote and proposed an interview for next day, and said that if I did not hear from him in the meantime I should take his silence for assent."

"Score five."

"I arrived at twelve sharp, and was given a chair in the anteroom and told to wait. I waited till half-past one; then I left, ashamed and angry. I waited another week, to cool down; then I wrote and made another appointment with him for next day noon."

"Score six."

"He answered, assenting. I arrived promptly, and kept a chair warm until half-past two. I left then, and shook the dust of that place from my shoes for good and all. For rudeness, inefficiency, incapacity, indifference to the army's interests, the Director-General of the Shoe-Leather Department of the War Office is, in my o—"

"Peace! I am very old and very wise, and have seen many seemingly intelligent people who hadn't common sense enought to go at a simple and easy thing like this in a common-sense way. You are not a curiosity to me; I have personally known millions and billions like you. You have lost three months quite unnecessarily; the inventor has lost three months; the soldiers have lost three—nine months altogether. I will now read you a little tale which I wrote last night. Then you will call on the Director-General at noon to-morrow and transact your business."

"Splendid! Do you know him?"

"No; but listen to the tale."

SECOND STORY:
How the Chimney-Sweep Got the Ear of the Emperor

I

Summer was come, and all the strong were bowed by the burden of the awful heat, and many of the weak were prostrate and dying. For weeks the army had been wasting away with a plague of dysentery, that scourge of the soldier, and there was but little help. The doctors were in despair; such efficacy as their drugs and their science had once had—and it was not much at its best—was a thing of the past, and promised to remain so.

The Emperor commanded the physicians of greatest renown to appear before him for a consultation, for he was profoundly disturbed. He was very severe with them, and called them to account for letting his soldiers die; and asked them if they knew their trade, or didn't; and were they properly healers, or merely assassins? Then the principal assassin, who was also the oldest doctor in the land and the most venerable in appearance, answered and said:

"We have done what we could, your Majesty, and for a good reason it has been little. No medicine and no physician can cure that disease; only nature and a good constitution can do it. I am old, and I know. No doctor and no medicine can cure it—I repeat it and I emphasize it. Sometimes they seem to help nature a little—a very little—but, as a rule, they merely do damage."

The Emperor was a profane and passionate man, and he deluged the doctors with rugged and unfamiliar names, and drove them from his presence. Within a day he was attacked by that fell disease himself. The news flew from mouth to mouth, and carried consternation with it over all the land. All the talk was about this awful disaster, and there was general depression, for few had hope. The Emperor himself was very melancholy, and sighed, and said:

"The will of God be done. Send for the assassins again, and let us get over with it."

They came, and felt his pulse and looked at his tongue, and fetched the drug-store and emptied it into him, and sat down patiently to wait—for they were not paid by the job but by the year.

II

Tommy was sixteen and a bright lad, but he was not in society. His rank was too humble for that, and his employment too base. In fact, it was the lowest of all employments, for he was second in command to his father, who emptied cesspools and drove a night-cart. Tommy's closest friend was Jimmy the chimney-sweep,[2] a slim little fellow of fourteen, who was honest and industrious, and had a good heart and supported a bedridden mother by his dangerous and unpleasant trade.

About a month after the Emperor fell ill these two lads met one evening about nine. Tommy was on his way to his night-work and of course was not in his Sundays, but in his dreadful work-clothes, and not smelling very well. Jimmy was on his way home from his day's labor, and was blacker than any other object imaginable, and he had his brushes on his shoulder and his soot-bag at his waist, and no feature of his sable face was distinguishable except his lively eyes.

They sat down on the curbstone to talk and of course it was upon the one subject—the nation's calamity, the Emperor's disorder. Jimmy was full of a great project, and burning to unfold it. He said:

"Tommy, I can cure his Majesty. I know how to do it."

Tommy was surprised.

"What! You?"

"Yes, I."

"Why, you little fool, the best doctors can't."

"I don't care; I can do it. I can cure him in fifteen minutes."

"Oh, come off! What are you giving me?"

"The facts—that's all."

Jimmy's manner was so serious that it sobered Tommy, who said:

"I believe you are in earnest, Jimmy. Are you in earnest?"

"I give you my word."

"What is the plan? How'll you cure him?"

"Tell him to eat a slice of ripe watermelon."

It caught Tommy rather suddenly, and he was shouting with laughter at the absurdity of the idea before he could put on a stopper. But he sobered down when he saw that Jimmy was wounded. He patted Jimmy's knee affectionately, not minding the soot, and said:

"I take the laugh all back. I didn't mean any harm, Jimmy, and I won't do it again. You see, it seemed so funny, because wherever there's a soldier-camp and dysentery, the doctors always put up a sign saying anybody caught bringing watermelons there will be flogged with the cat till he can't stand."

"I know it—the idiots!" said Jimmy, with both tears and anger in his voice. "There's plenty of watermelons, and not one of those soldiers ought to have died."

"But, Jimmy, what put the notion into your head?"

"It isn't a notion; it's a fact. Do you know that old gray-headed Zulu? Well, this long time back he has been curing a lot of our friends, and my mother has seen him do it, and so have I. It takes only one or two slices of melon, and it don't make any difference whether the disease is new or old; it cures it."

"It's very odd. But, Jimmy, if it is so, the Emperor ought to be told of it."

"Of course; and my mother has told people, hoping they could get the word to him; but they are poor working-folks and ignorant, and don't know how to manage it."

"Of course they don't, the blunderheads," said Tommy scornfully. "*I'll* get it to him!"

"You? You night-cart polecat!" And it was Jimmy's turn to laugh. But Tommy retorted sturdily:

"Oh, laugh if you like, but I'll *do* it!"

It had such an assured and confident sound that it made an impression, and Jimmy asked gravely:

"Do you know the Emperor?"

"Do *I* know him? Why, how you talk! Of course I don't"

"Then how'll you do it?"

"It's very simple and very easy. Guess. How would *you* do it, Jimmy?"

"Send him a letter. I never thought of it till this minute. But I'll bet that's your way."

"I'll bet it ain't. Tell me, how would you send it?"

"Why, through the mail, of course."

Tommy overwhelmed him with scoffings, and said:

"Now, don't you suppose every crank in the empire is doing the same thing? Do you mean to say you haven't thought of that?"

"Well—no," said Jimmy, abashed.

"You *might* have thought of it, if you weren't so young and inexperienced. Why, Jimmy, even a common *general,* or a poet, or an actor, or anybody that's a little famous gets

Above: *Mark Twain about 1907. (From Franklin J. Meine collection.)* Left: *Mark Twain as caricatured in the New York Times of March 1, 1908.*

sick, all the cranks in the kingdom load up the mails with
certain-sure quack-cures for him. And so, what's bound to
happen when it's the Emperor?"

"I suppose it's worse," said Jimmy, sheepishly.

"Well, I should think so! Look here, Jimmy; every single
night we cart off as many as six loads of that kind of letters
from the back yard of the palace, where they're thrown.
Eighty thousand letters in one night! Do you reckon anybody reads them? Sho! not a single one. It's what would
happen to your letter if you wrote it—which you won't, I
reckon?"

"No," sighed Jimmy, crushed.

"But it's all right, Jimmy. Don't you fret; there's more
than one way to skin a cat. *I'll* get the word to him."

"Oh, if you only *could,* Tommy, I should love you forever."

"I'll do it, I tell you. Don't you worry; you depend on
me."

"Indeed I will, Tommy, for you do know so much.
You're not like other boys; they never know anything.
How'll you manage, Tommy?"

Tommy was greatly pleased. He settled himself for
reposeful talk, and said:

"Do you know that ragged poor thing that thinks he's a
butcher because he goes around with a basket and sells cat's
meat and rotten livers? Well, to begin with, I'll tell *him.*"

Jimmy was deeply disappointed and chagrined, and said:

"Now, Tommy, it's a shame to talk so. You know my
heart's in it, and it's not right."

Tommy gave him a love-pat, and said:

"Don't you be troubled, Jimmy. *I* know what I'm about.
Pretty soon you'll see. That half-breed butcher will tell the
old woman that sells chestnuts at the corner of the lane—
she's his closest friend, and I'll ask him to; then, by request,
she'll tell her rich aunt that keeps the little fruit-shop on the
corner two blocks above; and that one will tell her particular friend, the man that keeps the game-shop; and he will
tell his friend the sergeant of police; and the sergeant will
tell his captain, and the captain will tell the magistrate, and

the magistrate will tell his brother-in-law the county judge, and the county judge will tell the sheriff, and the sheriff will tell the Lord Mayor, and the Lord Mayor will tell the President of the Council, and the President of the Council will tell the—"

"By George, but it's a wonderful scheme, Tommy! How ever *did* you—"

"—Rear-Admiral, and the Rear will tell the Vice, and the Vice will tell the Admiral of the Blue, and the Blue will tell the Red, and the Red will tell the White, and the White will tell the First Lord of the Admiralty, and the First Lord will tell the Speaker of the House, and the Speaker—"

"Go it, Tommy; you're 'most there!"

"—will tell the Master of the Hounds, and the Master will tell the Head Groom of the Stables, and the Head Groom will tell the Chief Equerry, and the Chief Equerry will tell the First Lord in Waiting, and the First Lord will tell the Lord High Chamberlain, and the Lord High Chamberlain will tell the Master of the Household, and the Master of the Household will tell the little pet page that fans the flies off the Emperor, and the page will get down on his knees and whisper it to his Majesty—and the game's made!"

"I've *got* to get up and hurrah a couple of times, Tommy. It's the grandest idea that ever was. What ever put it into your head?"

"Sit down and listen, and I'll give you some wisdom—and don't you ever forget it as long as you live. Now, then, who is the closest friend you've got, and the one you couldn't and wouldn't ever refuse anything in the world to?"

"Why, it's you, Tommy. You know that."

"Suppose you wanted to ask a pretty large favor of the cat's-meat man. Well, you don't know him, and he would tell you to go to thunder, for he is that kind of a person; but he is my next best friend after you, and would run his legs off to do me a kindness—*any* kindness, he don't care what it is. Now, I'll ask you: which is the most common-sensible—for you to go and ask him to tell the chestnut-woman about

your watermelon cure, or for you to get me to do it for
you?"

"To get you to do it for me, of course. I wouldn't ever
have thought of that, Tommy; it's splendid!"

"It's a *philosophy*, you see. Mighty good word—and large.
It goes on this idea: everybody in the world, little and big,
has one *special* friend, a friend that he's *glad* to do favors
for—not sour about it, but *glad*—glad clear to the marrow.
And so, I don't care where you start, you can get at
anybody's ear that you want to—I don't care how low you
are, nor how high he is. And it's so simple: you've only to
find the *first* friend, that is all; that ends your part of the
work. He finds the next friend himself, and that one finds
the third, and so on, friend after friend, link after link, like a
chain; and you can go up it or down it, as high as you like or
as low as you like."

"It's just beautiful, Tommy."

"It's as simple and easy as a-b-c; but did you ever hear of
anybody trying it? No; everybody is a fool. He goes to a
stranger without any introduction, or writes him a letter,
and of course he strikes a cold wave—and serves him
gorgeously right. Now, the Emperor don't know me, but
that's no matter—he'll eat his watermelon to-morrow.
You'll see. Hi-hi—stop! It's the cat's-meat man. Good-by,
Jimmy; I'll overtake him."

He did overtake him, and said:

"Say, will you do me a favor?"

"*Will* I? Well, I should *say*! I'm your man. Name it and
see me fly!"

"Go tell the chestnut-woman to put down everything
and carry this message to her first-best friend, and tell the
friend to pass it along." He worded the message, and said,
"Now, then, rush!"

The next moment the chimney sweep's word to the
Emperor was on its way.

III

The next evening, toward midnight, the doctors sat
whispering together in the imperial sick-room, and they

were in deep trouble, for the Emperor was in very bad case. They could not hide it from themselves that every time they emptied a fresh drug-store into him he got worse. It saddened them, for they were expecting that result. The poor emaciated Emperor lay motionless, with his eyes closed, and the page that was his darling was fanning the flies away and crying softly. Presently the boy heard the silken rustle of a portiere, and turned and saw the Lord High Great Master of the Household peering in at the door and excitedly motioning him to come. Lightly and swiftly the page tiptoed his way to his dear and worshiped friend the Master, who said:

"Only you can persuade him, my child, and oh, don't fail to do it! Take this, make him eat it, and he is saved."

"On my head be it. He shall eat it!"

It was a couple of great slices of ruddy, fresh watermelon.

The next morning the news flew everywhere that the Emperor was sound and well again, and had hanged the doctors. A wave of joy swept the land, and frantic preparations were made to illuminate.

After breakfast his Majesty sat meditating. His gratitude was unspeakable, and he was trying to devise a reward rich enough to properly testify it to his benefactor. He got it arranged in his mind, and called the page, and asked him if he had invented that cure. The boy said no—he got it from the Master of the Household.

He was sent away, and the Emperor went to devising again. The Master was an earl; he would make him a duke, and give him a vast estate which belonged to a member of the Opposition. He had him called, and asked him if he was the inventor of the remedy. But the Master was an honest man, and said he got it of the Grand Chamberlain. He was sent away, and the Emperor thought some more. The Chamberlain was a viscount; he would make him an earl, and give him a large income. But the Chamberlain referred him to the First Lord in Waiting, and there was some more thinking; his Majesty thought out a smaller reward. But the First Lord in Waiting referred him back further, and he had to sit down and think out a further and becomingly and suitably smaller reward.

Then, to break the tediousness of the inquiry and hurry the business, he sent for the Grand High Chief Detective, and commanded him to trace the cure to the bottom, so that he could properly reward his benefactor.

At nine in the evening the High Chief Detective brought the word. He had traced the cure down to a lad named Jimmy, a chimney-sweep. The Emperor said, with deep feeling:

"Brave boy, he saved my life, and shall not regret it!"

And sent him a pair of his own boots; and the next best ones he had, too, They were too large for Jimmy, but they fitted the Zulu, so it was all right, and everything as it should be.

Conclusion to the First Story

"There—do you get the idea?"

"I am obliged to admit that I do. And it will be as you have said. I will transact the business to-morrow. I intimately know the Director-General's nearest friend. He will give me a note of introduction, with a word to say my matter is of real importance to the government. I will take it along, without any appointment, and send it in, with my card, and I shan't have to wait so much as half a minute."

That turned out true to the letter, and the government adopted the boots.

1. *This is an allusion to the Boer War. As a result of disputes in South Africa, the semi-independent republics of Orange Free State and the Transvaal declared war on Great Britain in 1899. The Boers, capitalizing on their knowledge of the terrain and the ineptitude of royal commanders, won victories that year and in 1900, but the tide slowly turned when the British, aided by troops from Canada, Australia, and New Zealand, eventually committed 250,000 men, commanded by Lord Roberts. The Boers were finally subdued, but guerrilla warfare continued until 1902, when hostilities ceased. England annexed the republics, promised future self-government, and loaned large sums to rehabilitate Boer farms. In Britain the war was not generally popular, and in the United States, Mark Twain and*

other prominent Americans were outspoken in opposition to British policy in South Africa.

2. The two boys faintly resemble Tom Sawyer and Huck Finn. The name "Tommy" may not be accidental, for he is the organizer and manager, like his earlier namesake. Tommy's remark, "I know what I'm about," is an echo of Tom Sawyer's confident assertion to Huck, "Don't you reckon I know what I'm about? Don't I generly know what I'm about?"

The Saint Louis World's Fair, officially known as the Louisiana Purchase Exposition, was supposed to open in 1903, but it was delayed a year. In the interim, Sir Thomas Lipton, internationally famous for his tea and his yachts, suggested staging steamboat races as a Fair attraction. Mark Twain endorsed the idea, adding details recalled from his days as a pilot on the river.

RACES ON THE MISSISSIPPI
New York *Times*, March 31, 1903

New York City, March 30 [1903]

Dear President Francis:[1] As regards the suggestion of Sir Thomas Lipton,[2] it seems to me that an old-fashioned Mississippi steamboat race, as a feature of the fair,[3] would be a very good specialty indeed. As to particulars, I think that the race should be a genuine reproduction of the old-time race, not just an imitation of it, and that it should cover the whole course. I think the boats should begin the trip at New Orleans, and side by side, (not with an interval between), and end it at North St. Louis, a mile or two above the Big Mound.

I think they should have ample forecastle crowd[s] of negro chantey singers, with able leaders to do the solo and conduct the chorus from the capstan. I should reinstate the torch basket[4] and use the electric for business only. I should extinguish the Government lights in every crossing throughout the course, for where boats are equally matched in the matters of speed and draught, it is the quality of the piloting that decides the race.

Have you a couple of six-day boats? Then you have a continuous six-day world advertisement, for you would have wireless operators and Associated Press representatives on both boats, and they would report the positions of the contestants hourly, day and night, and describe the succeeding or failing jockeyings and stratagems of the pilots. This would be an innovation and dreadfully modern, but the value of it would condone it. It would keep the boats quite vividly in sight straight along a stretch of 1,400 miles, and for the first time the world would see a six-day boat race from start to finish.

The fair would issue the great War Department map of the Mississippi, and every citizen would buy a copy and check off the progress of the race hour by hour and arrange his bets with such judacity as Providence had provided him withal. This map is a yard wide and thirty-six feet long. It might be well to reduce it a little.

As a fair advertisement it would be difficult to beat the boat race; as a spectacle, nothing could add to it, except an old-time blow-up as the boats finished the home stretch. But this should not be arranged; it is better left to Providence and prayer.

Truly yours,
Mark Twain

1. *David Rowland Francis (1850–1927), a merchant who went into politics, became mayor of Saint Louis (1885), then governor of Missouri (1889–93). Appointed secretary of the interior (1896), he was a strong conservationist who battled to protect forest reserves. As president of the corporation promoting the Saint Louis World's Fair, he was successful in persuading foreign governments to take part. He published* The Universal Exposition of 1904 *(1913) and ended his political career as ambassador to Russia (1916), where he served creditably during a difficult time of revolution and confusion. A friendly man, he had an engaging personality that was an asset in politics as well as in human affairs generally.*

2. *Although generally thought of as an importer of tea, Thomas Johnstone Lipton (1850–1931) acquired, in his native Glasgow and elsewhere, shops that offered all sorts of foodstuffs, supplying them from his own tea, coffee, and cocoa plantations, also from his fruit farms, jam factories, and bakeries.*

He operated bacon-curing establishments and a packing house in Chicago. Equally well known as a member of the Royal Ulster Yacht Club, he made five unsuccessful attempts to lift the America's Cup between 1899 and 1930 with his yachts, Shamrock I to V. Knighted in 1898, he was made a baronet in 1902.

3. Another proposed feature, to be sponsored by an embryonic Mark Twain Association, was a Mark Twain Week; one day of that week was to be designated as Mark Twain Day, on which there would be a gathering of literary notables. He disapproved, saying that such honors were not proper for the living and that he hoped no association would be named for him because he might do something to make its members regret their action. When urged to reconsider, he said he relished spontaneous honors but shrank from distinctions that had to be arranged beforehand and thus made him a party to his own aggrandizement.

4. This was a basket-like container of iron mesh, which held a small bonfire. Usually there were two torch baskets, attached to long rods that extended from the lowest deck of the steamboat on both sides near the bow. The burning baskets made a spectacular show, and when the river rose they were also useful in silhouetting stumps and other obstructions to navigation. On Mark Twain's trip down the river in 1882, as he recounts in Life on the Mississippi, he found that the "flickering, smoky, pitch-dripping, ineffectual torch-baskets" had been replaced by "a blinding glory of white electric light."

Mark Twain began writing about Christian Science and Mary Baker Eddy when he was in Vienna in 1898. Having faith in the power of mental healing, he had no quarrel with the doctrine, which he called "a noble philosophy," but only with Mrs. Eddy, whom he believed to be incapable of writing the book Science and Health that bore her name. The facts came out after the death in 1900 of James Henry Wiggin, a Unitarian clergyman who had been asked to edit the sixteenth edition of Science and Health. He told his literary executor, Livingston Wright, that he found Mrs. Eddy's manuscript chaotic, contradictory, full of misspellings, poor punctuation, and inaccurate references to historical facts. He revised the whole thing, clarified the thought, deleted irrelevancies, restated vague generalities in simpler language, and added a chapter of his own, "Wayside Thoughts," which was retained in several subsequent editions. The popularity of the book dated from the revision of Wiggin, who was again called upon to work over another edition in 1890. Asked to read Wright's account of these matters, "How Rev. Wiggin Rewrote Mrs. Eddy's Book," Mark Twain responded in the following letter. The whole story was not made public until 1906, when Wright's article was finally published.

"MARK TWAIN" INDORSES EXPOSURE OF MRS. EDDY
New York *Times*, November 5, 1906

Riverdale, New York City, April 17, 1903

Dear Sir: The MS., with your letter of yesterday, arrived in my bedroom with my breakfast two hours ago, and I have already read the MS. through. I wonder why you have kept it two years without publishing it, for I find it exceedingly interesting and valuable, and with only one weak place in it that I can discover—the same one that is in Mr. Peabody's[1] pamphlet; the presenting (on your Page 27) of that grotesque irruption of Mrs. Eddy's[2] in print form instead of (at least partly) in facsimile reproduction of her hand. With that defect cured your essay would gain great strength. But it is convincingly strong—strong enough, in my belief, to prove to every intelligent non-Scientist that Mrs. Eddy and God did not write "Science and Health." All the world and God added could not convince a Scientist (intelligent or otherwise) that Mrs. Eddy's claim to the authorship is a lie and a swindle.

The first paragraph of your letter requires me to make instant decision or return your MS.; therefore, as I am not able to act so quickly (I am in bed these days with bronchitis and barred from work), I will make the return per to-day's next mail, as in honor bound.

I am puzzled. In the new part of my book I take up a great deal of space with an elaborate argument, reinforced by extracts from Mrs. Eddy's literature, to prove that she couldn't write "Science and Health," and must have stolen it[3]—circumstantial evidence, the whole of it—and now comes your essay and proves the same points by what the world would consider much better evidence. It's like a man trying to prove by labored and finespun logic that there has been a murder, and then, when he gets through, remarking to the stage manager, "Ask Mr. Wright to fetch in that corpse."

A reader might properly say: "Why did you make me read all that stuff, when you might have introduced Mr. Wright and the corpse in the first place and saved my time?"

Either process would do in a book, but doubtless to use one would bar the other from the book. I learn by a letter from a stranger that my book has been withdrawn until Autumn. It is true; I did it myself. I wonder how he knows. I have not said it publicly.

Very truly yours,
S. L. Clemens

1. *Frederick William Peabody (b. 1862) was a member of the New York law firm of Peabody, Baker, and Peabody. He was an outspoken critic of Christian Science. Besides publishing* Eddyism, or Christian Science, *the pamphlet mentioned by Mark Twain, Peabody was co-author, with Professor Woodbridge Riley and Charles E. Humiston, of* The Faith, the Falsity and the Failure of Christian Science *(1926).*

2. *Mary Morse Baker Eddy (1821-1910), preoccupied from childhood with the delicate state of her health, was healed by Phineas Parkhurst Quimby of Portland, Maine, who professed to achieve cures without medication or surgery. She maintained, however, that she discovered Christian Science when she recovered from a bad fall in 1866 by reading the New Testament. The new belief was formalized in the first edition of* Science and Health *(1875), a book that claimed divine revelation and that was published in many subsequent editions. Organizing the First Church of Christ Scientist (1879), she founded a Massachusetts Metaphysical College (1881) for the instruction of Scientist practitioners, dedicated the Mother Church of Boston (1895), and promulgated a church manual that prescribed a rigid organization under her sole control. In a long life marked by a number of lawsuits and increasing veneration, she was married three times: to George Washington Glover, Dr. Daniel Patterson, and Asa Gilbert Eddy. Among the tenets she proclaimed were such doctrines as "Disease is caused by mind alone," and "Mind controls the body, and with its own materials instead of matter; hence no broken bones or dislocations can occur."*

3. *In* Christian Science *(1907), Mark Twain pays tribute to the power of Christian Science in such statements as "No one doubts—certainly not*

I—that the mind exercises a powerful influence over the body." Without questioning the validity of the belief of Scientists, he devotes most of his text to a strong criticism of Mrs. Eddy as a writer and as a person. Examining her miscellaneous prose and verse, he finds her prevailing manner marred by clumsy English, lack of thought, puerility, sentimentality, "insane" metaphors, meaningless words, and wandering statements. "She is easily," he says, "the most baffling and bewildering writer in the literary trade." The more compact and orderly style of Science and Health makes him conclude that she could not have written that book: "Mrs. Eddy is not capable of thinking upon high planes, nor of reasoning clearly nor writing intelligently upon low ones." Explaining her tight control of every aspect of church organization, which he calls "the Trust," he characterizes her as a woman of "devouring ambition," of "limitless selfishness," possessed of "a hunger for power such as has never been seen in the world before."

Of Mark Twain as a literary critic, William Dean Howells said in an essay, "Mark Twain: an Inquiry": "It does not so much matter whether you agree with the critic or not; what you have to own is that here is a man of strong convictions, clear ideas, and ardent sentiments, based mainly upon common sense of extraordinary depth and breadth." The statement also applies to Mark Twain as commentator on politics, religion, society, and the human race generally. The following article on, of all things, seduction and its consequences is an illustration. In the late twentieth century, sociologists, psychologists, sociobiologists, psychiatrists, and other behavioral analysts, professional and amateur, may complain that his treatment of the subject is over-simplified, but none can doubt his strong convictions and ardent sentiments. That he published his views on the topic in the near-Victorian times of 1903 is worthy of remark. In those far-off days, the vagaries of sex had not yet become a commonplace of public discussion.

WHY NOT ABOLISH IT?
Harper's Weekly, MAY 2, 1903

We have many good laws. They embody the wisdom and the common sense of the ages. There is one very striking feature about these laws. Let me point it out. Among them—

1. There is not a law which says that if you consent to the robbery of your family, the robber's crime is reduced to a mere impropriety by that consent.

2.   There is not a law which says that if you consent to the burning of your father's house, the incendiary's crime is reduced to a mere impropriety by that consent.

3.   There is not a law which says that if you consent to let a man starve your mother to death, that man's crime is reduced to a mere impropriety by that consent.

4.   There is not a law which says that if you consent to let an assassin cut your throat, the assassin's crime is reduced to a mere impropriety by that consent.

It is strange, but these statements are true. The law does not grant you the tremendous privilege of propagating, inviting, and encouraging crime by your caprice, and of minimizing the responsibility of its perpetrators by the interposition of your royal consent. The law sticks stubbornly to the position that robbers, incendiaries, and murderers are criminals, no matter who are the victims; and it would not concede that they were criminals in a lesser degree in cases where you or your kin were the victims, and you gave your personal consent.

But there is one crime which is more disastrous than all of these put together; more bitter, more cruel, more infamous, more shameful, more insupportable, more far-reaching, more diffusive in its crushing effects, than all of those combined—and over the perpetrator of this one crime the law holds the protecting shield of its mercy and its compassion.

A murder kills the body, but sets it free and ends its cares; it brings grief to the surviving kindred, but it is a grief which time can soften, and even heal. But this other crime, this crime of crimes, kills the mental and spiritual life of its victim, but leaves its body to drag on and on, the symbol and sufferer of a living death, despised of kindred, forsaken of friends; and upon family and friends descends a blight of humiliation which time cannot remove nor forgetfulness ease of its pain.

The law is stern with the assassin, but gentle with the seducer; stern with the murderer of the body, but gentle with the murderer of all that can make life worth the living—honor, self-respect, the esteem of friends, the adoring worship of the sacred home circle, father, mother, and the cradle-mates of the earlier and innocent years. You may drag down into the mud and into enduring misery and shame the trusting and ignorant young flower of this household, and crush the heart of every creature that loves it and lives in the light of its presence; you may murder the spirit and consign to a living death and intolerable wretchedness all these—and if in certain cases you can prove *consent* the law will not deal unkindly with you.

"Consent" necessarily argues previous persuasion. It indicates who the instigator of the trespass was—that is to say, the offender-in-chief. Instead of magnifying his crime, this actually diminishes it, in the eyes of the law. The law establishes an "age of consent"—a limit during which a child of sixteen or seventeen is not privileged to help commit a tremendous and desolating crime against herself and her family; but she is privileged to do it if she is twenty; and in that case the person that persuades her to it is regarded by the law as being substantially guiltless, and it puts upon him no punishment which can be called by that name except sarcastically.

There is no age at which the good name of a member of a family ceases to be a part of the *property* of that family—an asset, and worth more than all its bonds and moneys. There is no age at which a member of the family may by consent, and under authority of the law, help a criminal to destroy the family's money and bonds. Then why should there be an age at which a member, by consent, and under connivance of the law, may help a criminal to destroy that far more valuable asset, the family's honor?

There being no age at which the law places the lives of a family in the hands of any member of it to throw away at his whim—including his own life—I see no sound reason why the law should not be consistent—consistently wise—and abolish the age limit in the case of the other and greater crime.

If a man and wife are drowned at sea, and there is no proof as to which died first, the law—in some European countries and in two of our States—decides that it was the wife. She is the weaker vessel. It is usually so in the matter of seduction. She is young, inexperienced, foolish, trustful, persuadable, affectionate; she would harm no one herself, and cannot see why any one should wish to harm her; while as a rule the man is older and stronger than she is, and in every case without exception is a scoundrel. The law protects him now; it seems to me that it ought to protect her, instead.

I think it ought to abolish "consent"—entirely. I think it should say there is *no* age at which consent shall in the least degree modify the seducer's crime or mitigate its punishment. "Consent" means previous persuasion—and there the crime *begins*. It is the first step, and responsible for the whole, for without it there would be no second. I would punish the beginner, the real criminal, and punish him well; society and civilization can be depended upon to punish with a ten thousand times exaggerated and unjust severity his thoughtless victim. If I were a law-maker I should want to make this law quite plain.

I should want it to say nothing about "consent"—I should take the persuasion for granted, and that *persuasion* is what I would punish, along with the resulting infamy. I should say simply that commerce *with a spinster,* of whatever age or condition, should be punished by two years of solitary confinement or five years at hard labor; and let the man take his choice. He has murdered the honor and the happiness of a whole unoffending family, and condemned it to life-long shame and grief, and while he ought to be flayed alive,[1] and the law ought of rights to provide that penalty, I know that no jury would vote it; I could not do it myself, unless mine were the family. And so I would make the penalty as above. A jury would vote that, for the judge would be thoughtful enough to appoint upon it none but fathers of families—families with young girls in them, the treasures of their lives, the light of their homes, the joy of their hearts.

I find the following in this morning's *Herald.* Will you print it?

Rosie Quinn, who was convicted of murder in the second degree on April 8, for drowning her baby in the lake in Central Park, will be sentenced by Judge Scott to-day in the Criminal Branch of the Supreme Court. Only one sentence, that of life imprisonment, may be imposed, and, although her counsel, Moses A. Sachs, will ask for a new trial, it is not probable it will be granted.

The girl dreads her appearance in the court-room. She spoke of this yesterday with even more horror than that which the idea of a life sentence aroused in her mind.

She has written to the father of the dead child, but has received no response. "I don't know what he can be thinking of," is her only comment.

Not even his name has been told to the persons who have approached Rosie Quinn in connection with her trial. She is loyal in this.

For her sisters, who have not been near her since her arrest in November, she displays a surprising thoughtfulness.

"Don't put my sisters' names in the paper," she begged. "I don't want their names used. I didn't even want it known that I had sisters, but it got out somehow." Since her conviction, one of her sisters has called at the prison to caution her against telling their names.

The girl is a most pitiable creature. She seems crazed by the happenings of the last few weeks, and is utterly unable to comprehend the enormity of her crime, or the hopelessness of the doom which is hanging over her. She is like a child, docile, quiet, undemonstrative. She will only say:

"It was a dear love affair for me."

Immediately after her sentence persons who have become interested in the girl's sad fate will appeal to Governor Odell in her behalf.

I think many of us will like to sign that petition.

1. *Mark Twain's severe penalty for seduction may be partly accounted for by an over-protective concern for his daughters. They were carefully guarded, chaperoned, harassed about proper public behavior, and sheltered from normal companionship with young men. Indeed, their father seemed like a vigilant watchdog preventing them from getting acquainted with likely suitors and turning a resentful eye upon any youthful male the girls so much as smiled upon. Clara was discouraged from contemplating marriage,*

although she did escape parental supervision on trips to Europe and elsewhere, and she did get married at the age of thirty-five. The relationship of parents and children in the Clemens household is a provocative subject for a clinical analyst. Nevertheless, Mark Twain's vindictiveness against the seducer is apparent before the girls arrived. In The Innocents Abroad, *when telling the story of Abelard and Heloise, chapter 15, he calls Abelard "unmanly," a villain of "degraded instinct" who "seduced the niece of the man whose guest he was." After ruffians, hired by her father, have inflicted upon Abelard "a terrible and nameless mutilation," Mark Twain observes: "I am seeking the last resting-place of those 'ruffians.' When I find it I shall shed some tears on it, and stack up some bouquets and immortelles, and cart away from it some gravel whereby to remember that howsoever blotted by crime their lives may have been, these ruffians did one just deed, at any rate, albeit it was not warranted by the strict letter of the law." The attitude here is similar to the approval of flaying alive. Worth noting, too, is the seduction of Laura Hawkins in* The Gilded Age. *When she is brought to trial for shooting her seducer, the jury acquits her of the charge of murder. To Mark Twain, seduction was evidently always a one-way process.*

Olivia having been an invalid in failing health for more than a year, Mark Twain and his family sought the hoped-for recuperative virtues of foreign parts. They sailed on October 24, 1903, aboard the Prinzessen Irene *for Genoa, their eventual destination being a villa near Florence. On the morning of that day Henry W. Lucy,[1] a British humorist, had landed in New York, where he was handed a note from Mark Twain: "You arrive this morning, and I sail this afternoon, in order to avoid you." To reporters Lucy explained: "Some time ago Mark Twain and I were at a surprise dinner to E. A. Abbey . . . when he proposed to me that we start a paper called* The Obituary. *We were to print the life of every living man of prominence, send him the proof, and ask him for £50 for suppressing the story. I considered the matter and wrote to Twain that it was agreeable to me. Since then he has made every effort, and successfully, to keep out of my way." Mark Twain elaborated to newsmen who had trailed him aboard.*

MARK TWAIN MAKES SOME PARTING REMARKS
New York *Times,* October 25, 1903

That's true, we did talk it over, and I think there never was a better paying institution that could be devised. You see, the idea was to write the most scandalous things about a man while he was alive, and tell him it would be published at the time of his death unless he paid to have it kept out of the papers. If the man paid handsomely, we would allow him to alter the proof and cover up the spots on his career. There are very few men who have not some spots that can be artistically covered. He could cut the proof, add to it, or polish it as much as he wished, but he had to pay for that. He could have as many of the copies of the paper in which the article was printed as he wished, and in the end he could, by paying enough money, get as good a reputation as he wanted, and one of which his family could be proud.

We had no circulation to our paper, for you see the circulation end is the losing end. When I got home I found I could make more money by Twain than by two, so I gently but firmly had to eliminate Lucy from the money proposition. I calculated that he would not land until to-morrow, or else I should not have sent the note until to-day. But he is a good fellow, and I hope he will do well. However, his situation reminds me of what St. Clair McKelway[2] said to me when he learned that the Harpers had promised me a pension for life in consideration of work I had promised to do for them.[3] "Col. Harvey[4] is living on hope," he said, "while you are living on a certainty."

A reporter observed that Mark Twain had his hands full shepherding Olivia, two daughters, their faithful servant Katie Leary, and Margaret Sherry, a nurse, besides seeing to the handling of eighteen pieces of baggage.

Well, I always was sorry for Father Noah; he had so much trouble getting all of his animals aboard the ark. But you see I'm peevish to-day. I have absorbed all of my wife's pugnacity, and all of my daughters' audacity.

A reporter said that the New York Times Saturday Book Review *had grouped Mark Twain with Rabelais and Aristophanes.*

Rabelais, yes. Aristophanes, no. I never knew Aristophanes personally. All of what I know of him was told me by William Dean Howells. I get quite a confused idea of what he was like. Sometimes I think of him sailing up the English Channel with Sir John Hawkins; again, I think of Aristophanes as the Greek physician, and again as an Italian virtuoso. If I had lived in the fifteenth century I should have been Rabelais. I know him from top to bottom.

A reporter asked whether Mark Twain had Dowie[5] in mind when he wrote about the Royal Nonesuch in Huckleberry Finn.

I can't trace the slightest resemblance, for I have never seen Dowie disrobing. I have a presentiment that I am to meet Dowie in the next world, but I do not know where. If I find him in one place I will go to the other. I don't care how hot or how cold it is, but I do not want to be in the same place where he is. I want society in the next world, but not that of Dowie or Mrs. Eddy.

1. *Henry William Lucy (1845–1924), a British journalist, joined the staff of the* Pall Mall Gazette *(1870), then of the* Daily News *as parliamentary reporter (1873). In 1881 he became a writer for* Punch *for which until 1916 he contributed a weekly synopsis, "Essence of Parliament," signed "Toby, M.P.," that made his name well known. He was*

knighted in 1909. Among his books are the autobiographical Sixty Years in the Wilderness (1909) and the three-volume Diary of a Journalist (1920).

2. McKelway (1845–1915) was a reporter for the New York World (1866), then Washington correspondent for the World and the Brooklyn Eagle (1868). He became chief editor of the Eagle in 1884. A fearless, independent man whose acquaintance with public men gave him an insight into domestic affairs, he made the paper influential nationally, his editorials being widely quoted. Having a high regard for the craft of the newsman, he said that journalism "is served as loyally, bravely, unselfishly, intelligently and honestly as Church or State, army or navy, university or sovereign." A gifted speaker, he was a dependable banqueter with whom Mark Twain enjoyed exchanging verbal thrusts.

3. Harper and Brothers, which became Mark Twain's exclusive publisher in October 1903, guaranteed him a minimum return of $25,000 a year for five years.

4. George Brinton McClellan Harvey (1864–1928) was an American political journalist, editor, and diplomat. After reporting experience on the staffs of the Springfield Republican, Chicago News, and New York World (1882–86), he made a fortune with William C. Whitney, bought the North American Review (1899), and became president of Harper and Brothers (1900). Editor of Harper's Weekly until 1913 and of the North American Review until 1928, he founded Harvey's Weekly in 1918 as a short-lived journal of political satire. Well known to politicos of both parties, he was ambassador to Great Britain (1921–23). As an enthusiastic banqueter and skillful toastmaster, Harvey stage-managed the sixty-seventh birthday dinner for Mark Twain and the more elaborate seventieth birthday dinner.

5. John Alexander Dowie (1847–1907) was the founder of the Christian Apostolic Church of Zion. In early life, he became convinced that he had been singled out as a special object of God's care. As a widely traveled evangelist, he was a fanatical forerunner of Billy Sunday, delivering vituperative harangues against sin in rhythmic language that had an effect like hypnosis on susceptible listeners. Claiming divine inspiration, he was also a faith healer whom clergymen and physicians vainly tried to suppress. In 1901 he proclaimed himself the prophet Elijah, and in 1905 he announced that he was the first apostle. He is probably best remembered for founding Zion City, forty-two miles from Chicago, a place where no theaters, dance halls, secret lodges, drug stores, or doctors' offices were allowed. Smoking and drinking were prohibited, and whistles blew frequently for public prayers. Obviously, Mark Twain would shun the society of such a man, whether in this world or the next.

The Clemens residence in the valley of the Arno near Florence was the Villa di Quarto, leased from the American-born Countess Rebaudi-Massiglia. It was a huge pile two hundred feet long with more than sixty rooms, none of them comfortable. From the start, owner and tenant were at odds. The countess imposed finicky restrictions, shut off the water supply, stopped telephone service, and allowed a vicious donkey to roam at large. Mark Twain brought suit against her for breach of contract and failure to maintain cesspools properly. The raw, rainy winter was no help to Olivia, who did not improve, nor to his own sporadic attacks of rheumatism and bronchitis. He dismissed two doctors attending his wife, then complained bitterly of the outrageous charges of the Austrian physician who replaced them. There was a lawsuit about that, too. Attended by such diversions, the stay in Italy conformed to the normal Twainian pattern of unrest, which was apparent in a crowded social program for everybody except the invalid—going to teas and dinners, receiving a parade of visitors on Thursday "at homes," Clara taking voice lessons and giving concerts. Mark Twain, resorting to creative work as he generally did under emotional pressure, wrote thousands of words for Harpers, besides experimental and unfinished fragments, and renewed his interest in autobiographical dictation. When a New York Times man sought him out early in 1904, he seemed cheerful enough, his outward demeanor giving no hint of inner distress over the precarious condition of Olivia.

MARK TWAIN TO REFORM THE LANGUAGE OF ITALY[1]
New York *Times,* April 10, 1904

Reporter: And how do you like Italy again after your long absence from here?

Oh, Italy is right enough. The best country in the world to live in. Perhaps England runs it rather close, but here all is quiet, town and country alike. In England there is always London with its great unquiet pulse.

Reporter: And the Italians?

Right enough, too. I love to watch them, and to study their gestures and their ways. That is why I do not object to the slow pace of our horses, like my daughter there, even if they do take a time to land us in town.

Reporter: And the language?

I never get hold of an entire sentence. Just a word here and there that comes in handy, but they never stay with me more than a day.

There is one person who always understands me, and that is our old kitchen scrub. She was with us last time, too.[2] We have quite long talks together and exchange no end of compliments. I talk English; she rattles along in her own lingo; neither of us knows what the other says; we get along perfectly and greatly respect each other's conversation.

When the talk turned to books, the reporter said that he had never been able to read a novel by Sir Walter Scott.

Just so. I was once ill and shut up and there was nothing but Scott's novels to read, so I had another try. Well, when I got through *Guy Mannering* I wrote to Brander Matthews and asked him if he would be good enough to point out to me the literary and stylistic merits of the work, for I could not find them.

Fact is, nothing is eternal in this world, and literature is as much subject to the character of the times as any other intellectual manifestation. Books reflect the mental atmosphere in which they were born, and on that account cannot expect to live forever. Every generation has its own authors. Look at Dickens. At one time nothing went down that was not a little tinted with the Dickens style; now who would allow that? And the same for all the others. Is there a more tiresome and unnatural book than *Pendennis*? All the people are exaggerated, caricatures, with no intention of being so. It's like when they show us some weird old picture and say it's wonderful. I dare say it is wonderful, for its time; but its time is past.

1. *The title of the interview refers to a speech of Mark Twain, "Italian Without Grammar," given for the benefit of the Florentine British Relief Fund. According to the* Times *of foregoing date, he said he intended to write a rational Italian grammar and sell it to the government. "They had for verbs too many ways of expressing themselves; even the regular verbs were irregular. Take the simple verb 'I love.' There were fifty-seven ways of*

conjugating this verb, and not one is able to convince a girl who wanted to marry a title. . . . That unnatural way of saying 'e' stato,' (has been), which is literally 'is been,' wouldn't do, anyhow. As for himself, he got on very well. When conversing with a stranger he was always taken for an Italian, but not so when he speaks with friends, for the friends were jealous." So he continued in a lengthy summary that tells how he puzzled the natives with Italian locutions that did not mean what he thought they meant.

2. *Italy was a stop on the European hegira that began in 1891, when the Hartford house was given up as a gesture of economy. In September 1892, Mark Twain, Olivia, Susy, and Jean had settled in the Villa Viviani at Florence. At the time, Mark Twain's publishing company was about to go into receivership and the Paige typesetter was close to failure. While the family remained in Italy, Mark Twain nervously commuted back and forth across the Atlantic in frantic attempts to stave off financial disaster. The crash came nevertheless, and they all returned home in the spring of 1895 to prepare for the round-the-world speaking tour to pay off the creditors.*

Mark Twain was generally fascinated by mechanical contrivances, especially when they seemed to promise substantial returns to an investor—the Paige typesetter, envelope-making machine, carpet-making machine, to name a few—but in the last decade of his life he did not rhapsodize over technological inventions. His nineteenth-century faith in machinery as the symbol of progress and civilization had disappeared in disillusion, and perhaps his speculative mania was, at long last, subdued. He should have been interested in pictures taken of him by Alvin Langdon Coburn, a famous photographer who used a camera equipped with Lumiere Autochrome plates, the first successful device for taking photographs in color, but there is no recorded Twainian comment about the remarkable new process. (One of Coburn's shots of Mark Twain wearing the gray and scarlet gown of Oxford appears in the National Geographic *of September, 1975.) Nor did he manifest enthusiasm for the motor car, which was beginning to pollute the air and to terrify pedestrians as well as horses. Still, he was aware of these newfangled monsters that were becoming a menace to unwary citizens. His letter deals with the kind of driver who is still with us, faster now and far more deadly.*

OVERSPEEDING

Harper's Weekly, NOVEMBER 5, 1905

Dublin, N. H., October 18, 1905

To the Editor of *Harper's Weekly*

Sir: Equal laws for all. It is good in theory, and I believe it would prove good in practice, if fairly and dispassionately tried. The law dresses a convict in a garb which makes him easily distinguishable from any moving thing in the world at a hundred and twenty-five yards, except a zebra. If he escapes in those clothes, he cannot get far. Could not this principle be extended to include his brother criminal the Overspeeder, thus making the pair fairly and righteously equal before the law? Every day, throughout America, the Overspeeder runs over somebody and "escapes." That is the way it reads. At present the 'mobile numbers are so small that ordinary eyes cannot read them, upon a swiftly receding machine, at a distance of a hundred feet[1]—a distance which the machine has covered before the spectator can adjust his focus. I think I would amend the law. I would enlarge the figures, and make them readable at a hundred yards. For overspeeding—first offence—I would enlarge the figures again, and make them readable at three hundred yards—this in place of a fine, and as a warning to pedestrians to climb a tree. This enlargement to continue two months, with privilege of resuming the smaller figures after the first thirty days upon payment of $500. For each subsequent offence, reenlargement for six months, with privilege of resuming the smaller figures upon payment of $1000 at the end of three. With auto numbers readable as far as one could tell a convict from a barber-pole none of these criminals could run over a person and "escape."

Two months ago a touring 'mobile came within an indeterminable fraction of killing a member of my family; and its number was out of sight range before the sharpest eyes present could make it out, it was so small and the spectators so dazed by momentary fright. I have had two narrow escapes in New York, and so has everybody else. None of us has succeeded in capturing the auto number. I feel a sort of personal interest in this suggested reform.

I am, sir,
M. T.

1. *License numbers are still hardly large enough to be clearly visible to people with poor eyesight, especially when the car is traveling sixty to seventy miles per hour. Mark Twain might be pleased to know, however, that the penalty for hit-and-run is stiffer than the one he recommends—if, that is, the driver is apprehended. Unfortunately, a good many continue to "escape."*

As Mark Twain's seventieth birthday approached, he was the center of much attention in the press and elsewhere. A New York Times man recorded a long interview carried on in the stately old-fashioned house Mark Twain had leased at 21 Fifth Avenue. The reporter described him: "Straight and spare as a New England pine, his great mane of thick white hair falling shaggily back from his brow, his thin, mobile upper lip covered

with a heavy drooping mustache that is yet only shading toward grayness, his eyes always clear, now reflective and now flashing with the fire of the thoughts that leap like lightning behind them, though the words fall . . . in that deliberate drawl which tens of thousands will never be able to forget . . . his face unlined and his cheeks touched with a ruddy glow, and only about the corners of his eyes the little tell-tale crow's feet that seventy years have scratched there—nobody who saw him thus could ever possibly think of Mark Twain as old. No, there is nothing of the 'last leaf' effect about Samuel L. Clemens."

A HUMORIST'S CONFESSION
NEW YORK *Times,* NOVEMBER 26, 1905

No, Sir, not a day's work in all my life. What I have done I have done, because it has been play. If it had been work I shouldn't have done it.

Who was it who said, "Blessed is the man who has found his work"? Whoever it was he had the right idea in his mind. Mark you, he says his work—not somebody else's work. The work that is really a man's own work is play and not work at all. Cursed is the man who has found some other man's work and cannot lose it. When we talk about the great workers of the world we really mean the great players of the world. The fellows who groan and sweat under the weary load of toil that they bear never can hope to do anything great. How can they when their souls are in a ferment of revolt against the employment of their hands and brains? The product of slavery, intellectual or physical, can never be great.

I'm glad you came to see me today, as I'm up and about, which I shouldn't have been if I had been doing anything of consequence. You're surprised at that, are you?

Well, I've found that whenever I've got some work to do—

Reporter: You mean play, of course.

Of course, of course; but we're all slaves to the use of conventional terms and I'll stick to them to avoid confusing you. Whenever I've got some work to do I go to bed. I got into that habit some time ago when I had an attack of bronchitis. Suppose your bronchitis lasts six weeks. The first two you can't do much but attend to the barking and so on, but the last four I found I could work if I stayed in bed, and when you can work you don't mind staying in bed.

I liked it so well that I kept it up after I got well. There are a lot of advantages about it. If you're sitting at a desk you get excited about what you are doing, and the first thing you know the steam heat or the furnace has raised the temperature until you've almost got a fever, or the fire in the grate goes out and you get a chill, or if somebody comes in to attend to the fire he interrupts you and gets you off the trail of that idea you are pursuing.

So I go to bed. I can keep an equable temperature there without trying and go on about my work without being bothered. Work in bed is a pretty good gospel—at least for a man who's come, like me, to the time of life when his blood is easily frosted.

Reporter: A good many people would think that the immense amount of labor you went through to pay the debts of . . . C. L. Webster & Co. . . . was entitled to be called by the name of hard work.

Not at all. All I had to do was write a certain number of books and deliver a few hundred lectures. As for traveling about the country from one place to another for years—the nuisances of getting about and bad hotels and so on—those things are merely the incidents that every one expects to meet in life. The people who had to publish my books, the agents who had to arrange my lecture tours, the lawyers who had to draw up the contracts and other legal documents—they were the men who did the real work. My part was merely play. If it had been work I shouldn't have done it. I was never intended for work—never could do it—can't do it now—don't see any use in it.

The reporter asked about the secret of Mark Twain's firm hold upon the public mind.

Well, I know it is a difficult thing for a man who has acquired a reputation as a funny man to have a serious

thought and put it into words and be listened to respectfully, but I thoroughly believe that any man who's got
anything worth while to say will be heard if he only says it
often enough. Of course, what I have to say may not be
worth saying. I can't tell about that, but if I honestly believe
I have an idea worth the attention of thinking people it's my
business to say it with all the sincerity I can muster. They'll
listen to it if it really is worth while and I say it often
enough. If it isn't worth while it doesn't matter whether
I'm heard or not.

Suppose a man makes a name as a humorist—he may
make it at a stroke, as Bret Harte[1] did, when he wrote those
verses about the "Heathen Chinee."[2] That may not be the
expression of the real genius of the man at all. He may have
a genuine message for the world. Then let him say it and say
it again and then repeat it and let him soak it in sincerity.
People will warn him at first that he's getting a bit out of his
line, but they'll listen to him at last, if he's really got a
message—just as they finally listened to Bret Harte.

Dickens had his troubles when he tried to stop jesting.
The "Sketches by Boz" introduced him as a funny man, but
when Boz began to take him seriously people began to
shake their heads and say: "That fellow Boz isn't as funny as
he was, is he?" But Boz and his creator kept right on being
in earnest, and they listened after a time, just as they always
will listen to anybody worth hearing.

I tell you, life is a serious thing, and, try as a man may, he
can't make a joke of it. People forget that no man is all
humor, just as they fail to remember that every man is a
humorist. We hear that marvelous voice of Sembrich[3]—a
wonderful thing—a thing never to be forgotten—but nobody makes the mistake of thinking of Sembrich as merely a
great, unmixed body of song. We know that she can think
and feel and suffer like the rest of us. Why should we forget
that the humorist has his solemn moments? Why should we
expect nothing but humor of the humorist?

My advice to the humorist who has been a slave to his
reputation is never to be discouraged. I know it is painful to
make an earnest statement of a heartfelt conviction and

then observe the puzzled expression of the fatuous soul who is conscientiously searching his brain to see how he can possibly have failed to get the point of the joke. But say it again and maybe he'll understand you. No man need be a humorist all his life. As the patent medicine man says, there is hope for you.

The quality of humor is the commonest thing in the world. I mean the perceptive quality of humor. In this sense every man in the world is a humorist. The creative quality of humor—the ability to throw a humorous cast over a set of circumstances that before had seemed colorless is, of course, a different thing. But every man in the world is a perceptive humorist. Everybody lives in a glass house. Why should anybody shy bricks at a poor humorist or advise him to stick to his trade when he tries to say a sensible thing?

Reporter: Even the English?

The English don't deserve their reputation. They are as humorous a nation as any in the world. Only humor, to be comprehensible to anybody, must be built upon a foundation with which he is familiar. If he can't see the foundation the superstructure is to him merely a freak—like the Flat-iron building without any visible means of support—something that ought to be arrested.

You couldn't, for example, understand an English joke, yet they have their jokes—plenty of them. There's a passage in Parkman that tells of the home life of the Indian—describes him sitting at home in his wigwam with his squaw and papooses—not the stoical, toy Indian with whom we are familiar, who wouldn't make a jest for his life or notice one that anybody else made, but the real Indian that few white men ever saw—simply rocking with mirth at some tribal witticism that probably wouldn't have commended itself in the least to Parkman.[4]

So you see, the quality of humor is not a personal or a national monopoly. It's as free as salvation, and, I am afraid, far more widely distributed. But it has its value, I think. The hard and sordid things of life are too hard and too sordid and too cruel for us to know and touch them year after year without some mitigating influence, some kindly veil to draw over them, from time to time, to blur the craggy outlines, and make the thorns less sharp and the cruelties less malignant.

The talk got around to Mark Twain's summer homes, native and foreign, and his recent sojourn in Dublin, New Hampshire.

Yes, I have tried a number of summer homes, here and in Europe together. Each of these homes had charms of its own; charms and delights of its own, and some of them—even in Europe—had comforts. Several of them had conveniences, too. They all had a "view."

It is my conviction that there should always be some water in a view—a lake or a river, but not the ocean, if you are down on its level. I think that when you are down on its level it seldom inflames you with an ecstasy which you could not get out of a sand flat. It is like being on board ship over again; indeed it is worse than that, for there's three months of it. On board ship one tires of the aspects in a couple of days and quits looking. The same vast circle of heaving humps is spread around you all the time, with you in the center of it and never gaining an inch on the horizon, as far as you can see one; for variety, a flight of flying fish, a flock of porpoises throwing summersaults afternoons, a remote whale spouting Sundays, occasional phosphorescent effects nights, every other day a streak of black smoke trailing along under the horizon; on the single red-letter day, the illustrious iceberg. I have seen that iceberg thirty-four times in thirty-seven voyages; it is always that same shape, it is always the same size, it always throws up the same old flash when the sun strikes it; you may set it on any New York doorstep of a June morning and light it up with a mirror flash and I will engage to recognize it. It is artificial, and is provided and anchored out by the steamer companies. I used to like the sea, but I was young then, and could easily get excited over any kind of monotony, and keep it up till the monotonies ran out.

Last January, when we were beginning to inquire about a home for this summer, I remembered that Abbott Thayer[5] had said, three years before, that the New Hampshire highlands was a good place. He was right—it is a good place. Any place that is good for an artist in paint is good for an artist in morals and ink. Brush[6] is here, too; so is Col. T. W. Higginson;[7] so is Raphael Pumpelly;[8] so is Mr. Secretary Hitchcock;[9] so is Henderson;[10] so is Learned; so is Sumner;[11] so is Franklin MacVeagh;[12] so is Joseph L. Smith; so is Henry Copley Greene, when I am not occupying his house, which I am doing this season. Paint, literature, science, statesmanship, history, professorship, law, morals- —these are all represented here, yet crime is substantially unknown.

The summer homes of these refugees are sprinkled, a mile apart, among the forest-clad hills, with access to each other by firm and smooth country roads which are so embowered in dense foliage that it is always twilight in there and comfortable. The forests are spider-webbed with these good roads, they go everywhere; but for the help of the guideboards the stranger would not arrive anywhere.

The village—Dublin—is bunched together in its own place, but a good telephone service makes its markets handy to all those outliars. If you spell it right it's witty. The village executes orders on the Boston plan—promptness and courtesy.

The summer homes are high perched, as a rule, and have contenting outlooks. The house we occupy has one. Monadnock, a soaring double hump, rises into the sky at its left elbow—that is to say, it is close at hand. From the base of the long slant of the mountain, the valley spreads away to the circling frame of hills, and beyond the frame the billowy sweep of remote great ranges rise to view and flow, fold upon fold, wave upon wave, soft and blue and unworldly, to the horizon fifty miles away. In these October days Monadnock and the valley and its framing hills make an inspiring picture to look at, for they are sumptuously splashed and mottled and betorched from sky line to sky line with the richest dyes the autumn can furnish; and when they lie flaming in the full drench of the mid-afternoon sun, the sight affects the spectator physically, it stirs his blood like military music.

These summer houses are commodious, well built, and

well furnished—facts which sufficiently indicate that the owners built them to live in themselves. They have furnaces and wood fireplaces, and the rest of the comforts and conveniences of a city home, and can be comfortably occupied all the year round.

We cannot have this house next season, but I have secured Mrs. Upton's house, which is over in the law and science quarter, two or three miles from here, and about the same distance from the art, literary, and scholastic groups. The science and law quarter has needed improving this good while.

The nearest railway station is distant something like an hour's drive; it is three hours from there to Boston, over a branch line. You can go to New York in six hours per branch line if you change every time you think of it, but it is better to go to Boston and stop over and take the trunk line next day; then you do not get lost.

It is claimed that the atmosphere of the New Hampshire highlands is exceptionally bracing and stimulating, and a fine aid to hard and continuous work. It is a just claim, I think. I came in May, and wrought thirty-five successive days without a break. It is possible that I could not have done it elsewhere. I do not know; I have not had any disposition to try it before. I think I got the disposition out of the atmosphere this time. I feel quite sure, in fact, that that is where it came from.

I am ashamed to confess what an intolerable pile of manuscript I ground out in the thirty-five days; therefore I will keep the number of words to myself. I wrote the first half of a long tale—"The Adventures of a Microbe"—and put it away for a finish next summer, and started another long tale—"The Mysterious Stranger"; I wrote the first half of it and put it with the other for a finish next summer. I stopped then. I was not tired, but I had no books on hand that needed finishing this year except one that was seven years old. After a little I took that one up and finished it. Not for publication, but to have it ready for revision next summer.

Since I stopped work I have had a two months' holiday.

Above: *A caricature in* McNaught's Monthly *circa 1908 captured (left) Andrew Carnegie's reaction to Mark Twain's wit.* Below: *Mark Twain about 1908–09. (From an unknown source.)*

The summer has been my working time for thirty-five years, to have a holiday in it (in America) is new to me. I have not broken it, except to write "Eve's Diary" and "A Horse's Tale"—short things occupying the mill twelve days.

This year our summer was six months long and ended with November and the flight home to New York, but next year we hope and expect to stretch it another month and end it the first of December.

1. *Francis Brett (he dropped one t) Harte (1836–1902) was a leader in the literary circles of San Francisco in the early 1860s. As such, he was a mentor to Mark Twain, schooling the wild humorist of the Pacific slope not only in writing, but also, by example at least, in dress, Harte's elegant turnouts contrasting sharply with the other's bohemian carelessness. The pair struck up a friendship that endured for about fifteen years, during which Mark Twain's literary reputation rose as Harte's declined. Not long after they had collaborated on* Ah Sin *(1877), an unsuccessful play, Mark Twain, suspecting his collaborator of shady dealing with the American Publishing Company, began denouncing Harte as a fraud and a cheat, also as a shoddy writer, insincere and sentimental. Off and on thereafter he took potshots at Harte, concentrating his fire in a climactic barrage of autobiographical dictations (February 1–4, 1907) devoted to the shortcomings, as man and writer, of his erstwhile friend.*

2. *It appeared as "Plain Language From Truthful James" (1870) in the* Overland Monthly, *which Harte, as first editor, made the leading literary journal on the Pacific coast. The story goes that publication of the poem was an accident, Harte fishing the discarded manuscript out of a wastebasket to fill unused space. He had already gained attention with "The Luck of Roaring Camp," "The Outcasts of Poker Flat" and other western tales, but the doggerel "Chinee" so enhanced his reputation that he accepted the* Atlantic Monthly's *sensational offer of $10,000 for a year's work or twelve contributions. Returning to the East, he was a disappointment, none of his later work living up to the promise of his writing in California. In 1878 he departed for Europe and a consulship in Germany, leaving wife and children behind. Transferred to Glasgow, he spent his last years in England, never returning to the United States and continually finding reasons why his family should not join him abroad.*

3. *Marcella Sembrich (1858–1935) was an Austrian-born operatic soprano who had studied in Vienna and Milan and who made her debut in Athens in Bellini's* Puritani *(1877). She sang in Paris, Dresden, and*

London, also in Spain, Russia, and the United States. In 1895 she was engaged by the Metropolitan Opera of New York, where she remained until she retired in 1917, then lived in New York thereafter. Her voice, with a range from middle C to the third octave above, has been described as "a combination of beautiful tone with musical intelligence."

4. *Francis Parkman (1823-93) was a historian who allied thorough research with literary skill. He followed the Oregon Trail in 1846, lived with the Sioux Indians, and gathered material for his first book,* The California and Oregon Trail *(1849). Then came* The Conspiracy of Pontiac *(1851). Partial blindness and violent head pains slowed him down but did not stop him from exploring regions that played a part in his narratives. Aware of the beauty of nature as well as the variables of human nature, he used the technique of the novelist to make history come alive in* The Jesuits in North America *(1867),* La Salle and the Discovery of the Great West *(1869),* Montcalm and Wolfe *(1884), and others.*

5. *Abbott Henderson Thayer (1849-1921) was an American landscape painter who exaggerated light and shadow to gain monumentality, as in "Winter Sunrise, Monadnock," now in the Metropolitan Museum of New York. Interested in the coloration of animals, he formulated Thayer's Law: "animals are painted by nature darkest on those parts which tend to be most lighted by the sky's light, and vice versa." This principle, it has been said, was applied to camouflage devices in World War I. In 1901 he settled in New Hampshire, where he lived like a hermit, yet he was apparently not too hermit-like to be well acquainted with Mark Twain. Thayer's idealization of women should have encouraged rapport. Another aid was his wife, the former Emma Beach, who had been a passenger on the* Quaker City *excursion in 1867.*

6. *George de Forest Brush (1855-1941) was an American painter, chiefly of landscapes with figures. He had studied at the National Academy of Design and the Ecole des Beaux Arts of Paris. Representative canvases are hung in the Metropolitan Museum of New York, the Boston Museum, Chicago Art Institute, and elsewhere.*

7. *Thomas Wentworth Storrow Higginson (1823-1911) was a reformer, soldier, and author. A graduate of the Harvard Divinity School (1847), he had been a Unitarian clergyman who was removed from his pulpit because of extreme views on temperance, slavery, and women's rights. An ardent abolitionist, he aided escaping slaves, supported John Brown in Kansas and at Harper's Ferry, and advocated breaking up the Union. When war came, however, he raised and drilled troops in Massachusetts and became colonel of the First South Carolina Volunteers composed of former slaves, the first black regiment in the Union Army. After the war he ran for Congress on the Free Soil ticket and wrote voluminously for the* Atlantic, Harper's,

North American Review, *and others. Among his books are* Army Life in a Black Regiment *(1869), the autobiographical* Cheerful Yesterdays *(1898),* Part of a Man's life *(1905), and biographies of Margaret Fuller, Longfellow, and Whittier.*

8. *Pumpelly (1837–1923), a geologist and mining engineer, was an explorer who had traveled widely: in Japan as geologist for the Japanese government, in China studying coal deposits on the Yangtze-kiang River, then through Siberia to Saint Petersburg, Russia. Appointed (1875) to investigate mineral resources of the United States for the tenth census, he was later (1884–89) in charge of the New England Division of the United States Geological Survey and in 1903–1904 went on expeditions to Central America to look for traces of prehistoric civilizations. Described as "a great blue-eyed giant, with long, flowing beard," he was a man of taste and culture, a humane gentleman who should have got on famously with Mark Twain.*

9. *Ethan Allen Hitchcock (1835–1909) amassed a fortune in an international commission business. After retiring (1869), he engaged in various enterprises in Saint Louis, then became minister to Russia (1897). As secretary of the interior (1898–1907), he investigated land office frauds, finding evidence of bribery, collusion, espionage, and undue political influence, which he made public despite the strong opposition of opponents who wished to stifle inquiry. An austere man impervious to pressure, Hitchcock removed corrupt officials and secured over a thousand indictments with 126 convictions—a record more impressive than the box score of Watergate. He had met Mark Twain when they were both candidates for honorary degrees at the University of Missouri commencement in 1902.*

10. *Ernest Flagg Henderson (1861–1928) a student of European history, had published* History of Germany in the Middle Ages *(1894) and* History of Germany *(1902). Later came* Symbol and Satire in the French Revolution *(1912) and* Germany's War Machine *(1914). Henderson was much younger than most of the eminent men of the Dublin community, yet he evidently felt at home intellectually and socially.*

11. *William Graham Sumner (1840–1910) was an educator, economist, publicist, and social scientist, who had studied at Yale, Geneva, Oxford, and Göttingen. As professor of political and social science at Yale (1872–1909), he taught the doctrine of individual liberty and of innate inequalities among men, propounding a social Darwinism, or survival of the economically fit. Endorsing the middle-class ethic of hard work, thrift, and sobriety, Sumner opposed paternalism in government. In his view, the "forgotten man" was not the deprived citizen of late twentieth century interpretation, but the self-supporting taxpayer who shouldered the burden of political bungling and social quackery. A man of prodigious industry, he*

wrote essays with such provocative titles as "The Absurd Attempt to Make the World Over" and "Protectionism, the Ism Which Teaches That Waste Makes Wealth." In a different vein, Folkways (1906) deals with the origin of customs in response to the stimuli of hunger, sex, vanity, and fear. As a teacher with a roving mind, Sumner was no doubt a lively conversational match for Mark Twain.

12. Isaac Wayne MacVeagh (1833–1917) was a lawyer, diplomat, and political reformer. As district attorney of Chester County, Pennsylvania (1859–64), he was a leader of state Republicans opposed to boss Simon Cameron and soon rose to party prominence nationally. MacVeagh was minister to Turkey (1870–71), head of the commission (1877) that ended reconstruction in Louisiana, briefly attorney general (1881) under Garfield, and ambassador to Italy (1893–97). Advocating government reform and condemning machine politics, he was confidential advisor to presidents and useful consultant in troublesome situations. One of his major achievements was arbitration of the long and costly strike of anthracite coal miners in 1902. Mark Twain, who admired MacVeagh as a man and as a responsible public official, knew him well enough to make joshing remarks about him in dinner speeches.

If Mark Twain did not accept all modern contrivances, he at least gave them a trial run now and then. He quickly adopted the telephone, then cursed the faulty service and frequent breakdowns. He bought a typewriter but found it less satisfactory than longhand, although typists transcribed his dictations. He tried dictating into a gramaphone, but after filling a number of cylinders with talk—and where are they now?—he gave that up, too. In late middle age, he learned to ride one of those difficult old high-wheeled bicycles. But the automobile seems not to have excited him, as numerous inventive marvels had in the past. He rode in Henry Rogers's big touring car, but there are no comments about the experience nor any hint that he thought of having a car of his own. We might think that he should have been attracted by an impressive Pierce Arrow or Locomobile or Packard, bright red with black fenders and huge brass headlights. Apparently not. When he settled at Stormfield, Connecticut, in 1908, he still used the carriage that had transported him and his bride to their home on Delaware Avenue, Buffalo, in 1870.

ADIEU, "CHAUFFEUR"!
Harper's Weekly, JANUARY 13, 1906

New York, December 24, 1905

To the Editor of *Harper's Weekly.*

Sir: Scarcely had Watchman Fowler taken his post at the gate when a procession of strange creatures appeared.

"Halt! Who goes there?" ejaculated the watchman when a fat negro approached, laboriously leading a thin, bow-legged goat.

"Dis heah beast is Ole Ironsides, suh," explained the goat's mahout.—From "Dan'l the Bulldog," in the *Times.*

When I read it I recognized, with a thrill, that the right word has been found at last—mahout. The 'mobile, that majestic devil, that impressive devil, is our elephant, he is in a class by himself, like the jungle monarch; to be his master, pilot, and compeller is a post of solemn and awful dignity and danger, and it does seem to me that that measly word "chauffeur" does not properly fit the occupant of it. Chauffeur is a good enough word when strictly confined to its modest and rightful place—as you will see by what Littre says about it.[1] I translate: "A chauffeur is the firer-up on the street-corner peanut-roaster; in English, *stoker*." A good enough word, you see, in its own place; but when we come to apply it to the admiral of the thunderous 'mobile or of the mighty elephant, we realize that it is inadequate. No, stoker is not the thing, chauffeur is not the thing, mahout is the thing—mahout is the word we need. Besides, there is only one way of saying mahout, whereas there are nine ways of saying chauffeur, and none of them right. With ever-increasing respect, dear sir, as the ages roll on, I am yours,

Mark Twain

1. *Maximilien Paul Emile Littre (1801–81) was a French lexicographer. More recent dictionaries designate* chauffeur *as a driver, and American editions acknowledge the usual native pronunciation as "shó-fer."*

In 1903, Brander Matthews, professor of dramatic literature at Columbia, and Melvil Dewey, inventor of the Dewey Decimal System of library classification, interested Andrew Carnegie[1] in a crusade to reform English spelling. Believing that simplified English could foster world peace as an international language, Carnegie agreed to contribute $25,000 a year to aid the work of a National Simplified Spelling Board. It was a twenty-eight-man body composed of Matthews as chairman and eminent men from all over the country: William James, David Starr Jordan, Nicholas Murray Butler, Richard Watson Gilder, Mark Twain, and others. From an office on Madison Avenue, the board issued letters and pamphlets urging news-papers and authors to adopt the revised spelling. Proposed changes dropped the final e in words like have *and* love, *the* u *in such words as* honour *and* labour, *and substituted* f *for* ph *in* phantom, sulphur, *and so forth. The crusade had the enthusiastic support of President Roosevelt and the qualified approval of such well-known writers as Howells and Cable, but the most noticeable response in America and Britain was protest and derision. In the New York* Times *a wag suggested that the "Bored of Spelling" revise the names of its members to "Androo Karnage," "Brandr Mathooz" and so on. By 1915 the reform movement had sputtered out as one of Carnegie's few failures. As he withdrew his yearly subsidy, he announced: "I think I have been patient long enuf."*

THE CARNEGIE SPELLING REFORM
Harper's Weekly, APRIL 7, 1906

In a thoughtful examination of certain objections to Mr. Carnegie's proposed spelling reform, Professor Francis Hovey Stoddard, of New York University, makes the following remarks in the *Times*:

The first of these objections is a formidable one. . . . It is the objection that the changes necessary would . . . destroy all associations of words. So far as literature is concerned English has become through the universality of printing mainly an eye language. Changes in spelling would make our classics as antique to the eye as Anglo-Saxon and as unintelligible to the ear of the uneducated person as Chaucer. It is conceivable that in the process of time much of the literature could be rewritten in a modern form, etc.

I suspect that this regret at the destruction of association is the most formidable objection. It certainly appeals to me most, and does not readily suggest its own answer.

The second main objection is based upon the futility of all preceding efforts.

The fifth objection is that if any reform is made there will be a long, long time of transition through which weary people must pass before any good results come.

Like all the objectors, Professor Stoddard contemplates a *slow and gradual* change. With that position as a basis, the argument is unanswerable. It is my belief that an effort at a slow and gradual change is not worth while. I think the language might die of old age before the change achieved completeness. It is the *sudden* changes—in principles, morals, religions, fashions, and tastes—that have the best chance of winning in our day. Can we expect a sudden change in our spelling? I think not. But I wish I could see it tried.

"Literature," says Professor Stoddard, "is mainly an eye language." It is also true that many a thing which revolts the eye at a first glance, loses its unpleasantness after the eye has become accustomed to it. Consider the hoopskirt. When it intruded itself upon us fifty years ago it was odious to us, it was ugly, it was grotesque, it was unendurable. It revolted us, it maddened us, it provoked our scornful laughter, just as would, to-day a newspaper page printed in cramped and crabby phonetics. But we got used to the hoopskirt in a marvelously little while, and came to think it beautiful. We quickly turned against the slim gown which we had so admired before, and could not abide it.

The first time we saw a woman on a bicycle, the vulgar spectacle shocked us. But we got over it; and by and by, when we had gotten used to it it no longer offended us, and we bought cycles for our wives and daughters.

In Europe, the first time we see a parlor full of ladies smoking cigarettes we are revolted, we are self-righteously incensed, we are ashamed of the human race. Six months later we find no offence in it—in fact, we like it.

I suppose we can all remember the first time we saw

bare-armed, bare-legged young ladies paddling in the surf, and how confounded and affronted we were by that gross exhibition of indecency. But we can stand it now, can't we? Certainly—and like it, too.

All these things suggest—and insist—that there is a law back of them. What is the law? I think it is this: Commonly, it is merely the strangeness of a new thing that rouses our aversion, not its form or character; use abolishes the strangeness, and the aversion along with it.

A year and a quarter ago Mr. Foley[2] began to do school-boy poems in a fire-new and blood-curdling and criminal fashion of spelling which no self-respecting eye could endure at first. It was phonetics carried to the uttermost limit of exactness in the reproduction of sound-effects. The public felt deeply outraged, and there was a smell of insurrection in the air—a quite justifiable condition of things, too, for the poems looked like the alphabet hiccuping home in disorderly squads, a most painful and irritating spectacle—but I ask you, what has become of that insurrection? No man knows. It disappeared and left no sign. For the public had done the fatal thing: it kept on reading the poems in order to curse the spelling and of course the natural thing happened: familiarity with the spelling modified the reader's hostility to it, then reconciled him to it, and at last made him fall in love with it; and now—well, now Mr. Foley's schoolboy is a pet.

Suppose all the newspapers and periodicals should suddenly adopt a Carnegian system of phonetic spelling—what would happen? To begin with, the nation would be in a rage; it would break into a storm of scoffs, jeers, sarcasms, cursings, vituperation, and keep it up for months—but it would have to read the papers; it couldn't help itself. By and by, and gradually, the offensive phonetics would lose something of their strange and uncanny look; after another by and by they would lose all of it, and begin to look rather natural and pleasant; after a couple of years of this, the nation would think them handsome, sane, and expressive, and would prefer them to any other breed of spelling. For, unto the eye that can make a haystack-hoopskirt beautiful, any other conceivable horror is an easy job.

To what literature would we limit the change? Naturally—and unavoidably—to literature written *after* the change was established. It would not occur to any one to disturb the "associations." No book already existing would be put into the new spelling. We do not guess at this; we have history for it. We do not profane Chaucer's spelling by recasting it to conform to modern forms. One of its quaintest and sweetest charms would be gone, it would not be Chaucer's any more. We would not disturb the Bible's spelling, but leave it as it is—no one would ever think of Carnegieizing it. All the old books would naturally and necessarily remain as they are. Do we change Marjorie Fleming's[3] spelling? No. No one could meditate a vandalism like that. Marjorie, like Chaucer, would not be Marjorie without her enchanting depredations upon the spelling-book. For half a century we have possessed the journals of that immortal child of six years,[4] and to this day no one has been impious enough to change a syllable contrived by that dear little hand. Her spelling is the very bloom and fragrance of her expressed thought:

An annababtist[5] is a thing I am not a member of:—I am a Pisplikan [Episcopalian] just now & a Prisbeteren at Kercaldy my native town. . . . The Divel always grins at the sight of the bibles; bibles did I say? nay at the word virtue. . . . Love I think is in the fasion for every body is marring [marrying] there is a new novel published named selfcontroul[6] a very good maxam forsooth Yesterday a marrade [man] named Mr John Balfour Esg offered to kiss me, & offered to marry me though the man was espused [espoused], & his wife was present, & said he must ask her permission but he did not I think he was ashamed or confounded before 3 gentleman Mr. Jobson and two Mr. Kings. . . . I am now going to tell you about the horible and wretched plaege my multiplication gives me you cant concieve it—the most Devilish thing is 8 times 8 & 7 times 7 it is what nature itselfe cant endure

No, Marjorie's spelling will remain unprofaned while the language shall last. Its "associations" are safe: and so are the associations which bind us to the other old books which we love.

By a sudden and comprehensive rush the present spelling

could be entirely changed and the substitute spelling be accepted, all in the space of a couple of years; and preferred in another couple. But it won't happen, and I am as sorry as a dog.

For I do love revolutions and violence.[7]

1. *Carnegie (1835-1919) was a Scotch-American industrialist who believed that a man of great wealth was obligated to distribute his fortune for the benefit of humanity. His objectives were world peace and education. After consolidating various enterprises as the United States Steel Corporation, he retired (1901) to distribute his millions. Having founded the Carnegie Institute of Technology (1900), he established a pension fund for former Homestead employees (1901), gave money (1903) for a Temple of Peace at the Hague and a Pan-American building in Washington for the International Bureau of American Republics, endowed the Carnegie Foundation for the Advancement of Teaching (1905), and founded the Carnegie Corporation for the Advancement of Civilization (1911). He also set up trust funds to aid education in Scottish universities and contributed liberally to Booker T. Washington's Tuskegee Institute. He is probably best remembered by hundreds of Carnegie libraries in small towns of the United States and Great Britain. Although fond of associating with monarchs and members of the nobility, he refused to accept a title himself. Mark Twain was both amused and irritated by Carnegie's continual name-dropping, his reiterated stories of meeting and dining with people of position, yet he liked the man, sometimes mockingly referred to him as "Saint Andrew," and mildly joshed him in dinner speeches.*

2. *Probably this was James William Foley (b. 1874), a vernacular poet whose verses appeared in newspapers and periodicals. An example is "Stubbed His Toe": "It does a heap o' good sometimes, to go a little slow, / To say a word o' comfort to th' man that's stubbed his toe."*

3. *Marjorie (properly Marjory) Fleming (1803–1811) was a precocious and high-spirited child born in Kircaldy, Scotland, who began writing, in a clear round hand, journals, poems, and letters at the age of six. Her observations are an engaging blend of the factual and romantic, of narrative mixed with philosophical reflections affected by Scotch Presbyterianism that makes her conscious of the Devil and continually repenting sins of disobedience and petulance committed in a temper. Her life and writing have stimulated a good deal of research and comment. In 1858, H. B. Farnie, a London journalist, published a sixpenny booklet,* Pet Marjorie: a Story of Child Life Fifty Years Ago. *In 1863 Dr. John Brown, an Edinburgh physician with whom Mark Twain became well acquainted, brought out*

Marjorie Fleming: a Sketch, *a long essay that appeared in several editions. In 1904, Lachlan Macbean published* The Story of Pet Marjorie, *which included nearly all of her writing and which ran through four British editions and one American. In 1930, Arundell Esdaile issued a volume of Marjory's manuscripts printed in facsimile. In 1934, Frank Sidgwick edited* The Complete Marjory Fleming: her Journals, Letters & Verses. *In 1946, Oriel Malet published* Marjory Fleming, *a romanticized biography. Stevenson and Swinburne paid tribute, and she has a place as the youngest subject in the* Dictionary of National Biography, *the entry written by Leslie Stephen, who incorrectly identifies her as Margaret.*

4. *Mark Twain, who heard about Marjory from Dr. John Brown in 1873, was fascinated by her thereafter. Perhaps he felt akin because of her mettle, her quick temper, and her consciousness of sin and the Devil, all of which were characteristic of himself. Possibly he sensed parallels between Marjory and his eldest daughter, Susy, who, like Marjory, was precocious, had a fond father, was a poor speller, and died of meningitis at an early age.*

5. *Marjory was casual not only about spelling, but also about punctuation. But she did enter this note in one of her journals: "Isa [Isabella Keith, her cousin and mentor, eleven years older] is teaching me to make Simecolings nots of interrgations peorids & commoes &c"*

6. Self-control, *a novel by Mary Balfour Brunton, wife of an Edinburgh clergyman, was published in 1811. The first edition sold out within a month.*

7. *The statement accurately implies Mark Twain's pleasure at being in the middle of whatever excitement was going on. Hence his attachment to the controversial movement for spelling reform, although he was not a wholehearted crusader perhaps because, as he said, he knew that no startling changes would occur. His speech in favor of simplified spelling at a dinner of the Associated Press in September 1906 was distributed as a propaganda pamphlet by the Simplified Spelling Board. In a later speech, however, at a dinner for Carnegie in December 1907, Mark Twain was critical of the reform movement, concluding with the skeptical remark "Your simplified spelling is well enough, but like chastity—it can be carried too far."*

Mark Twain, scheduled to speak in Carnegie Hall on April 19, 1906, for the benefit of the Robert Fulton Memorial Association, announced that it would be his last appearance on the platform. Whereupon General Frederick D. Grant wrote to urge him to reconsider his decision to retire. Mark Twain replied.

MARK TWAIN TELLS
HOW TO MANAGE AUDIENCES
New York *Times*, April 15, 1906

I mean the pay platform;[1] I shan't retire from the gratis platform until after I am buried and courtesy requires me to keep still, and not disturb the others. What shall I talk about? My idea is this: To instruct the audience about Robert Fulton, and tell me—was that his real name, or was it his nom de plume?

However, never mind, it is not important; I can skip it, and the house will think I knew all about it and forgot. Could you find out for me if he was one of the signers of the Declaration, and which one? But if it is any trouble, let it alone, and I can skip it. Was he out with Paul Jones? Will you ask Horace Porter?[2] And ask him if he brought both of them home.

These will be very interesting facts, if they can be established. But never mind, don't trouble Porter, I can establish them, anyway. The way I look at it, they are historical gems—gems of the very first water.

Well, that is my idea, as I have said: first excite the audience with a spoonful of information about Fulton, and then quiet them down with a barrel of illustrations drawn by memory from my books—and if you don't say anything the audience will think they never heard it before, because people don't really read your books; they only say they do to keep you from feeling bad.

Next, excite the audience with another spoonful of Fultonian fact; then tranquilize them with another barrel of illustration. An so on all through the evening, and if you are discreet and don't tell that the illustrations don't illustrate anything they won't notice it. I will send them home as well informed about Robert Fulton as I am myself. Don't be afraid. I know all about audiences.[3] They believe everything you say—except when you are telling the truth.

P.S. Mark all the advertisements "Private and Confidential"; otherwise the people won't read them.

1. *Tendered $1,000 for the Fulton speech, Mark Twain donated the fee to the memorial association. According to the* Times *of above date, he said "he loved to hear himself talk, because he got so much instruction and moral upheaval out of it. But the bulk of such joy was lost to him when he got paid for talking."*

2. *Porter (1837–1921) a soldier, railroad executive, and diplomat, was a graduate of West Point (1860) who served in the Army of the Potomac and Army of the Cumberland, won the Congressional Medal of Honor for gallantry at Chickamauga, then became an aide to General Grant (1864) and brevet brigadier general (1865). He published the story of his war experiences in an informative book,* Campaigning With Grant *(1897). Porter acted as military aide during President Grant's first term but resigned (1872) to be vice president of the Pullman Company and to promote elevated railroads. As ambassador to France (1897–1905), he dealt tactfully with friction caused by the Spanish-American War. While abroad he discovered the remains of John Paul Jones, which he brought back to the United States for burial at the Naval Academy in Annapolis. A delegate to the Hague peace conference (1907), he was nevertheless a strong champion of preparedness and later opponent of the League of Nations. As a good speaker and an entertaining raconteur, he was in demand for banquets, where he sometimes exchanged barbed pleasantries with Mark Twain.*

3. *The* Times *reported that Mark Twain, asked how long he intended to talk, replied, "It is my custom to keep on talking until I get the audience cowed. Sometimes it takes an hour and fifteen minutes. Sometimes I can do it in an hour."*

Soon after the death of Carl Schurz[1] on May 14, 1906, Mark Twain wrote a eulogy. It was his tribute to a German-American patriot who had been a public servant of unmistakable convictions and integrity. As a person, he was a man of commanding presence and great charm, a willing and tireless talker possessed of a good sense of humor. The two had known each other since the bitter presidential campaign of 1884, when both had defected from the Republican party to join the Mugwumps supporting the Democratic

candidate, Grover Cleveland, Mark Twain having introduced Schurz at a
Mugwump rally in Hartford shortly before election day.

CARL SCHURZ, PILOT
Harper's Weekly, MAY 26, 1906

We all realize that the release of Carl Schurz is a heavy
loss to the country; some of us realize that it is a heavy loss
to us individually and personally. As a rule I have had a
sufficiency of confidence—perhaps over-confidence—in my
ability to hunt out the right and sure political channel for
myself, and follow it to the deep water beyond the reef
without getting aground; but there have been times, in the
past thirty years, when I lacked that confidence—then I
dropped into Carl Schurz's wake, saying to myself, "he is as
safe as Ben Thornburgh." When I was a young pilot on the
Mississippi nearly half a century ago, the fellowship numbered among its masters three incomparables: Horace
Bixby, Beck Jolly, and Ben Thornburgh.[2] Where they were
not afraid to venture with a steamboat, the rest of the guild
were not afraid to follow. Yet there was a difference: of the
three, they preferred to follow Thornburgh; for sometimes
the other two depended on native genius and almost inspira-
tional water-reading to pick out the lowest place on the
reef, but that was not Ben Thornburgh's way: if there were
serious doubts he would stop the steamer and man the
sounding-barge and go down and sound the several crossings[3] and lay buoys upon them. Nobody needed to search for
the best water after Ben Thornburgh. If he could not find it,
no one could. I felt that way about him; and so, more than
once I waited for him to find the way, then dropped into his
steamer's wake and ran over the wrecks of his buoys on half
steam until the leadsman's welcome cry of "mark twain"
informed me that I was over the bar all right, and could
draw a full breath again.

I had this same confidence in Carl Schurz as a political
channel-finder. I had the highest opinion of his inborn
qualifications for the office: his blemishless honor, his unas-
sailable patriotism, his high intelligence, his penetration; I

also had the highest opinion of his acquired qualifications as a channel-finder. I believed he could read the political surfaces as accurately as Bixby could read the faint and fleeting signs upon the Mississippi's face—the pretty dimple that hid a deadly rock, the ostentatious wind-reef that had nothing under it; the sleek and inviting dead stretch that promised quarter-less-twain and couldn't furnish six feet.[4] And—more than all—he was my Ben Thornburgh, in this: whenever he struck out a new course over a confused Helena Reach or a perplexed Plum Point Bend I was confident that he had not contented himself with reading the water, but had hoisted out his sounding-barge and buoyed the maze from one end to the other. Then I dropped into his wake and followed. Followed with perfect confidence. Followed, and never regretted it.

I have held him in the sincerest affection, esteem, and admiration for more than a generation. I have not always sailed with him politically, but whenever I have doubted my own competency to choose the right course, I have struck my two-taps-and-one ("get out the port and starboard leads"), and followed him through without doubt or hesitancy. By and by I shall wish to talk of Carl Schurz the man and friend, but not now; at this time I desire only to offer this brief word of homage and reverence to him, as from grateful pupil in citizenship to the master who is no more.

1. *Schurz (1829–1906), a journalist and reformer born in Germany, came to the United States in 1852, opposed slavery, and campaigned for Lincoln. Appointed minister to Spain (1861), he resigned to be brigadier general of volunteers, serving as division and corps commander during the Civil War. Striving for high standards of honesty in government, he fought against political fraud and thievery in postwar years of reconstruction. Editor of the* Detroit Post *(1866) and editor and part owner of the Saint Louis* Westliche Post, *he was United States senator from Missouri (1869–75), then secretary of the interior (1877–81), aiding civil service reform and improving Indian policy. In the 1880s he was editor of the New York* Evening Post *and in the nineties an editorial writer for Harper's* Weekly, *his journalism marked by vigor and boldness. His uncompromising stands on important issues made enemies and reduced his influence*

among professional politicians, yet he earned their respect as a devoted patriot untainted by corruption. As a social being, he was a man of winning manner, a lively conversationalist, and a competent amateur pianist.

2. Bixby, as Sam Clemens's teacher on the river, has a prominent place in *Life on the Mississippi*. *Jolly and Thornburgh are mentioned briefly a few times, but Mark Twain does not elaborate upon their piloting methods.*

3. *An upstream pilot hugged the shore where the current was less strong. When the slack water ended, he crossed to the other side. In Sam Clemens's steamboating days, pilots identified the crossings by natural objects on shore, but when he visited the river in 1882, he found the crossings marked by lights.*

4. *"Mark twain" is 2 fathoms or 12 feet. Quarter-less-twain is 10½ feet, safe water for a steamboat, which had a draft of about 7 feet.*

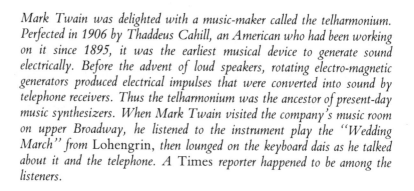

Mark Twain was delighted with a music-maker called the telharmonium. Perfected in 1906 by Thaddeus Cahill, an American who had been working on it since 1895, it was the earliest musical device to generate sound electrically. Before the advent of loud speakers, rotating electro-magnetic generators produced electrical impulses that were converted into sound by telephone receivers. Thus the telharmonium was the ancestor of present-day music synthesizers. When Mark Twain visited the company's music room on upper Broadway, he listened to the instrument play the "Wedding March" from Lohengrin, then lounged on the keyboard dais as he talked about it and the telephone. A Times reporter happened to be among the listeners.

TWAIN AND THE TELEPHONE
New York *Times,* December 23, 1906

The trouble with these beautiful, novel things is that they interfere so with one's arrangements. Every time I see or hear a new wonder like this I have to postpone my death right off.[1] I couldn't possibly leave the world until I have heard this again and again.

You see, I read about this in the New York *Times* last Sunday, and I wanted to hear it. If a great Princess marries, what is to hinder all the lamps along the streets on her wedding night playing that march together? Or, if a great man should die—I, for example—they could all be tuned up for a dirge.

Of course, I know that it is intended to deliver music all over the town through the telephone, but that hardly appeals as much as it might to a man who for years, because of his addiction to strong language, has tried to conceal his telephone number, just like a chauffeur running away after an accident.

When I lived up in Hartford, I was the very first man, in that part of New England at least, to put in a telephone, but it was constantly getting me into trouble because of the things I said carelessly. And the family were all so thoughtless. One day when I was in the garden, fifty feet from the house, somebody on the long distance wire who was publishing a story of mine, wanted to get the title.

Well, the title was the first sentence, "Tell him to go to hell." Before my daughter got it through the wire and through him there was a perfect eruption of profanity in that region. All New England seemed to be listening in, and each time my daugher repeated it she did so with rising emphasis. It was awful. I broke into a cold perspiration, and while the neighborhood rang with it, rushed in and implored her to desist. But she would have the last word, and it was "hell," sure enough, every time.

Soon after I moved to New York; perhaps that had something to do with my moving. When I got there and asked for a fire-proof telephone, the company sent up a man to me. I opened up all my troubles to him, but he laughed and said it was all right in New York. There was a clause in their contract, he said, allowing every subscriber to talk in his native tongue, and of course they would not make an exception against me. That clause has been a godsend to me.

1. *He was so much pleased with the device that he had it plugged into his telephone at 21 Fifth Avenue and entertained guests with telharmonium music at a New Year's Eve party.*

In 1907, Mrs. Jessamy Steele, daughter of Bret Harte and estranged wife of Frederick Dorr Steele, well-known illustrator, was living in an almshouse in Portland, Maine, without funds and mentally unbalanced. Eleanor Robson,[1] the actress, undertook to raise money for her by giving a benefit performance and enlisting the aid of Harte's publishers. She also sought the cooperation of Mark Twain. He responded with a kindly letter—the text given here probably being only an excerpt—in which praise of Harte sharply contrasted with previous harsh criticism of the man and his work. Probably out of compassion for the unfortunate daughter, Mark Twain suppressed his true opinion of the father.[2] Thus his remarks admirably illustrate the conclusion of his essay, "On the Decay of the Art of Lying" (1882): that one should lie "with a good object, and not an evil one . . . for others' advantage, and not our own . . . healingly, charitably, humanely, not cruelly, hurtfully, maliciously . . . gracefully and graciously, not awkwardly and clumsily . . . firmly, frankly, squarely, with head erect, not haltingly, tortuously, with pusillanimous mien."

AID FOR HARTE'S DAUGHTER
NEW YORK *Times*, JANUARY 30, 1907

I feel that the American people owe a debt of gratitude to Bret Harte, for not only did he paint such pictures of California as delighted the heart, but there was such an infinite tenderness, such sympathy, such strength, and such merit in his work that he commanded the attention of the world to our country, and his daughter is surely deserving of our sympathy.

1. *The actress was appearing at the Liberty Theatre in* Salomy Jane, *a play based upon a story by Harte. She gave a benefit matinee on February 14 and probably invited Mark Twain, but he did not attend because already booked up for afternoon and evening.*
2. *Evidently lying graciously for the advantage of others imposed a severe strain, for on February 1, 1907, Mark Twain began several days of autobiographical dictations devoted to the sins of Bret Harte as a perfidious human being and meretricious writer. These fulminations, by no means charitable, gracious, or humane, represented his private opinions, freely expressed because he intended that they should not be published until after everybody concerned was long since dead.*

In May 1907, Mark Twain was one of a party that sailed down to Norfolk, Virginia, on Henry Rogers's yacht, Kanawha, for the opening of the Jamestown Exposition. After a few days Rogers and others returned to New York by train, leaving behind Mark Twain and yacht. Fretting at being left alone, he said, "I declare that I feel like 'The Man Without a Country.' I pine for Fifth Avenue and the dear old coaches, to say nothing of the arch in Washington Square." Then the Kanawha with Mark Twain aboard was reported to have left Hampton Roads in heavy fog but had not been spoken off the capes. For a day or two friends in Virginia and elsewhere were disturbed by the rumor that he and the yacht had been lost at sea. In Norfolk clubs, as the Times put it, "servants were kept busy rushing messages to the telegraph offices, while the most expert of the julepers of the Southland worked their arms off cracking ice and plucking the tender leaves of the fragrant herb in the preparation of a certain famous concoction guaranteed to dispel sorrow and lighten hearts that are heavy." Mark Twain turned up safely in New York. Informed of the rumors about the disappearance of the Kanawha and himself, he issued a statement.

TWAIN AND YACHT DISAPPEAR AT SEA. MARK TWAIN INVESTIGATING
NEW YORK *Times*, MAY 4-5, 1907

You can assure my Virginia friends that I will make an exhaustive investigation of this report that I have been lost at sea. If there is any foundation for the report, I will at once apprise the anxious public. I sincerely hope that there is no foundation for the report, and I also hope that judgment will be suspended until I ascertain the true state of affairs.

To Milt Goodkind, a New York friend, he sent the following telegram.

Latitude 43 degrees 5 hours and 41 seconds west by southeast of Central Park West. Kanawha heading toward nowhere; terrific cyclone raging; all the houses down in our vicinity; vessel leaking badly; passed a school of whales and several elephants at dawn. Fire Department badly crippled; extension ladder out of commission; water very low; two of our crew lost overboard last evening. Please send airship and some bock beer at once, crew starving.

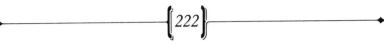
Deny report that I am dodging Mrs. Eddy or Actors'
Fund Fair.[1] Ship sinking; send financial relief at once.

Mark Twain

1. *Held in New York in May 1907, the fair was a ten-day combination
of entertainment and bazaars sponsored by theater people, social leaders, and
the press for the benefit of the Actors' Fund of America. Broadway
performers donated their talents, staging vaudeville acts and sideshows, and
clubs manned booths selling carnival commodities amd running low-powered
games of chance. Mark Twain, scheduled to assist at the Century Club
booth, unwittingly provoked a minor tempest. Mrs. Sidney Rosenfeld,
president of the club and a good Christian Scientist, announced that she
would not have him because of his hostility to Mrs. Eddy. Whereupon,
among ladies of the club, there were indignation meetings, a flurry of
correspondence, and rising tempers until Daniel Frohman, president of the
Actors' Fund, eased the tension by transferring Mark Twain to the Players'
Club booth.*

*In June 1907, when Mark Twain sailed for England to receive the honorary
degree of Doctor of Literature from Oxford, he announced that he did not
intend to doctor any literature. Over there he was immediately involved in a
swirl of social affairs, dinners, receptions, luncheons, and speeches that filled
his four-weeks' visit with a crowded schedule of engagements. Continually
trailed by reporters, he avoided the extended interview, but he always
exchanged a few words with newsmen when they managed to catch up with
him. The* New York Times *published remarks made to its London
correspondent and in the same issue collected some of his observations to
representatives of the London* Press, Chronicle, Express, *and other
papers.*

MARK TWAIN LIVING UP TO HIS DEGREE. MARK TWAIN'S EXPERIENCES IN THE HANDS OF BRITISH INTERVIEWERS

NEW YORK *Times,* JUNE 30, 1907

I was much impressed by my reception here. However, I
have refused to be interviewed up to this point, and don't
feel any more like it now than before. Naturally, I am much
impressed. "Naturally" is a good word. Take it down.

The ceremony was all most venerable and beautiful, and I was greatly moved by it. I have met hundreds of people here and have been touched, deeply touched, by their various welcomes. They have all greeted me with great heartiness. From the Sheldonian Theatre, where the degrees were conferred, to All Souls, where luncheon was served, the way was lined with spectators. Of all things, I was most moved to see how the walk was walled in with people of both sexes and all classes.

The actual number of my books circulating here may very well be greater than in America. The reason is the difference in price. A book costs a shilling or two here and a dollar or two in America.

Palmists, clairvoyants, seers and other kinds of fortune tellers all tell me that I am going to die, and I have the utmost admiration for their prediction. Perhaps they would convince me a little more of its truth if they told me the date. But I don't care so much about that. It was enough to know, on their authority, I was going to die. I at once went and got insured.

I think this funeral is going to be a great thing. I shall be there. I'm stopping for the Oxford pageant,[1] and I guess I shall pick up a few hints from it. I only wish I could make it last six days.

Shall I have a band. Land! I shall have fifty bands, falling over one another at every fifty yards, and each playing a different tune. It'll be a showy funeral, with plenty of liquor for the guests. I shall issue invitation cards something like this: "The late Mr. Mark Twain requests the pleasure of — ——'s company. Mourning dress." I haven't decided on the route yet, but it will be somewhere in a parallel latitude. Why, there was a lady on board asked me to come to her wedding. "Yes, I replied, "I will if you'll come to my funeral." I told her all about it, and now she's quite eager for it to happen.

No, I'm afraid I can't say anything more about Mrs. Eddy. I said it all five years ago. She was constituted like some people. When I say a thing I've no further use for it.

I get as much rest as I can. I'm doing very little writing now—nothing beyond my biography. When shall I have that written? When the undertaker calls. But most of my book is done through dictation.

I give it an hour and a half each day from 10 o'clock in the morning till 11:30. The arrangement has this advantage: One need not be out of bed to dictate. However, I'm always up for lunch, but it is not long before I am again resting.

For a man of my age rest is essential. I believe in giving way to the body as soon as it feels tired, just as I always obey my eyes when they suggest sleep. For dinner in the evening I always dress, but 11 o'clock generally sees me in bed, where I read and smoke till perhaps 1 o'clock in the morning.

In 1876, you know, they had a series [*of pageants*] at the hundredth anniversary of the Declaration of Independence, and then, just as it happened here, any town or place that had some events in its history that connected it with the American Revolution, they all followed one after the other. That was in our hundredth year; but you are in your thousands. It is good, you know, to revive history and impress the people. It does not take us long, for there is not much of it, but you have got to concentrate in six days the history of a thousand years.

1. *It was a historical panorama, town and gown thronging streets in the costumes of hundreds of years of history. Mark Twain was saluted by Henry II and Queen Elizabeth and shook hands with Henry VIII. Charles I, bowing gracefully, swept off his plumed hat with a flourish. Mark Twain said he hoped that the pageant would give him ideas about enlivening his own funeral procession.* See Albert Bigelow Paine, Mark Twain: A Biography (*New York: Harper, 1912*) 4:1395–96.

On his last day in England, Mark Twain was besieged by visitors calling to bid him farewell. For the press he expressed his pleasure in the warmth of his British reception and his regret over his departure.

TWAIN POSTPONES FUNERAL
NEW YORK *Times*, JULY 13, 1907

I have led a violently gay and energetic life here for four weeks, but I have felt no fatigue, and I have had but little desire to quiet down. I am younger now by seven years than I was, and if I could stay here another month I could make it fourteen.

This is the most enjoyable holiday I have ever had, and I am sorry the end of it has come. I have met a hundred old friends and made a hundred new ones. It's a good kind of riches—there's none better, I think.

For two years past I have been planning my funeral, but I have changed my mind and have postponed it.

I suppose I won't see England again, but I don't like to think of that.

Mark Twain enjoyed children, their guilelessness, and their frank manner of writing and talking. He knew a number of little girls, known as Angel Fish, who made up what he called his Aquarium. He corresponded with them, and some visited him at Stormfield, his new home in Connecticut. To this group we may surely add Marjory Fleming,[1] a child long dead yet as real to him as if she were alive, and the most remarkable of all his juvenile collection. In the last year of his life, he expressed his regard for Marjory in a sketch that is informative, gentle, and affectionate.

MARJORIE FLEMING, THE WONDER CHILD
Harper's Bazaar, DECEMBER, 1909

Marjorie has been in her tiny grave a hundred years; and still the tears fall for her, and will fall. What an intensely human little creature she was! How vividly she lived her small life; how impulsive she was; how sudden; how tempestuous, how tender, how loving, how sweet, how loyal, how rebellious, how repentant, how wise, how unwise, how bursting with fun, how frank, how free, how honest, how innocently bad, how natively good, how charged with quaint philosophies, how winning, how precious, how adorable—and how perennially and indestructibly interesting! And all this exhibited, proved, and recorded before she reached the end of her ninth year and "fell on sleep."

Geographically considered, the lassie was a Scot; but in fact she had no frontiers, she was the world's child, she was the human race in little. It is one of the prides of my life that the first time I ever heard her name it came from the lips of Dr. John Brown[2]—his very own self—Dr. John Brown of Edinburgh—Dr. John Brown of *Rab and His Friends*—Dr. John Brown of the beautiful face and the sweet spirit, whose friends loved him with a love that was worship—Dr. John Brown, who was Marjorie's biographer, and who had clasped an aged hand that had caressed Marjorie's fifty years before, thus linking me with that precocious child by an unbroken chain of handshakes, for I had shaken hands with Dr. John. This was in Edinburgh thirty-six years ago. He gave my wife his little biography of Marjorie, and I have it yet.

Is Marjorie known in America? No—at least to only a few. When Mr. L. MacBean's new and enlarged and charming biography of her was published five years ago it was sent over here in sheets, the market not being large enough to justify recomposing and reprinting it on our side of the water. I find that there are even cultivated Scotchmen among us who have never heard of Marjorie Fleming.

She was born in Kircaldy in 1803, and she died when she was eight years and eleven months old. By the time she was five years old she was become a devourer of various kinds of literature—both heavy and light—and was also become a quaint and free-spoken and charming little thinker and philosopher whose views were a delightful jumble of first-hand cloth of gold and second-hand rags.

When she was six she opened up that rich mine, her

journals, and continued to work it by spells during the remainder of her brief life. She was a pet of Walter Scott,[3] from the cradle, and when he could have her society for a few hours he was content, and required no other. Her little head was full of noble passages from Shakespeare and other favorites of hers, and the fact that she could deliver them with moving effect is proof that her elocution was a born gift with her, and not a mechanical reproduction of somebody else's art, for a child's parrot-work does not move. When she was a little creature of seven years, Sir Walter Scott "would read ballads to her in his own glorious way, the two getting wild with excitement over them; and he would take her on his knee and make her repeat Constance's speeches in *King John* till he swayed to and fro, sobbing his fill." [Dr. John Brown.]

"*Sobbing his fill*"—that great man—over that little thing's inspired interpretations. It is a striking picture; there is no mate to it. Sir Walter said of her: "She's the most extraordinary creature I ever met with, and her repeating of Shakespeare overpowers me as nothing else does."

She spent the whole of her little life in a Presbyterian heaven; yet she was not affected by it; she could not have been happier if she had been in the other heaven.

She was made out of thunder-storms and sunshine,[4] and not even her little perfunctory pieties and shop-made holinesses could squelch her spirits or put out her fires for long. Under pressure of a pestering sense of duty she heaves a shovelful of trade godliness into her journals every little while, but it does not offend, for none of it is her own; it is all borrowed, it is a convention, a custom of her environment, it is the most innocent of hypocrisies, and this tainted butter of hers soon gets to be as delicious to the reader as are the stunning and worldly sincerities she splatters around it every time her pen takes a fresh breath. The adorable child! she hasn't a discoverable blemish in her make-up anywhere.

Marjorie's first letter was written before she was six years old; it was to her cousin, Isa Keith, a young lady of whom she was passionately fond. It was done in a sprawling hand, ten words to the page—and in those foolscap days a page was a spacious thing:

> My dear Isa I now sit down on my botom to answer all your kind and beloved letters which you was so good as to write to me. This is the first time I ever wrote a letter in my Life. . . . Miss Potune a Lady of my acquaintance praises me dreadfully. I repeated something out of Deen Sweft and she said I was fit for the Stage and you may think I was primmed up with majestick Pride but upon my word I felt myselfe turn a little birsay⁵ birsay is a word which is a word that William composed which is as you may suppose a little enraged. This horid fat Simpliton says that my Aunt is beautifull which is intirely impossible for that is not her nature.

Frank? Yes, Marjorie was that. And during the brief moment that she enchanted this dull earth with her presence she was the bewitchingest speller and punctuator in all Christendom.

The average child of six "prints" its correspondence in rickety and reeling Roman capitals, or dictates to mama, who puts the little chap's message on paper. The sentences are labored, repetitious, and slow; there are but three or four of them; they deal in information solely, they contain no ideas, they venture no judgments, no opinions; they inform papa that the cat has had kittens again; that Mary has a new doll that can wink; that Tommy has lost his top; and will papa come soon and bring the writer something nice? But with Marjorie it is different.

She needs no amanuensis, she puts her message on paper herself; and not in weak and tottering Roman capitals, but in a thundering hand that can be heard a mile and be read across the square without glasses. And she doesn't have to study, and puzzle, and search her head for something to say; no, she has only to connect the pen with the paper and turn on the current; the words spring forth at once, and go chasing after each other like leaves dancing down a stream. For she has a faculty, has Marjorie! Indeed yes; when she sits down on her botom to do a letter, there isn't going to be any lack of materials, nor of fluency, and neither is her letter going to be wanting in pepper, or vinegar, or vitriol, or any of the other condiments employed by genius to save a literary work of art from flatness and vapidity. And as for judgments and opinions, they are as commodiously in her line as they are in the Lord Chief Justice's. They have weight, too, and are convincing: for instance, for thirty-six years they have damaged that horid Simpliton in my eyes; and, more than that, they have even imposed upon me—and most unfairly and unwarrantably—aversion to the horrid fat Simpliton's name; a perfectly innocent name, and yet, because of the prejudice against it with which this child has poisoned my mind for a generation I cannot see "Potune" on paper and keep my gorge from rising.

In her journals Marjorie changes her subject whenever she wants to—and that is pretty often. When the deep moralities pay her a passing visit she registers them. Meantime if a cherished love passage drifts across her memory she shoves it into the midst of the moralities—it is nothing to her that it may not feel at home there:

> We should not be happy at the death of our fellow creatures, for they love life like us love your neighbour & he will [love] you Bountifullness and Mercifulness are always rewarded. . . . In my travels I met with a handsome lad named Charles Balfour Esge, and from him I got ofers of marage. offers of marage did I say? nay plainly [he] loved me. Goodness does not belong [to the wicked] but badness dishonour befals wickedness but not virtue, no disgrace befals virtue, perciverence overcomes almost all difficulties no I am rong in saying almost I should say always, as it is so perciverence is a virtue my Cosin says pacience is a cristain virtue, which is true.

She is not copying these profundities out of a book, she is getting them out of her memory; her spelling shows that the book is not before her. The easy and effortless flow of her talk is a marvellous thing in a baby of her age. Her interests are as wide and varied as a grown person's: she discusses all sorts of books, and fearlessly delivers judgment upon them; she examines whomsoever crosses the field of her vision, and again delivers a verdict; she dips into religion and history, and even into politics; she takes a shy at the news of the day, and comments upon it; and now and then she drops into poetry—into rhyme, at any rate.

Marjorie would not intentionally mislead any one, but she has just been making a remark which moves me to hoist a danger-signal for the protection of the modern reader. It is this one: *"In my travels."* Naturally we are apt to clothe a word with its present-day meaning—the meaning we are used to, the meaning we are familiar with; and so—well, you get the idea: some words that are giants, to-day were very small dwarfs a century ago, and if we are not careful to take that vast enlargement into account when we run across them in the literatures of the past, they are apt to convey to us a distinctly wrong impression. To-day, when a person says *"in my travels"* he means that he has been around the globe nineteen or twenty times, and we so understand him; and so, when Marjorie says it, it startles us for a moment, for it gives us the impression that *she* has been around it fourteen or fifteen times; whereas, such is not at all the case. She had traveled prodigiously for *her* day, but not for ours. She had "traveled," altogether, three miles by land and eight by water—per ferry-boat. She is fairly and justly proud of it, for it is the exact equivalent, in grandeur and impressiveness, in the case of a child of our day, to two trips across the Atlantic and a thousand miles by rail.

> In the love novels all the heroins are very desperate Isabella will not alow me to speak about lovers & heroins & tiss too refined for my taste a lodestone is a curious thing indeed it is true Heroick love doth [never] win disgrace [this] is my maxium & I will follow it for ever Miss Egwards [Edgeworth's]⁶ tails are very good, particulay some that are very much adopted for youth as Lazy Lawrance & Tarelton False Key &c &c. Persons of the parlement house are as I think caled Advocakes Mr Cay & Mr Crakey has that honour, This has been a very mild winter, Mr. Banestors Budjet⁷ is tonight & I hope it will be a good one. A great many authors have expressed themselfes too sentimentaly. . . . The Mercandile Afares are in a perilious situation, sickness & a delicate frame I have not & I do not know what it is but Ah me perhaps I shall have it, Grandure reagns in London & in Edinburgh. . . .

Tomson[8] is a beautifull author & Pope but nothing is like Shakepear of which I have a little knolege of An unfortunate death James the 5 had for he died of greif. Macbeth is a pretty composition but an awful one Macbeth is so bad and wicked, but Lady Macbeth is so hardened in guilt she does not mind her sins & faults. . . . A sailor called here to say farewell, it must be dreadfull to leave his native country where he might get a wife or perhaps me, for I love him very much & with all my heart, but O I forgot Isabella forbid me to speak about love. . . . I wish every body would follow her example & be as good as pious & virtious as she is & they would get husbands soon enough, love is a very papithatick [pathetic] thing as well as troublesom & tiresome but O Isabella forbid me to speak about it.

But the little rascal can't *keep* from speaking about it, because it is her supreme interest in life; her heart is not capacious enough to hold all the product that is engendered by the ever-recurring inflaming spectacle of man-creatures going by, and the surplus is obliged to spill over; Isa's prohibitions are no sufficient dam for such a discharge.

Love I think is in the fasion for every body is marring [marrying]. . . . Yesterday a marrade [man] named Mr John Balfour Esge offered to kiss me, & offered to marry me though the man was espused [espoused], & his wife was present, & said he must ask her permision but he did not I think he was ashamed or confounded before 3 gentelman Mr Jobson & two Mr Kings.

I must make room here for another of Marjorie's second-hand high-morality outbreaks. They give me a sinful delight which I ought to grieve at, I suppose, but I can't seem to manage it.

James Macary[9] is to be transported for murder in the flower of his youth O passion is a terible thing for it leads people from sin to sin at last it gets so far as to come to greater crimes than we thought we could comit and it must be dreadfull to leave his native country and his friends and to be so disgraced and affronted.

That is Marjorie talking shop, dear little diplomat—to please and comfort mamma and Isa, no doubt.

This wee little child has a marvelous range of interests. She reads philosophies, novels, baby books, histories, the mighty poets—reads them with burning interest, and frankly and freely criticizes them all; she revels in storms, sunsets, cloud effects, scenery of mountain, plain, ocean and forest, and all the other wonders of nature, and sets down her joy in them all; she loves people, she detests people, according to mood and circumstance, and delivers her opinion of them, sometimes seasoned with attar of roses, sometimes with vitriol; in games, and all kinds of childish play she is an enthusiast; she adores animals, adores them all; none is too forlorn to fail of favor in her friendly eyes, no creature so humble that she cannot find something in it on which to lavish her caressing worship.

> I am going tomorrow to a delightfull place, Breahead by name,[10] belonging to Mrs Crraford [Crauford], where their is ducks cocks hens bublyjocks[11] 2 dogs 2 cats swine & which is delightful; I thing it is shoking to think that the dog & cat should bear them & they are drowned after [all]

She is a dear child, a bewitching little scamp; and never dearer, I think, than when the devil has had her in possession and she is breaking her stormy little heart over the remembrance of it.

> I confess that I have been more like a little young Devil then a creature for when Isabella went up the stairs to teach me religion and my multiplication and to be good and all my other lessons I stamped with my feet and threw my new hat which she had made on the ground and was sulky and was dreadfully passionate but she never whiped me but gently said Marjory go into another room and think what a great crime you are committing letting your temper git the better of you but I went so sulkely that the Devil got the better of me but she never never whips me so that I think I would be the better of it and the next time that I behave ill I think she should do it for she never does it. . . . Isabella has given me praise for checking my temper for I was sulkey when she was kneeling an hole hour teaching me to write

The wise Isabella, the sweet and patient Isabella! It is just a hundred years now (May, 1909) since the grateful child made that golden picture of you and laid your good heart bare for distant generations to see and bless; a hundred years—but if the picture endures a thousand it will still bring you the blessing, and with it the reverent homage that is your due. You had the seeing eye and the wise head. A fool would have punished Marjorie and wrecked her, but you held your hand, as knowing that when her volcanic fires went down she would repent and grieve, and punish herself, and be saved.

Sometimes when Marjorie was miraculously good, she got a penny for it, and once when she got an entire six-pence, she recognized that it was wealth. This wealth brought joy to her heart. Why? Because she could spend it on somebody else! We who know Marjorie would know that without being told it. I am sorry—often sorry, often grieved—that I was not there and looking over her shoulder when she was writing down her valued penny rewards: I would have said, "Save that scrap of manuscript, dear; make a will, and leave it to your posterity, to save them from want when penury shall threaten them; a day will come when it will be worth a thousand guineas, and a later day will come when it will be worth five thousand; here you are, rejoicing in copper farthings, and don't know that your magic pen is showering gold coin all over the paper." But I was not there to say it; those who were there did not think to say it; and so there is not a line of that quaint and precious cacography in existence to-day.[12]

I have adored Marjorie for six-and-thirty years; I have adored her in detail, I have adored the whole of her; but above all other details—just a little above all other details— I have adored her because she detested that odious and confusing and unvanquishable and unlearnable and shame-less invention, the multiplication table:

I am now going to tell you about the horible and wretched plaege [plague] that my multiplication gives me you cant concieve it—the most Devilish thing is 8 times 8 & 7 times 7 it is what nature itselfe cant endure

I stand reverently uncovered in the presence of that holy verdict.

Here is that person again whom I so dislike—and for no reason at all except that my Marjorie doesn't like her:

> Miss Potune is very fat she pretends to be very learned she says she saw a stone that dropt from the skies, but she is a good christian

Of course stones have fallen from the skies, but I don't believe this horid fat Simpliton had ever seen one that had done it; but even if she had, it was none of her business, and she could have been better employed than in going around exaggerating it and carrying on about it and trying to make trouble with a little child that had never done *her* any harm.

> The Birds do chirp the Lambs do leap and Nature is clothed with the garments of green yellow, and white, purple, and red. . . . There is a book that is caled the newgate Calender that contains all the Murders,—all the Murders [did] I say, nay all Thefts & Forgeries that ever [were] commited & fills one with horror & consternation

Marjorie is a diligent little student, and her education is always storming along and making great time and lots of noise:

> Isabella this morning taught me some Franch words one of which is bon suar the interpretation is good morning.

It slanders Isabella, but the slander is not intentional. The main thing to notice is that big word, "interpretation." Not many children of Marjorie's age can handle a five-syllable team in that easy and confident way. It is observable that she frequently employs words of an imposingly formidable size, and is manifestly quite familiar with them and not at all afraid of them.

> Isa is teaching me to make Simecolings nots of interrgations peorids & commoes &c; As this is Sunday I will Meditate uppon Senciable & Religious subjects first I should be very thankful that I am not a beggar as many are

That was the "first." She didn't get to her second subject,

but got side-tracked by a saner interest, and used her time to better purpose.

> It is Malancholy to think, that I have so many talents, & many there are that have not had the attention paid to them that I have, & yet they contrive to [be] better then me;
>
> Isabella is by far too indulgent to me & even the Miss Crafords say that they wonder at her patience with me & it is indeed true for my temper is a bad one

The daring child wrote a (synopsized) history of Mary Queen of Scots and of five of the royal Jameses in rhyme— but never mind, we have no room to discuss it here. Nothing was entirely beyond her literary jurisdiction; if it had occurred to her that the laws of Rome needed codifying she would have taken a chance at it.

Here is a sad note:

> My religion is greatly falling off because I dont pray with so much attention when I am saying my prayers & my character is lost a-mong the Breahead people I hope I will be religious again but as for reganing my charecter I despare for it

When religion and character go, they leave a large vacuum. But there are ways to fill it:

> I've forgot to say, but I've four lovers, the other one is Harry Watson, a very delightful boy. . . . James Keith hardly ever Spoke to me. he said Girl! make less noise . . . . Craky-hall . . . . I walked to that delightfull place with a delightfull young man beloved by all his friends and espacialy by me his loveress but I must not talk any longer about him for Isa said it is not proper for to speak of gentalman but I will never forget him
>
> The Scythians tribe lives very corsly for a Gluton Introdused to Arsaces the Captain of the Armey, 1 man who Dressed hair & another man who was a good cook but Araces said that he would keep 1 for brushing his horses tail, & the other to feed his pigs;
>
> On Saturday I expected no less than three well made Bucks the names of whom is here advertised Mr. Geo Crakey [Craigie] and Wm Keith and Jn Keith, the first is the funniest of every one of them Mr. Crakey & I walked to Crakyhall [Craigie-hall] hand by hand in Innocence and matitation sweet

thinking on the kind love which flows in our tender-hearted mind which is overflowing with majestick pleasure nobody was ever so polite to me in the hole state of my existence. Mr Craky you must know is a great Buck & pretty goodlooking

For a purpose, I wish the reader to take careful note of these statistics:

I am going to tell you of a malancholy story A young Turkie of 2 or 3 month Old would you believe it the father broak its leg & he kiled another I think he should be transported or hanged;

Marjorie wrote some verses about this tragedy—I think. I cannot be quite certain it is this one, for in the verses there are three deaths, whereas these statistics do not furnish so many. Also in the statistics the father of the deceased is indifferent about the loss he has sustained, whereas in the verses he is not. Also in the third verse, the *mother,* too, exhibits feeling, whereas in the two closing verses of the poem she—at least it seems to be she—is indifferent. At least it looks like indifference to me, and I believe it *is* indifference:

> Three Turkeys fair their last have breathed
> And now this worled for ever leaved
> Their Father & their Mother too
> Will sigh & weep as well as you
> Indeed the rats their bones have cranched
> To eternity are they launched
> . . . .
> A direful death indeed they had
> that would put any parent mad
> But she was more than usual calm
> She did not give a singel dam

The naughty little scamp! I mean, for not leaving out the *l* in the word "calm," so as to perfect the rhyme. It seems a pity to damage with a lame rhyme a couplet that is otherwise without a blemish.

Marjorie wrote four journals. She began the first one in January, 1809, when she was six years old, and finished it five months later, in June.

She began the second in the following month, and finished it six months afterward (January, 1810), when she was just seven.

She began the third one in April, 1810, and finished it in the autumn.

She wrote the fourth in the winter of 1810–11, and the last entry in it bears date July 19, 1811, and she died exactly five months later, December 19th, aged eight years and eleven months. It contains her rhymed Scottish histories.

Let me quote from Dr. John Brown:

> The day before her death, Sunday, she sat up in bed, worn and thin, her eye gleaming as with the light of a coming world, and with a tremulous, old voice repeated a long poem by Burns—heavy with the shadow of death, and lit with the fantasy of the judgment seat—a prayer in paraphrase, beginning:
>
> > Why am I loth to leave this earthly scene?
> > Have I so found it full of pleasing charms?
> > Some drops of joy, with draughts of ill between,
> > Some gleams of sunshine 'mid renewing storms.

It is more affecting than we care to say to read her mother's and Isabella Keith's letters written immediately after her death. Old and withered, tattered and pale, they are now; but when you read them, how quick, how throbbing with life and love! how rich in that language of affection which only women, and Shakespeare, and Luther can use—that power of detaining the soul over the beloved object and its loss.

Fifty years after Marjorie's death her sister, writing to Dr. Brown, said:

> My mother was struck by the patient quietness manifested by Marjorie during this illness, unlike her ardent, impulsive nature; but love and poetic feeling were unquenched. When Dr. Johnstone rewarded her submissiveness with a sixpence, the request speedily followed that she might get out ere New Year's day came. When asked why she was so desirous of getting out, she immediately rejoined, "Oh, I am anxious to buy something with my sixpence for my dear Isa Keith." Again, when lying very still, her mother asked her if there was anything she wished: "Oh, yes! if you would just leave the

room door open a wee bit, and play 'The Land o' the Leal,' and I will lie and *think,* and enjoy myself" (this is just as stated to me by her mother and mine). Well, the happy day came, alike to parents and child, when Marjorie was allowed to come forth from the nursery to the parlour. It was Sabbath evening, and after tea. My father, who idolised this child, and never afterwards in my hearing mentioned her name, took her in his arms; and while walking her up and down the room, she said: "Father, I will repeat something to you; what would you like?" He said, "Just choose yourself, Maidie." She hesitated for a moment between the paraphrase, "Few are thy days and full of woe," and the lines of Burns already quoted, but decided on the latter, a remarkable choice for a child. The repeating these lines seemed to stir up the depths of feeling in her soul. She asked to be allowed to write a poem; there was a doubt whether it would be right to allow her, in case of hurting her eyes. She pleaded earnestly, "Just this once;" the point was yielded, her slate was given her, and with great rapidity she wrote an address of fourteen lines, "To my loved cousin on the author's recovery."

The cousin was Isa Keith.

She went to bed apparently well, awoke in the middle of the night with the cry of woe to a mother's heart. "My head, my head!" Three days of the dire malady, "water in the head" followed, and the end came.

1. *For more information on the enchanting Marjory, see notes 3, 4, and 5 on pages 212–13.*

2. *Brown (1810–82), an Edinburgh physician, became a writer by accident, more or less, in middle age when he began contributing papers to a journal called* The Witness, *the first in 1846, others following at a leisurely pace. He had the essayist's charm and unhurried manner much admired in the nineteenth century, these attributes infusing discussions of medical subjects, art and literature, and the natural beauties of nature. Special regard for dogs produced his best known story,* Rab and His Friends *(1855).*

3. *According to Frank Sidgwick, Marjory's most meticulous editor, the avuncular relationship with Scott, the dandling on the knee, the sobbing and so forth, were romantic inventions of Dr. John Brown. Sir Walter was Marjory's aunt's husband's first cousin's son, but there is no positive evidence that he and Marjory ever met, and neither has left a record of the association. Mark Twain, however, evidently accepted Brown's account at face value.*

4. *Sidgwick praises this paragraph as part of Mark Twain's service in rescuing Marjory from "the fog of sentimentality" in which her Victorian editors beclouded her. The chief culprit was Dr. Brown, who not only gushed in such condescending expressions as "the warm, rosy, little wifie," but also pedantically edited her "prattle" to suit Victorian propriety and his own taste by deleting shockers like "botom" and "dam." Sidgwick calls Mark Twain's forthright treatment "a wholesome astringent."*

5. Birsy *is a Scotch word meaning "bristly" or "irritable," from* birse, *meaning "bristle" or "tuft of bristles."*

6. *Maria Edgeworth (1767–1849) wrote stories of children and of Irish life. Much of her work, written under the supervision of a censorious father, is burdened with oppressive moral teachings; but* Castle Rackrent *(1800) was a good first novel and* Belinda *(1801) was praised by Jane Austen, with whom Miss Edgeworth has often been compared. She was the creator of realistic children and well-balanced young women in* Moral Tales for Young People *(1801),* Popular Tales *(1804), and others.*

7. *John Bannister, a well-known comedian of London, gave a one-man performance of songs and jokes, which he called "Bannister's Budget." He toured England in 1808, visited Glasgow and Edinburgh early in 1809, and probably played return engagements in both cities a year or so later.*

8. *James Thomson (1700–48), a Scotch poet who migrated to London, is best known by the long blank verse poem* The Seasons *(1730), which marks a departure from the prevailing mode of closed heroic couplets and which shows genuine observation of nature and of country life.* The Castle of Indolence *(1748), written in Spenserian stanzas, is a burlesque metrical romance combined with conventional didacticism, praise of liberty, and so forth.*

9. *James McAra, convicted in January 1811 of the murder of his brother, was sentenced to banishment for life.*

10. *Braehead, across the Firth of Forth from Kircaldy, was the home of the Houison-Craufords, where Marjory spent part of her sixth, seventh, and eighth years with her aunt, Marianne Keith, and under the immediate care of her cousin and teacher, Isabella Keith.*

11. Bubblyjock *was a Scotch word for a male turkey. The name presumably comes from the bubbly sounds tom turkeys make.*

12. *Fortunately, the statement is an error. In 1880 Elizabeth Fleming, Marjory's younger sister, gave Marjory's manuscripts to the Very Rev. Dr. Macgregor of Saint Cuthbert's, Edinburgh, who kept them until his death in 1910. Then they passed into the custody of the Rev. Dr. Archibald Fleming of London, who presented them in 1930 to the National Library of Scotland in Edinburgh.*

Mark Twain Speaks for Himself *was phototypeset in 12-point Bembo by ParaGraphics, Inc., of Bloomfield, New Jersey. Printing by offset lithography on 60-pound wove finish Warren Olde Style paper and casebinding in Joanna Kennett were by Thomson-Shore, Inc., of Dexter, Michigan. James McCammack, graphic designer with Purdue University Press, designed the book and its jacket. Diane Dubiel and Verna Emery, former and present managing editors of the Press, edited the work and supervised its production.*